S

THE EDUCATION OF WOMEN DURING THE RENAISSANCE

By
MARY AGNES CANNON, M. A.

A DISSERTATION

Submitted to the Catholic Sisters College of the Catholic
University of America in Partial Fulfillment
of the Requirements for the Degree
Doctor of Philosophy

WASHINGTON, D. C.
THE CATHOLIC EDUCATION PRESS
1916

NATIONAL CAPITAL PRESS, INC., WASHINGTON, D. C.

To My Father

WHOSE ZEAL AND AFFECTION
FIRST GUIDED MY STEPS
INTO THE BY-PATHS OF
HISTORICAL TRUTH
THIS WORK
IS AFFECTIONATELY DEDICATED

PREFACE

In this dissertation is presented the result of an inquiry into the nature and extent of pedagogical endeavor in behalf of womankind during the period of the Revival of Learning, that is, from about 1350 to 1600. The subject here dealt with excludes the question of elementary training in the vernacular, and, generally, of all education in which the revived classics were not basic. Beginning with an examination into the origin and scope of the work of the humanistic theorists and practical educators in Italy, the center of the movement, the effort has been made to determine the results of similar endeavors in regions affected by the Italian Revival, that is, in Spain and Portugal, England, France, and the countries of northern Europe.

The history of the opportunities afforded woman in this particular phase of human activity can here be given but a passing review, but it is hoped that the few guide posts thus set up will invite investigation into the deeper mines of evidence bearing on other burning questions of woman's rights and privileges.

To the Reverend Patrick Joseph McCormick, Ph.D., under whose direction this dissertation has been written, the author owes grateful acknowledgment for encouragement and for the invaluable information afforded her through his lecture courses in the History of Education. She is also deeply indebted to the other professors in the Department of Education of the Catholic University of America, in a special manner, to the Very Reverend Doctor Shields, Dean of the Catholic Sisters College, her professor in the Psychology of Education; and to her professors in Philosophy, the Reverend Doctor Turner and the Very Reverend Doctor Pace.

Mary Agnes Cannon.

Washington, D. C.,
   February 25, 1916.

3

CONTENTS

CHAPTER I

ITALY

The political and social conditions in Italy during the period of the Renaissance, appear, at first sight, unfavorable to the advancement of intellectual interests. In the kingdoms and duchies the turmoil of foreign invasions and local wars kept prince and condottiere ever on the defensive or in the field, and in the republics party strife and the resulting family feuds were a constant menace to individual freedom.

While the fortunes of leaders rose and fell through political games of chance, the merchant class profited by the state of commercial activity and domestic patronage and rose to a condition of wealth and security.

Amid scenes of military triumphs and civic festivities, therefore, the Revival of Learning was ushered in, but we look in vain for signs of conflict between the apparent lust of power and greed of gain and the contradictory passion for the intellectual riches of antiquity.

From the first the nobles and the merchant princes encouraged the authors of the movement, placing at their disposal generous portions of their gains and founding libraries to receive the recovered manuscripts. The people as a nation welcomed the Renaissance and as individuals sought to make its wealth their own.[1]

In the general interest in classical learning, awakened by its re-birth into Italian life and letters, woman took no insignificant a part. From the beginning of the Revival we find the record of her literary tastes and accomplishments side by side with those of the leading men of her time. The history of Italian literature makes mention of many women proficient in Latin and Greek, languages which they spoke with ease and in which they wrote familiarly both in prose and poetry. Italian, too, was cultivated by them, especially in their correspondence with kindred and intimate friends, in hymns and the favorite form of the sonnet.

As early as 1405, scarcely more than thirty years after the death of Petrarch, Battista di Montefeltro, daughter of Antonio,

[1] Cf. Burckhardt, *The Civilisation of the Renaissance in Italy*, Translated by Middlemore, London, 1898; Symonds, *Renaissance in Italy*, London and New York, 1900.

Count of Urbino, and wife of Galeazzo Malatesta, besides exchanging Italian sonnets with her father-in-law, "Il Malatesta degli Sonetti," the reigning lord of Pesaro, was writing Latin epistles and composing complimentary Latin discourses which she pronounced before distinguished visitors at her father's court. One of these addresses made to the Emperor Sigismund, in 1433, when he passed through Urbino on the way from his coronation, is still preserved, as is also a letter to Pope Martin V and several sonnets.[2] One of these last is dedicated to her father-in-law and addressed to the Holy Spirit.[3]

Costanza da Varano, the grand-daughter of this Battista, was likewise a poet and a famous Latin scholar. Born in 1428, she was the daughter of Elisabetta Malatesta and Piergentile Varano, Lord of Camerino. She wrote Latin verse and, at the age of 14, composed a Latin address which she delivered before Francesco Sforza, Duke of Milan, on behalf of her brother, Rodolfo. On this occasion Guiniforte Barzizza sent her a congratulatory letter, and the fame of her eloquence spread throughout Italy. Costanza wrote also to Alfonso, King of Naples, begging his favor for her brother, and in 1444, when Rodolfo's rights as Lord of Camerino were restored to him, she made another Latin address before the populace of that city.[4]

Battista Sforza, who was the only daughter of this Costanza and of Alessandro Sforza, Count of Pesaro, and who became the wife of Federico, Duke of Urbino, in 1459, was even more gifted than her mother. After the death of the latter which took place when Battista was 18 months old, she was brought up at the

---

[2] Tiraboschi, *Storia della Letteratura Italiana*, Vol. VI, Pt. III, 844–846, Firenze, 1809; Dennistoun, *Memoirs of the Dukes of Urbino*, Ed. Hutton, Vol. I, 40; App. I, 428.   London and New York, 1909.

[3] "Clementissimo Spirto, ardente amore
     Dal Padre Eterno, e dal Verbo emanante;
     Somma Benignità, cooperante
     Quel mistero, ch' esolta il nostro cuore;
  Nella mia mente infondi il tuo timore,
     Pietà, consiglio: e poi, somma Creante,
     Dammi fortezza, e scienza fugante
     Dall' alma nazional ciaseuno errore.
  Solleva l'intelletto al Ben superno,
     Illuminando l'tanto che difforme
     Non sia da quella fe ch' al ciel ne scorge.
  Donami sapienza, con eterno
     Gusto di tua dolcezza, O Settiforme
     Si, ch' io dispregi ciò ch' il mondo porge."
                                   Dennistoun, *Ibid.*

[4] Tiraboschi, *op. cit.*, 846.

court of Milan under the care of Bianca Maria Visconti, wife of Francesco Sforza.

Of her talents and accomplishments Tiraboschi says: "There was no ambassador, prince nor cardinal who passed through Pesaro to whom she did not pay compliment in an extemporaneous address in true Latin fashion [latinamente]; and after she was Duchess of Urbino she once pronounced so eloquent an address to Pope Pius II that, learned and eloquent as he was, he protested that he was unable to make a like response."[5] Bernardo Tasso, in his "Amadigi" pays her a noted tribute.[6]

By the middle of the fifteenth century we find many other girls, who, like Battista Sforza, were remarkable for their early knowledge of Greek as well as of Latin.

Ippolita Sforza, daughter of Francesco, Duke of Milan, and Bianca Maria Visconti, and wife of Alfonso II, King of Naples, was proficient in Greek and in "all agreeable learning." During the Mantuan Congress when she was only 14, she made a Latin address to Pope Pius II and drew from this Pontiff a reply which is preserved together with her speech on this occasion and another address written by her in praise of her mother.[7]

Isotta Nogarola, of Verona, daughter of Leonardo Nogarola and Bianca Borromea, was noted from her tenderest years for her remarkable knowledge of Latin and Greek and of "all sciences." She corresponded in Greek with the scholars of her day and many of her Latin letters and other compositions are preserved. In 1437, when Isotta was in all probability 9 years old, she wrote a congratulatory letter to Ermolas Barbaro, the newly appointed protonotary apostolic. In 1451, when Lodovico Fascarini, a learned senator, was welcomed as mayor of Verona, she took part in the conferences held in his honor and won great distinction by her cleverness in discussion. One of the questions proposed on this occasion was whether the first sin was more the fault of

---

[5] *Ibid.*, 848.
[6] "La prima, che Demostene e Platone
Par ch'abbia avanti, e legga anche Plotino.
D'eloquenza e savere al paragone
Ben potrà star con l'Orator d'Arpino,
Moglie fia d'un invitto altro campione
Fedrigo Duca dell'antica Urbino."
                                                        Ibid.
[7] Pastor, *Geschichte der Päpste*, II, 43, Freiburg, 1889; Tiraboschi, *op. cit.*, Vol. VI, Pt. III, 849.

Adam or of Eve. The topic furnishes information on the nature of these assemblies and the triumph won by Isotta.[8]

Associated with Isotta were her sister, Genevra, another similarly gifted girl, who later married Brunoro Gambara, and Polissena de'Grimaldi, a Latin poet of Verona.[9]

Ferrara had her gifted women, preeminent among whom, in the early days, was Bianca d'Este, daughter of Niccolo III. She was born in 1440 and is characterized by her biographer as thoroughly accomplished in virtue and all learning. She wrote Latin and Greek in both prose and poetry, was proficient in music and dancing, in embroidery and other forms of needlework so popular in that day.

To her Tito Vespasiano Strozzi penned a glowing eulogy beginning:

> "Æmula Pieridum et magnae certissima cura
> Palladis, Estensem Virgo quae tollis ad astra
> Eximia virtute domum, cui non tulit aetas
> Nostra parem, quid primum in te mirabile dicam?"[10]

At the court of Mantua, Cecilia Gonzaga, daughter of the Marquis Gianfrancesco II and Paola Malatesta, was the admiration of Ambrosio Traversari for her precocity and her learning,[11] and in 1447, when she was 22, Pisanello made her the subject of one of his famous medals. On one side are her features in profile, with the inscription "Cecilia Virgo," and on the other her seated figure with the emblems of the unicorn and crescent moon.[12]

In Venice, as in Verona, learned women took part in the friendly disputations of social gatherings and distinguished themselves in philosophical discussions. Prominent among these is Cassandra Fedele, who was chosen by the Senate to make the address of welcome to the Emperor Frederick III in 1463.[13]

She was the daughter of Angiolo Fedele and Barbara Leoni, and wife of Giammaria Mapelli. Born in 1465, she lived far into the next century and won renown for her Latin and Greek scholarship and for her musical accomplishments, as well as for her proficiency in philosophy and Italian.

[8] Cf. Tiraboschi, *ibid.*, 850.
[9] *Ibid.*, 852.
[10] *Ibid.*
[11] "*Hodoeporicon*," quoted by Drane, *Christian Schools and Scholars*, II, 299, London, 1867.
[12] Gustave Gruyer, "Vittore Pisano," *Gazette des Beaux Arts*, 1894, 215–216.
[13] Yriarte, *Venice: histoire, art, industrie, la ville, la vie*, 191. Paris, 1878.

In reply to one of her letters, Poliziano, the great Florentine stylist, addressed her: "O decus Italiae virgo," praising her pure espistolary style and her skill in logic and in all philosophy.[14] Writing of her to Lorenzo de'Medici, the twentieth of June, 1491, this same scholar says: "Last evening I called on the famous Cassandra Fedele, and saluted her in your name. Truly, Lorenzo, she is something admirable, and learned no less in Italian than in Latin. She is exceedingly prudent [discretissima] and beautiful even to my eyes. I departed amazed. . . . Since she will certainly come some day to Florence to visit you, prepare to do her honor."[15]

In his Latin couplets, Poliziano characterizes many of the Florentine women of his day who devoted themselves to the classics.[16] One of these, Alessandra Scala, who played the rôle of Electra in Sophocles' drama given in the original, is thus described: "What an admirable Electra was the youthful Alessandra: admirable, being Italian, in the pronunciation of the language of Athens; in her correct intonation; in preserving the illusions of scene; in faithfully interpreting the character; in controlling expression, gesture and movement; in properly restraining the language of passion and awakening the pity of the audience by her tears."[17]

This Alessandra was the daughter of Bartolommeo Scala of Florence, and wife of Michelo Marullo, a native of Greece. She corresponded in Greek with the men and women of her time, and while she may not have written Latin and Italian verse she wrote Greek poetry, some of which is preserved.[18]

To these might be added the names of other women of the fifteenth century, all similarly gifted if not equally celebrated. Tiraboschi alone notes eight or ten others who wrote before 1500, and among the poets of the sixteenth century he mentions upwards of forty women who cultivated Italian verse and classical literature.

The history of one of these, Olimpia Morata, a daughter of Pelegrino Morata, of Ferrara, gives evidence that woman's

[14] Tiraboschi, op. cit., 855.
[15] Del Lungo, La Donna Fiorentina del Buon Tempo Antico, 230, note 29. Firenze, 1906.
[16] Ibid., 175–190.
[17] Ibid., 188.
[18] Tiraboschi, op. cit., 850.

interest in the classics did not abate when the vernacular became more widely cultivated.

Born in 1526, Olimpia was associated with Duchess Renée of France, at the court of Ferrara, as companion to her daughter, Anna Sforza. She wrote poetry in Latin and Greek and, when only 14, discoursed on Plato and Cicero before learned audiences at the University of Ferrara where her father was engaged as professor. With the latter she embraced the doctrine of Calvin and married Andrea Gruntero, a young German protestant, who came to Ferrara to study medicine. Retiring with her husband to Germany she taught in the University of Heidelberg, where her husband became professor of medicine. Here she died at the age of 29, and three years later her productions were collected and published at Basle.[19]

Among these poets of the sixteenth century, two of the most remarkable are the friendly rivals in the art, Vittoria Colonna and Veronica Gambara. Of them and of the other women of their time who wrote generally in Italian, Tiraboschi says: "Nothing shows us so well what was the common enthusiasm in Italy for the cultivation of vernacular poetry as the number of noble ladies who pursued it with such ardor and who valued nothing as much as the title of poet."[20]

Of Veronica Gambara this would appear to be literally true. Pietro Bembo (afterwards Cardinal), in his correspondence with this interesting woman, has left us the history of her aspirations and her successes in this field of literature. Writing to her from Padua, May 27, 1532, this "greatest Latinist of his day" says: "I am going to have my poems reprinted and I have collected two sonnets which I once wrote to you, and I want to put them with the others. One of mine, already printed, was an answer, rhyme for rhyme, to that sonnet which you wrote to me when you were a child, which begins thus: *S'a voi da me non pur veduto mai.* But it happens that I have lost that sonnet of yours and have nothing of it except the first line which I quote, nor can I find it anywhere. So I beg you to be kind enough to look for it among your papers and to send it to me, so that I may put it together with my own in the volume which will be reprinted, and I hope to make amends for the fault committed in the first edition, and that you

---

[19] Cf. Tiraboschi, *op. cit.*, Vol. VII, Pt. III, 1186–1191.
[20] *Ibid.*, 1167.

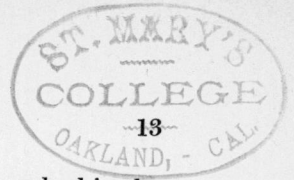

will no more have cause to complain of me as you have had in the past. I confess this that you may punish me the less."[21]

A year before the date of this letter Veronica had sent Bembo two sonnets for criticism, saying, "I send them to you as to my light and guide;" to which he replied: "As for the sonnets, both seem to be most beautiful. They are simple, they are lovely, and infinitely affectionate and graceful: I congratulate you upon them, . . . I cannot say for certain which is the more charming but the one which begins *Se a quella* takes my fancy most."[22]

Enclosing another sonnet, Veronica again writes in 1540: "You will see what I have meant, but have not known how to express, and when you have seen it, you will treat it as its simplicity deserves. It is enough for me that, as I dedicated my first fruits to your most reverend Lordship, I also send to you that which I think will be my last."[23]

The Cardinal replied from Rome on December 7, 1540: "I have not replied sooner to your Ladyship's most sweet letter, which I received through Signor Girolamo, your son, together with the sonnet of Our Lady, because I wanted first to give the sonnet to his Holiness, and then to write to you about it. But now that that has been delayed longer than I wished on account of his innumerable occupations I will at least answer you and tell you . . . As for the sonnet, it seems to me very beautiful, as I told the Reverend Monsignor, your brother. And, therefore, I would not have you abandon this art as you say, but rather not refrain from making others of them. I will give the sonnet to his Holiness by all means, at a time when he can read it more than once."[24]

Happily this sweet sonnet, which must have given pleasure to the great Pope Paul III, as well as to Cardinal Bembo, is still preserved, and it is gratifying to feel that on the nearing Christmas morning the Holy Father and the Cardinal borrowed the words of the Renaissance matron to express their prayer before the crib:

[21] Bembo, *Opere*, VIII, 61–62. Translated by Jerrold, "Vittoria Colonna," 142. London and New York, 1906.
[22] *Ibid.*, 141.
[23] Letter XIII, Correggio, October 29, 1540. Quoted in Jerrold, *op. cit.*, 144.
[24] *Ibid.*

"Turn then thy rays of grace, O Virgin fair,
On me, that so the comprehension may
Of this deep mystery to me be given."[25]

The admiration felt by Veronica for the gifts of her sister poet,
Vittoria Colonna, drew from her the expression of the esteem in
which this poet was held throughout Italy.   Veronica thus became
the laureate of this school of Vernacular Poets:

"O thou sole glory of our century,
Lady most admirable, wise, divine,
To whom today do reverently incline
All who deserve a place in history.
Immortal here shall be your memory;
Time that dooms all to ruinous decay,
Shall make of your fair name no impious prey,
But unto you shall be the victory.
To Pallas and to Phoebus shrines of old
Were raised, and such to you our sex should raise
Of richest marble and finest gold,
And, since in you is found all excellence,
In equal measure I would give you praise,
Lady, with worship, love, and reverence."[26]

[25] "Oggi per mezzo tuo, Virgine pura,
Si mostra in terra si mirabil cosa,
Che piena di stupor resta pensosa,
Mirando l'opra, e cede la natura.
Fatto uomo è Dio, e sotto umana cura,
Vestito di mortal carne noiosa,
Restò qual era, e la divina ascosa
Sua essenzia tenne in pueril figura.
Misto non fu, ne fu diviso mai;
Ma sempre Dio e sempre uomo verace,
Quanto possente in ciel, tanto nel mondo.
Volgi dunque ver me, Virgine, i rai
De la tua grazia, e'l senso mio capace
Fa'di questo misterio alto e profondo."
Trans. and quot. in Jerrold, *op. cit.*, 143.

[26] "O de la nostra etade unica gloria,
Donna saggia, leggiadra, anzi divina,
A la qual riverente oggi s'inchina
Chiunque è degno di famosa istoria,
Ben fia eterna di voi qua giù memoria,
Nè potrà 'l tempo con la sua ruina,
Far del bel nome vostro empia rapina
Ma di lui porterete ampia vittoria.
Il sesso nostro un sacro e nobil tempio
Dovria, come già a Palla e a Febo, alzarvi
Di ricchi marmi e di finissim' oro.
E, poichè di virtù siete l'esempio,
Vorrèi, Donna, poter tanto lodarvi,
Quanto io vi riverisco, amo ed adoro."
Quoted and trans. in Jerrold, *op. cit.*, 161.

A similar instance of one artist's appreciation of another is given in Michelangelo's verses to Vittoria. Here the strength of feeling which manifested itself in her letters, even more than in her verses, found response in his noble spirit:

"O Lady, who doth bear
    The soul through flood and fire to a bright shore,
    Unto myself let me return no more."[27]

There are other learned women, contemporaries of these poets, whose names do not appear on the pages of the history of Italian literature, but whose correspondence compares favorably with that of Vittoria Colonna and Veronica Gambara and betrays a literary power which they exercised in other forms of composition as occasion arose. They too wrote verses, but in their rigorous self-criticism they consigned them to oblivion.[28] Their extant letters, however, abundantly compensate for this loss.

While the sixteenth century women wrote Latin epistles and read both Latin and Greek,[29] their correspondence is, for the most part, in Italian. But here again language is stamped with the seal of culture. In this direct and simple prose the Renaissance mind is revealed to better advantage even then in the more studied productions of the poets.

Of Isabella d'Este's letters alone there are preserved upwards of two thousand,[30] which, with those of her numerous correspondents, bear unquestionable historical evidence as to woman's place in the Italian Revival. Through these heart to heart communications, too, these women became unconsciously the historians of their generation. Family joys and cares, social and political events, personal experiences and longings, all find a place here amidst the more serious business of life which was transacted through this same medium with merchants and artists and printers—always with admirable courtesy and skill.

Here we find no evidence of the formality of treatment or the artificial subject matter which the history of Ciceronianism would lead us to expect. On the contrary, unlike some of their brother

---

[27] "O donna, che passate
    Per acqua e foco l'alme a' lieti giorni,
    Deh fate ch'a me stesso più non torni!"
                    Ibid., 135.
[28] Cf. Cartwright, *Isabella d'Este*, I, 81. London, 1903.
[29] *Ibid.*, II, 21-26.
[30] Mantuan Archives. Cf. Cartwright, *op. cit.*, p. vi.

scholars of this century, whose letters are accessible, these women felt that they had something to say and they said it on paper as naturally and as frequently as women of our day converse over their telephones.[31]

In this particular the personal letters of Isabella d'Este contrast favorably with those written by her through her secretary, Equicola.[32]

In 1493, when on a journey to Venice, she wrote daily letters to Mantua, addressed to her husband, Federico Gonzaga, and to Elisabetta, Duchess of Urbino, her sister-in-law. In one of these letters to Elisabetta is the passage: "When I realized that I was all alone in the boat, without your dear company, I felt so lonely that I scarcely knew what I was doing or where I was. For my greater comfort, the wind and tide were against us all the way and I many times wished myself back in your room playing *scartino.*"[33]

And when returning she invites Elisabetta to meet her at Porto, saying "where we may enjoy the pure country air together and talk over all that has happened since we parted."[34]

Again, in 1502, when she visits Venice accompanied by Elisabetta, all the details of her journey are sent to her husband. Long and chatty letters, dated each successive day, contain descriptions of the city, accounts of friends and of ceremonies, of social parties and outings, and all end with the same affectionate farewells, each time differently expressed, and the request: "I beg you to kiss our boy," or "Please give our boy a hundred kisses for me so that when I return he won't think it strange to be kissed."[35]

In one of these letters is the sentence: "Tomorrow I will send some fish and oysters." And this from the collector of antiques, the patron of artists and booksellers, in whose famous "Grotto" the poets and painters of her day were honored in their persons and in their works.[36]

---

[31] Cf. Cartwright, *op. cit.*; Del Lungo, *Ibid.*

[32] Cf. Luzio e Renier, *Mantova e Urbino*, Toreno and Rome, 1893.

[33] "Appena me ritrovai in barca senza la sua dulcissima compagnia venni tanto bizarra, che non sapeva che volesse. Havendo per mio conforto aqua et vento sempre contrario . . . molte volte me agurai in camera de V. S. a giochare a scartino."—Luzio e Renier, *op. cit.*, 63.

[34] "a ció che de compagnia godiamo quello aere bono et stiamo in consolatione a rendere conto l'una a l'altra de quanto c' è occorso doppo siamo state separate."—*Ibid.*, 67.

[35] *Ibid.*, 307–315.

[36] Yriarte, "Isabella d'Este et les Artistes de son Temps." *Gazette des Beaux Arts*, 1895, 382.

Three years before the date of these matronly letters, Isabella was striving to restore the statue of Vergil to its place of honor in Mantua, and her name was proposed to accompany that of the poet on the base of the memorial. "At the base should be only a few words; such as, 'Publius Virgilius Mantuanus,' and 'Isabella Marchionissa Mantuae restituit,' as Your Excellency may desire," wrote the secretary of the commission, addressing Isabella.[37]

Although this project was not realized, yet the disappointment had not abated Isabella's zeal for the ancients nor diminished her love for the antique.

Three months after this visit to Venice, she wrote to her brother, Cardinal Ippolite d'Este, begging him to secure for her a torso of Venus, and a Cupid which had been carried off from Urbino by Caesar Borgia. The Venus seems to have been a genuine antique and the Cupid the famous Sleeping Cupid of Michelangelo.[38]

In keeping with this enthusiasm for art and letters is a certain physical power and a spirit of endurance which these women might call the "joy of living." This physical vigor and enjoyment frequently finds expression in their letters. One of Isabella's, addressed to Elisabetta, is characteristic: "By the love I bear you, my dearest sister, I must say this one thing, that I hope the first bath you take [Elisabetta had been ordered to Viterbo for her health] will be a steadfast resolve to avoid all unwholesome things and live on those that give health and strength. Above all I hope you will force yourself to take regular exercise on foot and horseback, and to join in pleasant conversation, in order to drive away melancholy and grief, whether they arise from mental or bodily causes. And you will, I hope, also resolve to think of nothing but your health in the first place, and of your own honor and comfort in the second place, because in this fickle world we can do nothing else, and those who do not know how to spend their time profitably allow their lives to slip away with much sorrow and little praise.

"I have said all this, not because Your Highness, being most wise yourself, does not know all this far better than I do, but only in the hope that, being aware of my practice, you may the more

---

[37] Baschet, "Recherches de Documents d'Art et d'Histoire dans les Archives de Mantue." *Gazette des Beaux Arts*, 1866, 481.

[38] Cartwright, *op. cit.*, I, 230.

willingly consent to live and take recreation as I do, and as the Castellan will be able to inform you."[39]

Isabella's favorite motto, "Nec spe, nec metu,"[40] explains her meaning.

Beatrice d'Este, Duchess of Milan, shared her sister's sentiments in regard to life's ills. Writing on one occasion to her husband, Lodovico Sforza, she says: "So we set out and reached the port of Chioggia, where the ships began to dance. I took the greatest delight in tossing up and down, and, by the grace of God, did not feel the least ill effects. But I can tell you that some of our party were very much alarmed, amongst others Signor Urbino, Niccolo de'Negri and Madonna Elisabetta."[41]

These sentiments of a marchioness and a duchess find an echo in the correspondence of a Florentine lady of a few decades later. In her letters to her husband, Isabella Sacchetti, the wife of Luigi Guicciardini and sister-in-law of the historian, thus formulates her philosophy of life: "I am sorry that you have so much trouble with the servants: it is a trying thing but you are not alone in it; it is the same for all. Something must be endured sometimes . . . we all have our faults and we must bear with one another until we die."

Then after long paragraphs of interesting information about the country home which she is keeping during the summer while her husband is serving the government, she compassionates him on his poor state of health and remarks: "I wish you would do as you advise me to do, look upon business as pleasure. Do you believe it is so pleasant for me here with only two maids to speak to, and to have to spend my time in writing and paying the workmen and keeping accounts? Those who would be happy in this world must find their pleasure in the things that annoy them, otherwise they will be always in sadness. I go to see Ser Antonio sometimes and when I see him in such pain, I feel myself blessed that I am able to sleep, to eat and to get some rest. So for this let us thank God."[42]

These letters are dated from 1535 to 1542. In her younger days Isabella doubtless took a zealous part in the festivities of

---

[39] *Ibid.*, 67.
[40] *Ibid.*, 280.
[41] Cartwright, *Beatrice d'Este*, 190. London, 1899.
[42] Del Lungo, *op. cit.*, 251–277.

her native city as we find them described by Poliziano, where graceful maidens danced in the afternoon sunshine to the music of the lute or viol.[43]

The evidences of taste and cheerfulness and outdoor freedom, which we find in all these letters, add to our faith in the representations of such types of physical beauty as the Renaissance artists produced, and dismiss from our minds any preconceived ideas of a vain artificiality, wholly incompatible with the keen aesthetic enjoyment with which these women speak of their own or their neighbors' personal ornamentation. In this, as in other material things, art ruled their habits and regulated their tastes. With intimate friends they borrow and lend home decorations and even jewels for special occasions and take pleasure in exchanging articles of toilet necessity of their own manufacture, such as the Renaissance drug store failed to supply.[44]

The writings of these women indicate, too, beyond a doubt, the nature of their love for the literature and art of the Revival. With none of them was this love an all-absorbing passion. Other interests claimed their share of attention in the daily lives of all these women. The domestic instinct is everywhere manifest in their correspondence with kindred or family friends; their letters addressed to scholars and artists have a tone of aesthetic feeling, of piety or cordial equality, in which good sense and propriety always predominate; and the same may be said of their poems.

With many the cares, not only of a family, but from time to time of the state, called them away from their classical pursuits. This was particularly the case in the kingdoms and duchies. Whenever this happened they proved themselves capable and prudent rulers, but their attitude in general towards public affairs and towards the obligations imposed by the frequent absence of their husbands on military duty, is well expressed by Vittoria Colonna:

> "Your mighty valor has proclaimed you kin
> To Hector and Achilles. But for me,
> Forlorn and weeping, what can this avail?
>
> .   .   .   .
>
> Others cried out for war, but I for peace.
> My speech was ever: it suffices me
> If my dear lord rest ever at my side.

---

[43] *Ibid.*, 175.
[44] Cf. Cartwright, *op. cit.*; Jerrold, *ibid.*

> You are not hurt by hazardous emprises,
> But rather we who, mournful and afflicted,
> Wait on sore wounded by our doubts and fears."[45]

However the preferences of these women may differ in choice or in degree of intensity in their love for literature and art, it is manifest that they have one sentiment in common. All, without exception, are deeply spiritual; and very nearly all stood the test of orthodoxy when the Reformation crossed the borders into Italy. Of the learned women above mentioned, several entered convents, some abandoning their earthly studies at the door of the contemplative cloister, and others entering the teaching orders.

Bettista di Montefeltro, after the death of her husband, became a Franciscan; Cecilia Gonzaga, with her mother, Paola Malatesta, entered the Franciscan convent founded by the latter at Mantua; Alessandra Scala joined the Benedictines in Florence, after her husband's death, and Isotta Nogarola also abandoned the world.[46]

The best efforts of all these Renaissance poets were on religious themes, and the letters all breathe a sincere piety. "I. H. S." stands at the head of every epistle of Isabella Guicciardini, and "May Christ keep you," or "May the Lord keep you and preserve your health," is the closing prayer.

The letters of Isabella d'Este give evidence of her solid piety. Those concerning her children reveal at once the mother and the woman of devout life: "Yesterday when I was saying my office," she writes to her husband, "he [Federico] came in and said he wanted to find his papa, and turned over all the cards till he found a figure with a beard, upon which he was delighted, and kissed it six times over saying 'Papa bello!' with the greatest joy."[47]

Isabella took special pains with her other children, notwith-

---

[45] "La vostra gran virtù s' e dimostrata
       D'un Ettor, d'un Achille, Ma che fia
       Questo per me, dolente, abbandonata!

     .   .   .   .   .   .

Attri chiedeva guerra, io sempre pace,
       Dicendo: assai mi fia se il mio marchese
       Meco quieto nel suo stato giace.
Non nuoce a voi tentar le dubbie imprese;
       Ma a noi, dogliose afflitte, che aspettando
       Semo da dubbio e da timore effese!"
Quoted and translated by Jerrold, op. cit., 68.
[46] Cf. Tiraboschi, op. cit.; Del Lungo, ibid.
[47] Lugio, "I Precettori d'Isabella d'Este." Quoted in Cartwright, op. cit., I, 225.

standing that she so much more often mentions the precious heir in her correspondence. The baby Leonora writes to her father, as any baby girl would, from the lap of her mother. Ippolita and Livia both were encouraged in their vocation to religion, while Ercole, afterwards Cardinal and famous in connection with the Council of Trent, owed much to his devoted mother whose good example his professors at Bologna encouraged him to follow.[48]

The history of the friendship of Vittoria Colonna and Michelangelo enables us to see the virtue and piety of this other great woman of the sixteenth century.

Speaking of the Pietà, Vittoria writes to the artist: "Your works forcibly awaken the judgment of whoever looks at them, and I spoke of adding goodness to things already perfect because I have seen actual instances of this in your work. . . . I had the greatest faith in God that He would grant you a supernatural grace to make this Christ, and when I saw it, it was so wonderful that it surpassed all my expectations in ever way. . . . I do not know how else to serve you than by praying for you to this sweet Christ, whom you have drawn so well and perfectly."[49]

Of Cardinal Pole, whose friendship meant so much to her amid the dangers attending her association with the reformers in Italy, Vittoria says to Cardinal Cervini: "The more opportunity I have had of observing the actions of the most reverend Monsignor of England, the more he seems to me a true and most sincere servant of God. So, when in his charity he condescends to answer any questions of mine, I think I am secure from error in following his advice."[50]

That the poems of this devout woman are not only spiritual but sincerely Catholic, is pointed out by her best critics. Such passages as the following are cited as evidence of this:

"Francis, in whom like wax our Lord imprest
His bitter wounds and sole elected thee,
Sealed with the seal of love thus vividly,
His image true to us to manifest.

. . . .

Saint in Paradise, I pray thee plead
That I may follow thy fair humble way,
In thought, in wish, in every holy deed."[51]

---

[48] Cf. Cartwright, *ibid.*, II, 216.
[49] Carteggio, Letter CXXIV. Translated by Jerrold, *op. cit.*, 129.
[50] *Ibid.*, Letter CXLIX. Jerrold, *op. cit.*, 262.
[51] *Ibid.*, 285.

The virtues that spring from religion enabled such women as these to keep steadily on their way, not only amid the dangers of error, but amid the more common dangers of adulation. In the early days of the Renaissance movement Bianca d'Este is commended for her virtue and good sense in spite of the praises of which she was the object,[52] and later on the gifted Florentine woman, Alessandra Seala, sends this reply to the laudatory epistles of Poliziano: "There is nothing better than the praises of a man of worth, and with what glory do thy praises cover me. But as for thy dreams, have a care that thou interpret them truly. Thou canst not possibly have found in me all that thou sayest. The divine Homer saith, 'A god should be approached only by those like unto him,' and between thee and me there is too great difference. For thou art like unto the Danube, which floweth from the west unto the south, and then towards the east in a mighty stream of water. Glorious philologist, thou dost disperse the darkness from works in many tongues, Greek, Roman, Hebrew, Etruscan. A Hercules of learning, thou art called upon to show thy strength in labors upon works of astronomy, physics, arithmetic, poetry, law and medicine. My childish writings are things as light as the flowers and the dew. Shall I stand by thy side because I have a little learning, or,—as saith the proverb,—shall we not be as the gnat beside the elephant, because both have a proboscis, or the cat beside Minerva on account of their coerulean eyes!"[53]

To be found in the correspondence of these Renaissance women are many letters written by religious, either monks or nuns, containing friendly advice and exhortations to perseverance in virtue and piety and in the fulfillment of duty.

One of these, written by Paola Antonia de'Negri (Sister Angelica), the daughter of Lazzaro de'Negri, a professor of literature in Milan, is addressed to Gaspara Stampa. Gaspara's ancestors were Milanese but she was born in Padua and, in 1544, was in Venice where she was greatly admired and sought after for her singular gifts as a musician and poet.

Writing from her convent of San Paolo in Milan, August 20, 1544, Sister Angelica says to her: "If the Creator loves you so

---

[52] Tiraboschi, *op. cit.*, 852.
[53] Del Lungo, *Women of Florence.* Translated by Steegmann, 183. London, 1907.

much, why should not I, a miserable creature, love you? If He
took such pleasure in you as to adorn you with His abundant
graces in order that He might better be able to take delight in you,
why should not I also take delight in the wonderful works that
He has wrought in you? Ah! if it might please His goodness to
make me worthy to see the beautiful work which He has begun in
you brought to perfection; and this I am sure He will do, you being
willing, as I trust you will be. For, if you are possessed of the
noble spirit that is announced to me by many, I cannot believe
that you will wish to imitate the folly of those who, arrogating to
themselves the gifts and graces bestowed on them, are so charmed
with themselves and become so proud that, making an idol of such
graces, they desire for themselves the praises that belong to God.
They want to be worshipped and praised and they make it their
whole study to please the world and men."[54]

When this letter was addressed to her, the youthful Gaspara was
basking in the sunshine of popular favor and wasting her spiritual
energies in composing daily verses to an indifferent lover. Her
later poems prove that she was not deaf to the warning.

In addition to the many devout Renaissance women who especially consecrated their lives to the service of God, either in religion
or, like Vittotia Colonna, among the poor and afflicted out in the
world, there is a long line of perfect mothers who, like Isabella
d'Este, wisely guided the inner life of the family, directing the care
of their children and the affairs of the household.

At Mantua, from the days of Paola Malatesta, all through the
critical period of the Revival, noble women ruled the Gonzaga
court. After this gifted woman had retired to the convent,[55]
Barbara von Brandenburg, the wife of Lodovico Gonzaga, with her
daughter-in-law, Margaret of Bavaria, kept alive her memory and
emulated her virtues,[56] until Isabella d'Este came from Ferrara to
guide the fortunes of Mantua for half a century.

The mother of Isabella, Leonora of Aragon, bringing from Naples
the best gifts of her race, took up the mission of good example at
Ferrara and handed it down to the days of her daughter-in-law,
Lucrezia Borgia, who found at this court and in the neighboring

[54] "Lettere Spiretuale della Devota Religiosa, Angelica Paola de'Negri,"
619–623. Translated by Jerrold, *op. cit.*, 179.
[55]Donismondi, *Dell'Istoria Ecclesiastica di Mantova*, Pt. I, 382.
[56] Kristeller, "Barbara von Brandenburg," *Hohenzollern Jahrbuch*, 1899.

convents, an element of piety in which her true nature blossomed forth in vindication of her name.[57]

Lucrezia's only daughter, Eleanora, inherited her mother's ripened virtues and entered a convent in her native city, while the foreign princess, Renée of France, who married Duke Ercole II, Lucrezia's eldest son, brought other phases of the new thought to old Ferrara and trained her daughters in other paths than those of Italian tradition.

From the days of Battista di Montefeltro, the court of Urbino fostered the spirit of the true Renaissance and sent forth devout women to rule the homes of Italy, or, after the example of Battista, to consecrate their talents and their virtues to the service of God in religion.

To this center of culture Battista Sforza, the great granddaughter of the first Battista, came from Milan as the wife of the "Good Duke Frederick." How Battista cared for her daughters, of whom she had eight, we can only conjecture, but when at length she gave to Urbino the long desired heir and passed away in fulfillment of her promise made to God, all Italy mourned her loss and sympathized with the grief expressed by the Good Duke: "For many reasons her death was a grievous vexation, for she was the beloved consort of my fortunes and domestic cares, the delight equally of my private and public hours, so that no greater misfortune could have befallen me."[58]

The spirit that reigned at Milan is evidenced by the piety of Bianca Maria Visconti, mother of Lodovico, of Ippolita and of six other children. When Lodovico was 5 years old and dangerously ill, his mother placed him under the protection of the Blessed Virgin and vowed rich offerings to the shrine of St. Anthony at Padua if her son should be spared. After his recovery she sent a life-sized silver image of Lodovico to Padua, with a set of vestments and altar plate for the Church of the Saint.[59]

The devotion of Bianca is in keeping with that of so many other Renaissance mothers whom we find making long journeys on pilgrimage to Loretto and other shrines to give thanks for favors obtained through the intercession of the Blessed Virgin and the Saints.

---

[57] Cf. Bertoni, *La Bib. Estense e la Coltura Ferraise.* Torino, 1903; Cath. Encyclopedia, *Alexander VI*; Gregorovius, *Lucrezia Borgia nach Urkunden und Korrespondenzen ihrer eigenen Zeit.* Stuttgart and Berlin, 1906.

[58] Dennistoun, *op. cit.,* I, 216.

[59] Cartwright, *Beatrice d'Este,* 14.

Long before the days of Savanorola, the Florentine mothers fulfilled the mission of apostles in their families. This is attested by one of his spiritual daughters in a letter written in May, 1496, in which she asks him to advise the maidens "whose judgment will lead them astray," as to the proper style of their new attire. After complaining that the zeal of the preacher has been directed more towards the welfare of the men and children than that of the women, she observes: "And since we have already labored and sown for a great while, it is needful to make sure that the enemy do not come and sow tares."[60]

The hymns composed by Lucrezia Tornabuoni, the wife of Piero de'Medici, and mother of Lorenzo, for her boys and girls, and for her devout friends, speak to us still of the care and affection with which she governed her household. Among these "laude" are two Christmas hymns, beginning: "Venite Pastori," and "Ecco il Re forte."[61]

Clarice Orsini, the wife of Lorenzo de'Medici, watched over her children with equal care as is plain from the complaint addressed to Lorenzo by Poliziano, the tutor of the future Pope Leo X. "As for Giovanni, his mother employs him in reading the Psalter, which I by no means commend. Whilst she abstained from interfering with him it is astonishing how rapidly he improved."[62]

That the virtues and graces of many of the Renaissance women were celebrated by Castiglione in the "Cortegiano," is more than fictitious evidence of their merits, if we consider the deep interest which this gallant historian of the Italian courts took in his own daughters and in their moral welfare.

After the premature death of his wife, Ippolita Torelli, he wrote to his children whom his mother was caring for at Mantua: "My Anna, who first taught me to use the sweet name of daughter, may your character be adorned with such moral graces that the beauties of your person may be excelled by that of your soul, and may be justly celebrated by posterity. And you, my Ippolita, whom I love so much for the sake of her whose name you bear, how pleasant it would be if, in the practice of virtue, you could surpass the sister who is so much your elder in years! But go on, both of you, as you have begun, and imitate the pattern held up

---

[60] Del Lungo, *op. cit.*   Translated by Steegmann, 227.
[61] Tiraboschi, *op. cit.*, Vol. VI, Pt. III, p. 848; Hare, *Most Illustrious Ladies of the Italian Renaissance*, 57.   London and New York, 1904.
[62] Hare, *ibid.*, 67.

before your eyes by her who has nurtured you since your mother
died, when you were too young to mourn her loss, so that all may
with one voice exclaim how close a likeness you bear to her."[63]

It was but natural that the Italian woman should take so active
a part in the Revival of Learning.   Her position in the home and
in society had secured a development of her mental and moral
powers sufficiently strong to render both safe and profitable to her
the new conditions brought about by the Renaissance.

Since the advent of Christianity man had treated her with
the respect and confidence inspired by his faith and all the great
teachers of the Church had labored for her spiritual and intellectual
advancement.   To her St. Peter imparted wisdom and knowledge
through his guidance of St. Petronilla and her companions;
St. Paul expressed Christ's attitude towards her in his Epistle to
the Galatians[64] and upheld her dignity by his example to the
Romans;[65] St. Ambrose, St. Jerome and St. Augustine devoted
themselves to her interests, especially in their literary labors.

Later ages inherited this spirit and passed it on to the Renaissance.   When Dante sings of the old Testament models of perfect
womanhood it is with the voice of St. Bernard[66] and his homage
to Beatrice is that of medieval knighthood, a homage inspired by
Catholicism.[67]

By responding to the teaching of the Church and reciprocating
the confidence placed in her, the Italian woman had become
worthy of her destiny and had handed down from generation to
generation the wealth of virtue and knowledge inherited through
the Gospel.

The numerous moral treatises addressed to the medieval woman

---

[63] Cartwright, *Baldassare Castiglione*, II, 394.   London, 1908.
[64] III, 28.
[65] *Rom.*, XVI.
[66] *Paradiso*, XXXII.
[67] "O Donna, in cui la mia speranza vige,
    E che soffristi per la mia salute
    In Inferno lasciar le tue vestige;
Di tante cose, quante io ho vedute,
    Dal tuo potere e dalla tua bontate
    Riconosco la grazia e la virtute
Tu m'hai di servo tratto a libertate
    Per tutte quelle vie, per tutti i modi,
    Che'di ciò fare avei la potestate."
                    Ibid., XXXI, 79.

reflect her condition and character and the trend of her mental activities, as well as the solicitude of her spiritual guides. The Houses of Anjou and Aragon found direction for every duty and occupation in such lessons as those contained in the "Speculum Dominarum" of Durand de Champagne[68] and the women of Northern Italy had for their guidance such teachings as we find expressed in the "Del Reggimento e Costumi di Donna" of Francesco da Barberino.[69] These and the many other "mirrors for ladies," published before the time of the Renaissance, treat for the most part of morals and manners, but they contain also advice on reading and on the acquisition of the knowledge suitable to their readers' station in life. That they were read and disseminated by the women, to whom they were addressed is evident from their wide circulation, but they did not constitute the entire library of the medieval household. The frequent mention in these treatises of topics from the Holy Scriptures and the Fathers, and from the Classics, supposed on the part of the reader a more or less familiar acquaintance with such topics, and the human element was further supplied by popular versions of the Carlovingian and Arthurian legends, afterwards cherished as heirlooms in the Renaissance household.[70]

The sympathy with the past greatness of neighboring nations which these medieval tales created, fostered the spirit of patriotism and, by turning attention to her own great past, helped to prepare Italy for the New Learning. At the same time these legends inspired a greater interest in the things that pertain to humanity, and this interest manifested itself in a taste for the heroic in literature and in life.

But the leaders of pedagogical thought, while realizing that a rich field of culture had been opened up in the revival of the classics, realized, too, that Arthur, in yielding place to Aeneas, had withdrawn the Christian element in which his humanity was steeped, and that that element had to be supplied by other means. Entering the movement with an earnest Catholic spirit, these humanists became the instruments in the hands of the Church for bringing about the adjustment to the new conditions. How to adapt the study of the classics to the needs of the Christian

---

[68] Manuscrits Latins 6784, Bibliothèque Nationale, Paris. Cited in Hentsch, *De la Littérature Didactique du Moyen Age*, 99. Halle, 1903.
[69] *Opere Volgari*, II. Bologna, 1875; Hentsch, *op. cit.*, 104.
[70] Cartwright, *Beatrice d'Este*, 38.

youth's mental and moral development and at the same time guard against its abuse, became, therefore, the question of first importance.

To aid in the solution of the problem the humanists hastened to give public expression to their personal views and at the same time to expound the principles of action adopted by the new system. All that was essential or useful in the older theories was to be retained. Like Dante and Petrarch, these men were of both the past and the future and their mission was to harmonize the two. Their work was not to be one of demolition but of repair and addition. To them the first essential in the old order was religion, with its accompanying code of Christian morality. This foundation undisturbed, the remedying of defects, the extending and beautifying, would be welcomed by them with enthusiasm.

The attitude of this school of humanists toward the new studies is defined by Pier Paolo Vergerio[71] in his treatise addressed to Ubertinus of Carrara, about the year 1405:

"We call those studies liberal which are worthy of a free man; those studies by which we attain and practice virtue and wisdom; that education which calls forth, trains and develops those highest gifts of body and of mind which enoble men and which are rightly judged to rank next in dignity to virtue only. For to a vulgar temper gain and pleasure are the one aim of existence, to a lofty nature moral worth and fame. It is, then, of the highest importance that even from infancy this aim, this effort, should constantly be kept alive in growing minds."[72]

The chief concern of the humanist was to gain control, not only of the first efforts of the child, but of the earliest influences brought to bear upon its development. To the practical educators of the system, the teaching profession was a noble vocation and they devoted their best energies to the training of children, even very young children, making no distinction of age or of sex. To them the child was a child of God, therefore there was "neither male nor female."

From this same principle sprang the choice of the initial field of action determined upon by the humanistic school. Previously existing conditions and the conditions peculiar to the Revival, led

[71] Professor at Florence and Padua. Cf. Woodward, *Vittorino da Feltre and Other Humanist Educators*. Cambridge, 1912.
[72] "De Ingenuis Moribus," Basileae, 1541. Translated by Woodward, *op. cit.*, 102.

the new system first to take up its labors among the daughters of the ruling classes, before passing on into the convents and down among the masses. The courts had become the centers of interest in the new studies through the patronage secured from the nobles by the initiators of the Renaissance.[73] It was consequently imperative for the educational system first to provide these courts with teachers who were alive to the dangers of the movement as well as to its advantages.

The custom of employing governors for the children of the household was a long established one in Italy.[74] This fact determined the nature of the new teaching body so far as it concerned the private domestic schools. In other private schools existing in the duchies and in the republics, like Venice and Florence, similar conditions obtained.

Men, therefore, and for the most part laymen, became the initial working factors of the system. These trained schoolmasters secured the positions of governor in the families of wealth and distinction, or established independent private schools. When the good will of the princes gave them an opportunity of extending their influence to families connected with the courts or dependent upon them, they established more pretentious palatial schools.[75] In these schools the instruction given to boys and girls had many features in common.

In his treatise[76] published in 1405, the same year as that of the appearance of Vergerio's, Leonardo Bruni D'Arezzo,[77] Chancellor of the City of Florence, announces the attitude assumed towards woman's education under the new system. Addressing his treatise to Battista di Montefeltro,[78] the author first commends her singular learning and exhorts her to further effort. He then outlines a course of study suitable for a woman moving in the society of scholars and sharing in their literary pursuits, and incidentally

---

[73] Cf. Burckhardt, op. cit.; Symonds, ibid.

[74] Cf. McCormick, Education of the Laity in the Early Middle Ages, 21. Washington, 1912.

[75] Cf. Tiraboschi, op. cit., Vol. VI, Pt. III; Rosmini, 'Idea Dell' ottimo precettore, nella vita e disciplina di Vittorino da Feltre e dei suoi discepoli, Libri quattro. Milano, 1845.

[76] "De studiis et literis," Parisiis, 1642. Translated by Woodward, op. cit., 119.

[77] Cf. Pastor, Geschichte der Päpste, I, 37; Tiraboschi, op. cit., Vol. VI, Pt. III, 845.

[78] Supra, 7ff.

formulates theories intended to guide the instructors of such girls as were under humanistic influence and training.

Public interest having been thus aroused by the theorists, the task of testing out in the classroom the general principles adopted by the system devolved upon the practical educators. The methods employed to this end by Vittorino da Feltre and Guarino da Verona[79] coincide with the aims of the leading theorists and seem to justify the conclusion that the general body of tutors trained like themselves in the universities or under famous scholars followed the same system of instruction.

In the humanistic schools thus founded, while boys and girls were taught side by side and by methods practically uniform, yet in the general choice of subject matter a marked distinction was made between them. This distinction was based on the fundamental principles of Humanism, prominent among which was that of deference to the claims of individuality.

Apart from the attention bestowed upon each girl in accordance with her special gifts or deficiencies, the humanist took into consideration, not only her future mission in Renaissance society, but her personal vocation as well, and to this end ministered to her intellectual and moral needs. Not unfrequently the girl's special vocation was early determined by her parents, who, in exercising the right of giving in marriage, destined her not only to a particular state of life but to definite surroundings and to a definite sphere of future activity.

To these considerations, more or less accidental, were added those arising from the peculiar interpretation given by Humanism to the universal principle that true education is preparation for life and for the life to come. With the humanist, such as we are considering him, life here must be lived "happily and beautifully," as well as "usefully," but, too, the happiness of the Future Life must not be lost sight of.

To attain this manifold end, therefore, the new system first provided for the girl a basic training in the classics, identical with that of the boy, as a means of similarly developing her faculties, and imparting to her the necessary power in the acquisition of further knowledge. This end reached, the nature and degree of exercise

---

[79] Cf. McCormick, "Two Catholic Medieval Educators," *Cath. Univ. Bulletin*, October, 1906, April, 1907; Woodward, *op. cit.;* Rosmini, *ibid.*

in other forms of mental activity should be determined by her peculiar needs.

In accordance with these views, a curriculum was gradually developed and universally adopted before the close of the first quarter of the fifteenth century. This plan, determined upon by the early humanists, was followed practically unmodified, throughout the Italian Revival.

In considering the special features of this curriculum we shall examine first the provision made for the fundamental training through the study of Latin, assisted and supplemented by that of Greek. From this viewpoint the attitude of the system towards the other prescribed disciplines is more readily appreciated.

LATIN

If we bear in mind that the Italian language was looked upon by the humanists as merely a form of Latin dialect and that for this reason its use in cultured society was to be discouraged, we shall realize that in the place assigned to Latin in the curriculum the first consideration was the restoration to popular usage of a mother tongue long confined to the use of scholars and to the business of diplomacy.

This motive explains why, in the schools of Humanism, the girl as well as the boy was to be trained from the cradle in the use of Latin as the medium of thought interpretation and expression under the direction of her tutor.

From this point of view, D'Arezzo[80] defines his position: "The foundation of all true learning must be laid in the sound and thorough knowledge of Latin: which implies study marked by a broad spirit, accurate scholarship, and careful attention to details. Unless this solid basis be secured it is useless to attempt to rear an enduring edifice. Without it the great monuments of literature are unintelligible and the art of composition impossible."

Grammar and Rhetoric

To secure this end the author counsels a thorough study of grammar; not as a feat of memory, but with constant interpretation of the usage of the best authors, and practice in the art of composition. "We may gain much from Servius, Donatus or Priscian, but more by careful observation in our own reading."

---

[80] *Op. cit.*

Treating of the authors to be read as models of correct grammatical construction, D'Arezzo first recommends Lactantius, St. Augustine, St. Ambrose, St. Cyprian, and translations of the Greek Fathers, if those translations are accurate.

Of the classical authors he says: "Cicero will be your constant pleasure: how unapproachable in his wealth of ideas and of language, in force of style, indeed in all that can attract in a writer! Next to him ranks Vergil, the glory and delight of our national literature.   Livy and Sallust and the chief poets follow in order. The usage of these authors will serve you as your test of correctness in choice of vocabulary and of constructions."

Reading or Elocution

To gain an understanding of an author, the humanist would have the student frequently read aloud, noting the rhythm of the prose and the quantity and meter of the poetry, and by this means more rapidly seize upon the thought and interpret the feeling of the passage.   These recommendations show us the importance of the study of elocution in the humanistic schools.

"I commend therefore to you as an aid to understanding an author the practice of reading aloud with clear and exact intonation.   By this device you will seize more quickly the drift of the passage, by realizing the main lines on which it is constructed. And the music of the prose thus interpreted by the voice will react with advantage upon your own composition, and at the same time will improve your own reading by compelling deliberate and intelligent expression. . . .   The laws of quantity are more important, since in poetry scansion is frequently our only certain clue to construction. . . .   A skillful orator or historian will be careful of the effect to be gained by spondaic, iambic, dactylic or other rhythm in arousing different emotions congruous to his matter in hand.   To ignore this is to neglect one of the most delicate points of style.   You will notice that such refinements will apply only to one who aspires to proficiency in the finer shades of criticism and expression."

Composition

The insistence on "thought getting" as the first requisite in the art of composition is frequent in the writings of all the early humanistic theorists.   Each gives his own peculiar application to Horace's

rule: "Scribendi recte sapere est et principium et fons."[81] Vergerio despairs of the student who has only "words" at his command: "Where the power of talk alone is remarkable I know not what advice to give."[82] And D'Arezzo says: "Proficiency in literary form, not accompanied by broad acquaintance with facts and truths, is a barren attainment."

In estimating the value of careful attention to form and the practice of oral and written composition, he remarks: "Information, however vast, which lacks all grace of expression, would seem to be put under a bushel or partly thrown away. Indeed one may fairly ask what advantage it is to possess profound and varied learning if one cannot convey it in language worthy of the subject. Where, however, this double capacity exists—breadth of learning and grace of style—we allow the highest title to distinction and to abiding fame." This breadth of learning which the author calls 'Knowledge of realities—Facts and Principles'— is attained only by one "who has seen many things and read much."

Among the forms of oral expression to be acquired by practice, D'Arezzo recommends the art of clever conversation and the formal discussion of topics of interest in books and in life, but he discourages for the girl the study of what he styles "Rhetoric," by which we are to understand "Oratory." He explains that his motive is the obvious one—what is fitting for a woman: "To her neither the intricacies of debate nor the oratorical artifices of action and delivery are of the least practical use, if indeed they are not positively unbecoming. Rhetoric in all its forms—public discussion, forensic argument, logical fence and the like—lies absolutely outside the province of woman."

This passage throws light on the peculiar merits of those public addresses so often mentioned in connection with the Renaissance girl's literary attainments. The occasions which called them forth and the themes of these addresses explain their nature as to form and content, but D'Arezzo's treatment of the question of delivery lets us into the secret of the charm cast over their audiences by the women trained in the schools of humanistic culture.

Penmanship

In his discussion of so elementary a subject as that of handwriting the humanist doubtless had in mind the important consideration

---

[81] *Ars Poetica*, 309.
[82] *Op. cit.*

that to the accuracy of the copyist was intrusted the preservation
of the true meaning of the classical writings, at this early day, before
the invention of the printing press.   But the artist's passion for the
perfection of detail also appears in D'Arezzo's recommendation:
"The art of Writing is not limited to the mere formation of letters,
but it concerns also the subjects of the diphthongs, and of the
syllabic division of words, the accepted usage in the writings of each
letter, singly and in cursive script, and the whole field of abbrevia-
tions.   This may seem a trivial matter, but a knowledge of educated practice on these points may fairly be expected of us."

Literature

Literature as a study apart from grammar and composition is
treated by D'Arezzo under three heads: History, Oratory, Poetry.
This study he ranks with those which conduce to the "profitable
enjoyment" of life.   It is characteristic of the humanist that the
enjoyment to be sought in study must be profitable to the mind;
must conduce to intellectual pleasure worthy of the "lofty nature."

Of these three forms of profitable enjoyment, *History* holds the
first place in the estimation of D'Arezzo.   He makes this distinction
from the point of view of utility.   He reminds the girl that it is her
duty to understand the origin of the history of her own country
and its development, and the achievements of peoples and kings:
"For the careful study of the past enlarges our foresight in contemporary affairs and affords to citizens and to monarchs lessons
of incitement or warning in the ordering of public policy."

This recommendation hints at the interest taken by the Renaissance women in questions of the day and the necessity of preparation for occasional responsibilities of governing which the times
imposed.

But apart from the information to be derived from the study of
the historians, the humanists would have them read for enjoyment;
a true possibility at this stage of the girl's progress, after she has
acquired facility in reading and a taste for her authors such as the
humanist's masterly discipline in grammar and rhetoric secured to
her.[83]

In the choice to be made among historians, D'Arezzo says: "We
equally prize such authors as Livy, Sallust and Curtius, and,
perhaps, even above these, Julius Caesar; the style of whose Com-

---

[83] Cf. Woodward, *op. cit.*, 44–49.

mentaries, so elegant and so limpid, entitles them to our warm admiration."

In recommending the *Orators*, D'Arezzo lays stress upon their help as models of style, and is satisfied with a general statement of their merits, as if again to draw the distinction between the study of oratory for a girl and for a boy.

By the place which he assigns to *Poetry* he makes his strongest appeal to the humanistic instinct. In his enthusiasm, however, he fails to solve the problem raised through the indiscriminate use of texts in teaching the young. But the men who organized the humanistic schools warded off the danger which threatened the new system from this lack of judgment on the part of the theorist and of a few among the practical educators.[84] Such men as Vittorino da Feltre understood the necessity of careful selection and prudent expurgation and in consequence the girl was given in the classroom only "worthy thoughts worthily expressed."[85]

D'Arezzo counsels the study of poetry first for information, for "profitable" enjoyment. To encourage the girl in this motive he cites the example of Aristotle, Plato, Cicero, Seneca, and the early Fathers, all of whom show by their writings their profound knowledge of the poets. "Hence my view," he says, "that familiarity with the great poets of antiquity is essential to any claim to true education."

Speaking of the value of poetry in training the emotions, the humanist proposes the psychological theories based on the principles of affective consciousness and formulates, though not in our modern terminology, the fundamental doctrine of Humanism: Through the beautiful to the good and the true: "Have we not felt the sudden uplifting of the Soul when in the solemn Office of the Mass such a passage as the 'Primo dierum omnium' bursts upon us. It is not hard for us, then, to understand what the Ancients meant when they said that the Soul is ordered in special relation to the principles of Harmony and Rhythm, and is, therefore, by no other influence so surely moved. Hence I hold my conviction to be securely based, namely, that Poetry has by our very constitution a stronger attraction for us than any other form of expression."

The poets are to be chosen for study from the standard of art,

---

[84] Cf. Dominici, *Regola del Governo di Cura Familiare*, 133–136. Edited by Donato Salvi, Firenze, 1860.
[85] Woodward, *ibid.*, 57.

rather than for the content of their writings. Thus considered, D'Arezzo distinguishes two classes, the aristocratic and the vulgar. The latter he counsels the lady to pass by. Such are the comic dramatist, who may season his wit too highly; and the satirist, who may describe too bluntly the vices he scourges. But Vergil, Seneca, and Statius, and their school, must be the trusted companions of all who aspire to culture.

GREEK

In the schools of Humanism Greek was not only studied as the key to the richest treasures of the Revival; in these schools the use of Latin as the colloquial language afforded still another motive for the thorough study of the older language; namely, the close relation existing between the Latin and the Greek. In addition to this, Greek was for the Italian the living language of a neighboring and kindred nation. This explains the nature of the training in this language proposed by the humanist for girls and boys indifferently. The study of Greek was to the Renaissance woman what the study of any modern foreign language, and Latin and Greek all combined, is for the student of today. Hence its importance as a branch of learning in the Italian schools of the Revival.

That as early as 1405, D'Arezzo makes no provision in his treatise for the teaching of Greek is in all probability due to the fact that this language was then only beginning its struggle for a place in the New Learning and facilities for its study were still, for the most part, confined to the universities. Whether the hope of the humanist to restore the language and literature of Greece to a place of honor in the grammar school should be realized, still remained to be seen.

As late as 1405 Vergerio complained of the lack of zeal for this restoration[86] and affirmed that there were only one or two who were tardily endeavoring to rescue from oblivion something of "that noble tongue once well nigh the daily speech" of the Italian race.

But the girl did not have to wait for the influx of native teachers after the fall of Constantinople, in 1453, to share in the advantages of the Greek Revival. The "one or two" to whom Vergerio gives credit for exceptional zeal in this respect, soon succeeded in persuading others to join them. Of the three famous lecturers in

---

[86] *Op. cit.*

Greek, Manuel Chrysoloras, Theodore Gaza and George of Trebizond, two, Gaza and Trebizond, were later employed by Vittorino da Feltre in his school at Mantua, and three others, Guarino Veronese, Francesco Filelfo and Giovanni Aurispa, traveling to Greece or Constantinople to make the better progress, returned to Italy to give an impulse to the movement which, in consequence, spread rapidly before the close of the first half of the fifteenth century.

In 1431, the little 6-year-old pupil of Vittorino, Cecilia Gonzaga, was making such progress in both Latin and Greek that her tutor ordered for her use, the next year, a copy of the four Gospels in Greek together with two Latin grammars for immediate use.[87]

In the schools of Guarino da Verona, the girls received a similar training. Isotta Nogarola and her sister, Genevra, attended his classes in Verona,[88] and at Ferrara the Este family benefited not only by his personal teaching, but by that same teaching through his son, Battista Guarino, who continued his father's labors at Ferrara well into the sixteenth century. Battista gave Isabella d'Este her first lessons, as we learn from a letter which he addressed to Federico Gonzaga in 1482, when Isabella was 8 years old. In this year there was a famine in Ferrara and Guarino begged the Marquis of Mantua for a grant of wheat in order that he might the better instruct Donna Isabella, who, two years before, had been betrothed to Francesco Gonzaga, the heir of Mantua. She "is now," he adds, "thank God, in perfect health and learns with a marvelous facility far beyond her years."[89]

This account of the tutor agrees with that of the Mantuan envoy at the time of the betrothal: "Madonna Isabella was then led in to see me and I questioned her on many subjects, to all of which she replied with rare good sense and quickness. Her answers seemed truly marvelous in a child of 6, and although I had already heard much of her singular intelligence, I could never have imagined such a thing to be possible."[90]

When sending to Mantua her portrait, painted by Cosimo Tura, the envoy adds: "I send the portrait of Madonna Isabella so that your Highness and Don Francesco may see her face, but I can

[87] Woodward, *op. cit.*, 70.
[88] Sabbadini, "Vita di Guarino Veronese, 123," Geneva, 1891. Cited by Woodward, *ibid.*, 120.
[89] Cartwright, *op. cit.*, I, 9.
[90] Cartwright, *Isabella d'Este*, I, 3.

assure you that her marvelous knowledge and intelligence are far
more worthy of admiration."[91]

While no special mention is made of Greek, the presence of
Battista Guarino as instructor at this Court, and of his father,
Guarino da Verona, would indicate the parallel teaching of Latin
and Greek at Ferrara as a matter of course.   As late as the days of
Isabella a child's "marvelous knowledge" would need no speci-
fication as to the subjects commonly taught her.

In a treatise published in 1459 one year before the death of
Guarino da Verona, Battista Guarino expounds his methods
which he affirms are precisely those of his father.[92]

Of the study of Greek he says: "I have said that the ability to
write Latin verse is one of the essential marks of an educated
person. I wish now to indicate a second, which is of at least equal
importance, namely familiarity with the language and literature of
Greece. . . .   I can allow no doubt to remain as to my conviction
that without a knowledge of Greek, Latin scholarship itself is in
any real sense impossible."

He then points out the importance of Greek scholarship
for the proper understanding of Latin, and the desirability
of even studying Greek before Latin, notwithstanding the
necessity of giving it the second place since it must be "for us . . .
a learned and not a colloquial language, and that Latin itself needs
much more elaborate and careful training than was requisite to a
Roman of the imperial epoch.   On the other hand," he continues,
"I have myself known not a few pupils of my father—he was, as
you know, a scholar of equal distinction in either language—who
after gaining a thorough mastery of Latin, could then in a single
year make such progress with Greek that they translated accurately
entire works of ordinary difficulty from that language into good
readable Latin at sight."

After giving directions for the careful and systematic teaching
of the rudiments of *Grammar*, Guarino recommends in the choice
of texts simple narrative prose for the beginning that the attention
may be concentrated upon vocabulary and constructions.   He
would then gradually increase the intricacy of the text to lead the
student from difficulty to difficulty.

---

[91] *Ibid.*, 4.
[92] "De ordine docendi et studendi," Modena, 1496.   Translated by Woodward, *op. cit.*, 159.

Of *Poetry* he says: "Our scholar should make his first acquaint-ance with the poets through Homer, the sovereign master of them all." And this because of the dependence of the Latin poets, notably Vergil, on Homer and the other Greeks. From Homer he would pass on to the other heroic poets and to the dramatists.

The women of the republics and those under private instructors in the family circle must have had equal opportunities for the study of Greek with the pupils in the palace schools. We cannot be certain who Alessandra Scala's teacher was, but her husband was a native of Greece,[93] and Greek had been cultivated at Florence since the coming of Chrysoloras in 1397. At Venice the presence of both Vittorino and Guarino[94] would give such women as Cassandra Fedele, though indirectly, the opportunities less evident here than at the centers of culture created by the great humanistic schools.

Ippolita and Battista Sforza, at Milan, had not only Lascaris to teach them Greek, but later Baldo Martorelli, a pupil of Vittorino da Feltre. Under this tutor Ippolita made remarkable progress in Latin and there is preserved in Rome in the Monastery of the Holy Cross in Jerusalem a little manuscript of hers on the "De Senectute" written when she was 13.[95] Her knowledge of Greek warrants the belief that she made similar progress in that language under Martorelli. This tutor later became the secretary of Ippolita at Naples and in all probability tutor to her daughter Isabella d'Aragona.[96]

The many instances of Greek learning which we find among the Renaissance women, enable us to conjecture what were the re-sults obtained in the education of girls through the instrumen-tality of the various tutors trained in the schools of Vittorino and Guarino. The statement made through the filial pride of Battista Guarino holds equally for the Mantuan school in the days of Vittorino:[97] "For as from the Trojan Horse of old the Greek heroes spread over the captured city, so from that famous Academy of my father has proceeded the greater number of those scholars who have carried learning, not merely throughout Italy, but far beyond her borders."

---

[93] *Supra*, 11
[94] Tiraboschi, *op. cit.*, Vol, VI. Pt. III, 968–989.
[95] *Ibid.*, 849.
[96] Rosmini, *op. cit.*, 268.
[97] Cf. Tiraboschi, *op. cit.*; Rosmini, *Ibid.*

The anxiety not to overcrowd the curriculum, or to give too wide a scope to subjects purely objective, to the detriment of the more important "humanities," is a characteristic feature of the new system. In his general treatment of the choice of subject matter, Vergerio[98] would have educators beware of this danger. In keeping with his theories for general application on the part of the pupil, are those of D'Arezzo for the choice of studies proper to a woman, even one "of keen and lofty aspirations to whom nothing that is worthy in any learned discipline is without its interest."

On this subject he says: "In some branches of knowledge I would rather restrain the ardor of the learner, in others, again, encourage it to the uttermost. Thus there are certain subjects in which, whilst a modest proficiency is on all accounts to be desired, a minute knowledge and excessive devotion seems to be a vain display."

Science and Mathematics

Among the studies deemed by the humanist "not worthy to absorb a cultivated mind" are "astrology," by which we are given to understand "astronomy" as well, and the "subtleties" of arithmetic and geometry. We may not infer from this that the humanist dismissed all interest in science and mathematics in a girl's study. In treating of the information to be derived from the poets the same author says: "For in their writings we find deep speculations upon Nature and upon the Causes and Origins of things." His assertion that a modest proficiency in such subjects as science and mathematics is on all accounts to be desired, and the general trend of his thought in treating of the character of true learning lead us to read his meaning in the expression of a nineteenth century theorist: "A woman in any rank of life, ought to know whatever her husband is likely to know, but to know it in a different way. . . . Speaking broadly a man ought to know any language or science he learns, thoroughly, while a woman ought to know the same language or science only so far as may enable her to sympathize in her husband's pleasures and in those of his best friends. Yet, observe, with exquisite accuracy as far as she reaches. There is a wide difference between elementary knowledge and superficial knowledge—between a firm beginning

---

[98] *Op. cit.*

and a feeble smattering. A woman may always help her husband by what she knows, however little; by what she half knows, or mis-knows, she will only teaze him."[99]

Christian Doctrine and Ethics

"What Disciplines then are properly open to her?" D'Arezzo asks. And he answers: "In the first place she has before her as a subject peculiarly her own the whole field of religion and morals." Under the head of the Literature of the Church the author here prescribes the study of Christian Doctrine as a formal branch of necessary knowledge: "The literature of the Church will thus claim her earnest study. Such a writer, for instance, as St. Augustine affords her the fullest scope for reverent yet learned inquiry."

Of the formal study of ethics, apart from religion, he says: "Moreover, the . . . Christian lady has no need in the study of this weighty subject to confine herself to ecclesiastical writers. Morals indeed, have been treated of by the noblest intellects of Greece and Rome. What they have left us upon Continence, Temperance, Modesty, Justice, Courage, Greatness of Soul, demands your sincere respect. You must enter into such questions as the sufficiency of Virtue to Happiness, or whether, if Happiness consists in Virtue, it can be destroyed by torture, imprisonment or exile; whether, admitting that these may prevent a man from being happy, they can be further said to make him miserable. Again, does Happiness consist (with Epicurus) in the presence of pleasure and the absence of pain; or (with Xenophon) in the consciousness of uprightness; or (with Aristotle) in the practice of Virtue? These inquiries are of all others, most worthy to be pursued by men and women alike; they are fit material for formal discussion and for literary exercise."

And he concludes: "Let religion and morals, therefore, hold the first place in the education of a Christian lady."

Thus the humanist anticipates by five hundred years the doctrine of the English social reformer, John Ruskin: "And, indeed, if there were to be a difference between a girl's education and a boy's, I should say that of the two the girl should be earlier led, as her intellect ripens faster, into deep and serious subjects; and that her range of literature should be, not more, but less frivolous, calculated

---

[99] Ruskin, *Sesame and Lillies*.

to add the qualities of patience and seriousness to her natural poignancy of thought and quickness of wit; and also to keep her in a lofty and pure element of thought."[100]

Music

Of the further forms of discipline suitable to a girl, D'Arezzo makes no mention, but his associates treat of other subjects and methods, in a general way, which were evidently adopted in the system for training girls.   Among the branches of study thus provided for, music holds a place of distinction.   The attitude of Humanism towards this art is very definite.   Like poetry and all the other forms of harmony and rhythm, it must be classical, not sensuous or sentimental.   The example of the Greeks was a conclusive argument with the Renaissance educator: "As to music," says Vergerio, "the Greeks refused the title of 'Educated' to any one who could not sing or play. . . .   In so far as it is taught as a healthy recreation for the moral and spiritual nature, music is a truly liberal art, and, both as regards its theory and its practice, should find a place in education."[101]

Under the careful supervision here recommended music was taught in the school of Vittorino da Feltre [102] and it is very probable that Cecilia Gonzaga and her companions were trained in this art, although we find no special mention of the musical education of the girls at the court of Mantua until the days of Isabella d'Este. It would appear that in the beginning of the movement Naples and Ferrara offered the best opportunities to girls in this respect. In the first half of the fifteenth century, the daughters of Niccolo d'Este were proficient in music[103] and Leonora, daughter of King Ferrante of Naples, was an accomplished musician when she came to Ferrara in 1473 as the bride of Ercole d'Este.   Here she kept up her practice on the harp while her daughters learned to play the clavichord, lute and viol.

Don Giovanni Martino, a priest whom Duke Ercole had invited from Constance to direct the chapel choir of Ferrara, taught the Este girls and after Isabella's marriage he went occasionally to Mantua to give her lessons.   Giralomo da Sestola taught her singing, an accomplishment for which she became famous.[104]   Beatrice d'Este

---

[100] *Ibid.*
[101] *Op. cit.*
[102] Woodward, *op. cit.*, 43.
[103] *Supra*, 10.
[104] Cf. Cartwright, *Isabella D'Este, I; Beatrice d'Este*, 35, London, 1899.

was specially gifted in music and at the court of Milan, after her marriage with Lodovico Sforza, she engaged Lorenzo Gusnasco of Pavia to make her calvichords and viols of the rarest workmanship.[105]

It was as a musician more than as a poet, that Gaspara Stampa won renown at Venice. With Cassandra Fedele[106] this gifted girl exemplifies the nature of the musical education afforded in the classical circles of this city of all sweet harmonies.

Chorus singing was carefully cultivated among the children at all these schools as we learn from the accounts of the public plays and pageants so frequent and so artistic, in Renaissance society;[107] and the child's musical appreciation was early developed through the solemn chant of the court chapel and the classical performances in the theater attached to the palace.[108]

Art

Drawing, as a subject of special study, even for the boy, seems not to have found favor with the humanists. The judgment expressed by Vergerio, in 1405, appears to have been followed out in practice in the schools of the Revival: "We are told that the Greeks devised for their sons a course of training in four subjects: letters, gymnastics, music and drawing. Now, of these drawing has no place among our liberal studies; except in so far as it is identical with writing (which is in reality one side of the art of Drawing), it belongs to the Painter's profession: the Greeks, as an art-loving people attached to it an exceptional value."[109]

Even though Italy was soon to become intensely art-loving, the geniuses that suddenly transformed her into a paradise of beauty were, in all truth, "born, not made." They cultivated their gifts independently of the schools, and helped themselves by the private study of geometry and the practice of drawing.[110]

The Italian girl might not prove her genius in this practical way, but she gave at least proof of her artistic sense by her just

---

[105] Cartwright, *Beatrice d'Este*, 37.
[106] *Supra*, 10ff.
[107] Cf. Cartwright *op. cit.*; Ady, *His. of Milan under the Sforza*, 290. London, 1907.
[108] *Ibid.*
[109] *Op. cit.*
[110] Cf. Rio, *De l'Art Chrétien*, Paris, 1874; Vasari, *Le Vite de' più eccellenti pittori, scoltori et architetti*. Bologna, 1647.

appreciation of the works of the great masters.   The Renaissance court became a veritable art gallery through the patronage extended to painters and sculptors and to the master-architects of the Revival.[111]

In such an environment the girl found inspiration and developed the conscious power of interpreting the thoughts and feelings embodied in the forms of beauty that surrounded her.   This aesthetic education produced such keen critics and enthusiastic patrons as Vittoria Colonna and Isabella d'Este.

But there was still another branch of art open to the girl—one in which she possessed peculiar advantages over her brother; for in the Renaissance days beautiful needlework was not only prized and procured at much cost and trouble but it was taught in the household as a branch of domestic science and as a fine art.

When we find the little girl deftly plying the embroidery needle before she is 6, we understand the skill with which the maiden in her teens planned the patterns for her gowns and for the ornamental designs upon them in which she took so much pure pleasure.[112]

In the occasional glimpses into the Italian household which the family records afford us we see the girl diligently occupied with her sewing when not busy with her books or taking exercise in the open air.

The little Piero de'Medici, son of the great Lorenzo, while practicing his Latin under the eye of Poliziano, thus gives his father an account of his sisters: "Maddelena knocks her head against the wall but does not hurt herself.   Lucia can already say a few things.   Contessina makes a great noise all over the house. Lucrezia sews, sings and reads."[113]

At Mantua, the great Elisabetta Gonzaga, the future Duchess of Urbino, and her sister Maddelena are still mere children when their governess writes to the Marquis Federico, their father: "You will be glad to hear that both your illustrious daughters are well and happy and very obedient, so that it is a real pleasure to see them with their books and embroidery."[114]

[111] Ibid.
[112] Cartwright, Isabella d'Este.
[113] Hare, op. cit., 68.
[114] Luzio e Renier, Mantova e Urbino, 6.

In the household entries of Ferrara is the significant item: "Two bone needles and one gold needle for Madonna Isabella's embroidery."[115]

Physical Culture

While this spirit of quiet industry and premature seriousness would seem to indicate an undue physical and mental restraint, it is evident from parallel records that this was far from being the case. The Renaissance girl enjoyed freedom and liberty, and her physical needs were carefully provided for.

On this important subject of physical training, in so far as it concerns the education of girls, the theorists are silent. But the harmonious development of body and mind is a principle strongly insisted upon in the general treatises of the humanist educators. Here we find counsels on the practice of self-restraint and self-denial from motives of virtue, and advice on the cheerful endurance of privation as a means of securing to the boy the hardihood becoming the future soldier.

For the girl, like principles held. While she was spared the hardships attendant on wars, she was not exempt from the inconveniences occasioned by political changes, and even in peaceful times, necessary journeys alone called for the spirit of heroic endurance.[116] Hence her need of discipline in the power of physical resistance.

Physical training in both these aspects was advocated by the humanist in common with his immediate predecessors in the field of education, but to these two ideas he added a third; namely, the Greek system of regular exercise to secure grace and freedom of movement, with health and strength of limb.[117] For the girl this end was attained by means of ample outdoor exercise and by the assiduous cultivation of the classical dance.

The Greek dance was evidently cultivated at Ferrara in the days of Niccolo d'Este, but we find no record of a regular dancing master at this court until 1480, nearly thirty years after Strozzi's account of the graces exhibited by Bianca in this art.[118] In this year a Jewish master, who had previously taught dancing at the court of Urbino, was employed by Ercole d'Este to give his

[115] "Registro de' Mandati," 48. Cited in Cartwright, *Isabella d'Este*, I, 10.
[116] Cf. Cartwright, *op. cit.*; Ady, *op. cit.*
[117] Cf. Aeneas Sylvius, "De Liberorum Educatione." Translated by Woodward, *op. cit.*, 138; Vergerio, *Ibid.*, 113.
[118] Tiraboschi, *op. cit.*, Vol. VI, Pt. III, p. 853.

daughters lessons, as we learn from a letter to the Marquis Federigo Gonzaga in which his envoy says that he had seen Isabella dance with her master, Messer Ambrogio, a Jew in the Duke of Urbino's service, and that the grace and elegance of her movements were amazing in one of her tender age. When this letter was written Isabella was six.[119]

Another dancing master, Lorenzo Lavagnola, was employed by Ercole d'Este for some time, after he had taught in Mantua and Milan. This teacher was commended to Bona, Duchess of Milan, by Barbara, the wife of Lodovico Gonzaga, who, from the age of ten, was brought up at the court of Mantua and educated with Cecilia, her future sister-in-law.[120]

Whether Cecilia and Barbara had these systematic dancing lessons in the school of Vittorino, does not appear, but Barbara recommended this teacher of her grand-daughters, and very probably of her daughters, to Bona of Savoy as superior to all other masters of the art of dancing.[121]

Lavagnola not only taught dancing but directed the theatricals given on family festive occasions and arranged little plays for the children. In these theatricals the dance was a feature of special interest and received careful preparation. In these dances the children attached to the court took part as they did in the choruses and processions,[122] so frequent on Church festivals and other state occasions.

The importance attached to physical culture, purely as culture, is manifest in the value set on its possession as we find it expressed not only by the poets and painters of the time, to whom must of necessity be allowed a certain license, but in the intimate correspondence of serious men and women.

Lucrezia Tornabuoni, wife of Piero de'Medici, writing to her husband from Rome where she is seeking the acquaintance of Clarice Orsini, the future bride of her son Lorenzo, says: "She doesn't carry her head well as our girls do, but lets it droop a little forward, which I think is due to her timidity." And in her maternal pride she concludes that Clarice is "far above the ordinary, but not to be compared to Maria, Lucrezia and Bianca."[123]

---

[119] Cartwright, *Isabella d'Este*, I, 12.
[120] Kristeller, "Barbara von Brandenburg" in *Hohenzollern Jahrbuch*, 1899, 66.
[121] Cartwright, *Beatrice d'Este*, 37.
[122] *Ibid.*
[123] Del Lungo, *op. cit.*, 233, note 41.

The Italian humanists were so fortunate in climatic conditions and in the location of their buildings, that the problem of indoor gymnasiums would have been an anomalous one. Free open-air life was the precious inheritance of the Italian child and the Renaissance educators had but to leave him in possession of his freedom. The obligatory exercises were consequently held on the grounds allotted to the schools.

The girl enjoyed the same rights as the boy in this respect. In the days of Vittorino da Feltre we find the little Cecilia Gonzaga with her brothers, riding out in the pleasant air and sunshine in the company of their beloved tutor;[124] and later on other Gonzaga children roved over the same spacious meadows on foot or on horseback in the company of their pet dogs and fawns. Writing of two of these, Elisabetta and Maddelena, the grand-nieces of Cecilia, their governess says: "They enjoy riding the new pony, one on saddle, the other on pillion. . . . They are quite delighted with it and your Excellency could not have sent them anything which would please them more."[125]

In the family group outside of Florence, the Medici girls must have had a share in the joy brought by the gifts which Lorenzo made to the young Piero after receiving his begging letters: "I wish you would send me some of the best setters that there are, I do not desire anything else. . . . Something must have happened to the horse because if it had been all right you would have sent it to me as you promised. In case that one cannot come please send me another."[126]

The girls of Naples and Ferrara enjoyed their outdoor sports if one may judge from the zest with which Beatrice d'Este entered into the life of Milan in company with Isabella d'Aragona, the daughter of Ippolita Sforza. When Beatrice was married to Lodovico Sforza she was only fifteen and her girlhood exercises were very naturally continued. Expeditions on horseback, fishing, hunting, playing ball for recreation after the refection at the water's edge, and the chorus singing on the way, are all in keeping with the spirit of the Revival as we find it expressed in the writings of the theorists and exemplified at Florence and Mantua.[127]

---

[124] Woodward, *op. cit.*, 66.
[125] Luzio e Renier, *op. cit.*, 6.
[126] Hare, *op. cit.*, 68.
[127] Cartwright, *Beatrice d'Este*, 81.

Morality and Religious Practice

But while mind and body were thus harmoniously developed the girl's moral and religious training was not neglected.   Although the Church did not directly establish these private domestic schools she governed them by right of her spiritual authority, a right not questioned by the men who founded these schools or by those whose patronage or labor maintained them.

Nor was her jurisdiction over them merely temporal.   Her rule was exercised through the moral influence of her teaching and by means of the encouragement and assistance arising from the patronage extended by the Soverign Pontiffs and other churchmen to the promoters of the true Renaissance, as well as from their attitude towards the educated women of their day.[128]

Enlightened by faith and directed by supernatural motives, such humanist schoolmasters as Vittorino da Feltre promoted religious practice among their pupils and stimulated devotion, both by precept and example.   The court chapel or the near-by church was regularly attended by the entire body of teachers and students. Daily Mass and the frequentation of the sacraments, sermons and instructions and prayers recited in common, all helped to form habits of virtue and piety.[129]

In these schools, Religion was queen.   Her court was graced by the presence of the New Learning, but she was far from abdicating in favor of her honored guest.   The regrets expressed by educators laboring under less happy conditions are not to be found in the writings of the Italian humanists.   The cooperation of parents and of the Church created obligations and granted liberties by virtue of which the work in the classroom was not limited, either by choice or by necessity, to an aim which could find "no higher purpose than that of determining for each individual the things in this life best worth living for."[130]

While their study of the ancients showed these humanists the futility of attempting to substantiate the claims of knowledge, when defined in terms of virtue, yet they had other convictions which taught them that morality must either drop out of a girl's life or be fostered by religion.

---

[128] Cf. Pastor, *op. cit.*
[129] Cf. Vespasiano, *Vite de Uomini Illustri del secolo XV.*   Firenze, 1859.
[130] Monroe, *Text Book in Hist. of Ed.*, 59.   New York, 1912.

By means of the teaching of Christian Doctrine and Ethics the humanists determined for her the things in both this life and the next best worth living for, but they were not satisfied with this. That they might secure the application of this knowledge in right doing they saw to it that the essential elements of religion and morality were bound up with her mental and physical development. To this end stress was laid upon the cultivation of moral and religious sentiments in the study of the classical languages and other related subjects, just as in the teaching of music and in physical culture.

In his enthusiasm for ancient literature, D'Arezzo did not lose sight of this. Summing up his theories he says: "None have more urgent claim than the subjects and authors which treat of Religion and of our duties in the world; and it is because they assist and illustrate these supreme studies that I press upon your attention the works of the most approved poets, historians and orators of the past."[131]

But beyond the strength of the theory was the personal power of the teacher, who understood how to mingle philosophy and religion with his lessons in Latin and Greek, and by means of the study of men and things to "lead the soul back to God."

This loyalty of the Renaissance schoolmaster to the standard of morals raised by the early theorists, enabled later humanistic writers to express their convictions on this point with greater assurance.

In 1450, Aeneas Sylvius takes for granted that Humanism has produced perfectly cultured mothers to serve as models for their sons, whose educational interests he is considering:[132] and in 1460, Maffeo Vegio could appeal to experience when he asserted that the study of the classics should be a help rather than a hindrance to the girl in her study and practice of virtue and religion.[133]

Added to these powerful influences of the Church and the schoolroom was that of family environment in which the young Renaissance girl found peculiar inspiration. The daily companionship of brothers and sisters tempered her nature and strengthened her character, while the watchful love of a wise and tender mother and a devoted father directed her progress in

---

[131] *Op. cit.*
[132] *Op. cit.*
[133] Cf. Kopp, "Mapheus Vegius und Aneas Sylvius," in *Bibliothek der katholischen Pädagogik*, II. Freiburg, 1889.

virtue and knowledge.   For her coeducation was thus stripped of
its disadvantages and robbed of its dangers.   With the safeguards
provided by this combination of happy circumstances she could
lend herself to every intellectual and human interest without
sacrificing the peculiar graces of her feminine nature not endanger-
ing her spiritual well-being.

At the passing away of the larger home schools, when the
ducal families declined, the convent became the natural center of
the new influence.   The tendency among the women educated
under humanism to embrace the life of the cloister was not diminished in Italy during the sixteenth century.   The older orders of
nuns thus strengthened their efficiency in the work of education,
while new orders sprang up.   Early in this century St. Angela de
Merici founded the Order of Ursulines for the express purpose of
educating girls.   This was the first exclusively teaching order
established in the Church, and it took its spirit from the attitude
of the times towards the higher education of women.[134]

---

[134] Catholic Encyclopedia, *The Ursulines*; Cf. Heimbucher, *Die Orden und
Kongregationen der katholischen Kirche*, Paderborn, 1907-08; Hèlyot, *Histoire
des Ordres Monastiques, Religieux et Militaires*, Paris, 1714-19.

CHAPTER II

In the history of the Italian Revival is seen woman's perfect equality with man in the Republic of Learning—an equality to which the princes of that republic generously invited her, notwithstanding their power to withhold from her the traditional rights of her social inheritance. In Spain this same equality characterized the movement, but with this difference, that here the power of patronage rested more largely with woman herself—that through her were extended to the martial lords of dying feudalism the advantages of the revived culture when it first passed on from Italy to the Peninsula.

That the age of Isabel of Castile should correspond to the Golden Age of Italian humanism is significant. Had the pioneer humanists of Spain lacked the attitude of the true Revival toward womankind, they would have met with an insurmountable obstacle to success in the opposition of a powerful sovereign, but, in the spirit of the Italian Renaissance, the school of Spanish humanists proudly placed at their head, in reverence and honor, her who was at one and the same time the Queen-Leader of the nation's armies and the Queen-Mother of its fondest hopes.

The history of the Peninsula Renaissance makes it evident that, if Isabel the Catholic stands forth in the world's annals as the type of womanly perfection during the Quattrocento, that fact is due less to her superiority of intellect over her contemporary sisters than to her superiority of inherited position. Intellectual she was and learned—as gifted in mind and heart as were the daughters of more favored Italy, but the duties of queenhood, in calling forth her many-sided genius, gave her the added advantage of a strong and gifted personality reinforced by the power of delegated authority. Profiting by these favorable conditions, the student queen worked hand in hand with those humanists who were, either by birth or by education, possessed of Italian sympathies and who sought, under her patronage, to spread the blessings of the Revival throughout united Spain.

It is true that Isabel neither founded universities nor established public colleges, as did her immediate successors on the throne, yet

51

it is equally true that she gave to the dawning Revival that which
conditions imperatively demanded—liberty to propagate itself and
adequate means for such propagation.   To her fostering was due
the hardy rooting and steady growth of humanistic learning among
the nobility of Spain.   Her patronage extended to individual
humanists, both in the existing universities and in the private
schools, which here as elsewhere were the natural centers of pioneer
humanistic endeavor.[135]

It is to one of these humanists, the Italian, Marineo of Sicily,
that we are indebted for the record of the literary accomplishments
of Queen Isabel, as well as for the best testimony of the esteem in
which she was held by men of learning and the influence which she
exercised over the labors of the humanists of Spain.

"She spoke the Castilian," he says, "with ease and elegance and
with much gravity, and although she lacked the Latin tongue she
listened with pleasure to Latin sermons and discourses."   With
the true humanistic touch he adds: "She loved to hear the Latin
eloquently rendered."[136]   When the cares of war were over, Isabel
applied herself to the study of grammar and such was her progress,
says the chronicler, that "In quibus per unius anni spacium tantum
profecit, ut non solum Latinos oratores intelligere, sed etiam libros
interpretari facile poterat."[137]

This account is corroborated by the statement of Peter Martyr
of Anghiera, that, as Ferdinand had been obliged to go to the wars
when he was about to take up the study of grammar, Isabel did him
the service of translating the letters addressed to him by that
savant.[138]

In view of the fact that Isabel was herself so enthusiastic a
humanist it is not surprising to find a long line of truly famous
women—teachers, writers, poets, scientists, artists, and musicians
who flourished throughout the history of the Peninsular Revival.
The works of modern writers have not extended the fame of these
Iberian women of the fifteenth and sixteenth centuries far beyond
the borders of Spanish territory; with the exception of the makers

---

[135] *Supra.*   Cf. Marineo, *De Rebus Hispaniae Memorabilibus*, Alcalá, 1533.
Ibid., Spanish Ed., Alcalá, 1539; Florez, *Mem. de las Reynas Católicas*,
Madrid, 1790; *Mem. de la Real Acad. de la Hist.*, VI, Madrid, 1821; Altimira
y Crevea, *Hist. de España y de la Civilización Española*, II, Barcelona, 1902.
[136] Marineo, *De Rebus Hispaniae Memorabilibus*, Lib. XXI, Fol. 122.
Alcalá, 1533.
[137] *Ibid.*
[138] Mariéjol, *Pierre Martyr D'Anghera*, 35ff, IV, Paris, 1887.

of history, Isabel of Castile and Catherine of Aragon, and the world-renowned saint, Teresa of Jesus, little has been printed concerning them outside their native land. But true to the chivalrous instinct inherited from Christian tradition, Spanish historians have kept alive the memory of the achievements attained by the noble daughters of their race, and Spanish poets have sung their praises with the reverence born of candid admiration.

As types of all that was noblest and best in these followers of the great Queen Isabel, her own illustrious daughters should hold the first rank. But as their history belongs rather to the lands of their adoption we shall first consider here the life and character of the woman famous in Spanish annals as the Queen's Latin tutor and cherished companion, Beatriz Galindo, surnamed from her scholarship, *La Latina*. Born in Salamanca in 1475, Beatriz was descended from the Galindos of Andalusia, her biographers agreeing that she had her name from the family of her mother, her father being a "cabellero" named Gricio, who, after the death of his wife, took the habit in the Order of St. Augustine. It is also shown that Beatriz was sister to Gasper de Gricio, secretary of Ferdinand and Isabel.

At court, as tutor to the Queen, La Latina won general esteem for her virtues and learning. In 1495 she was given by the sovereigns in marriage to Don Francisco Ramirez, a widower, whose first wife was Isabel of Oviedo, and who was then lord of the house of Ramirez of Madrid. In 1501 he was killed in battle against the Moriscos, and Beatriz hastened to complete the founding of projected institutions of mercy perpetuating her memory and that of her husband.

Among these is the Hospital of the Conception of Madrid, and a school for poor young ladies, similar to Madame de Maintenon's foundation of Saint-Cyr. This school Beatriz herself directed after the death of the Queen, until she finally handed it over to the Franciscan Sisters in 1512. From her estates she founded other institutions, as the monastery of nuns of the Concepcion Jerónima, in the street of that name, and the convent of Trinitarians of Malaga, a city which owed its conquest to the valor of her husband.

While occupied with these works of charity and zeal, La Latina continued to study and teach, personally directing the work, not only in the first school, in Toledo Street and the plaza of the Cebada, but also in the convent of the Concepcion Jerónima, which she made

her home until her death.   She was interred in the chancel of the
church of this convent, beside her husband.[139]

Both her tomb and that which she had built for Lord Ramirez
are sumptuous marble sepulchres, monuments of Renaissance style
which surpass in beauty and richness all others of the kind in
Madrid.   The inscription reads: "Here lies Beatriz Galindo, who,
after the death of the Catholic Queen, retired, into this monastery
and into the Franciscan monastery of the Conception, of this city,
where she spent herself in good works until her death, in 1534."[140]

But few of the writings of La Latina have been preserved.
Among the collection of the Dukes of Rivas are mentioned, *Anno-
tations on the Ancient Classical Writers: a Commentary on Aristotle*:
and *Miscellaneous Poems*.[141]

Among the many eulogies of La Latina's virtues and talents,
that of Lope de Vega is unique:

> "Like to Latina
> Whom scarcely the gaze can determine
> Whether pure mind
> Or woman indeed as it seemeth.
> Learned, with modesty clothèd
> And holy in courts all too human.
> To what heights will she venture unaided
> Whose end is the God of her being![142]

Another teacher by profession, like La Latina, but unlike her, a
lecturer in the University, was Francisca de Lebrija.   This gifted
daughter of the great Spanish humanist of that name, enjoys the
distinction of a history briefly told but full of significance.   Her
father's right hand in his literary labors, she proved her claim to
learning by acting as substitute for him in his chair of humanities at
Alcalá whenever his infirmities or preoccupations rendered it
desirable.   This fact has led her biographers to conjecture that she
may have had a share in the authorship of the works produced by

---

[139] Parada, *Escritoras y Eruditas Españolas*, 127 ff. Madrid, 1881.
[140] Rada y Delgado, *Mugeres célebres de España y Portugal*, II., 351.
Barcelona, 1868.
[141] Parada, *Ibid.*; Cf. Antonio, *Bibliotheca Hispana Nova*, II, 346, Matriti,
1788; *Mem. de la Real Acad. de la Hist.*, Vol. VI, Il. XVI.
[142] *Laurel de Apolo*, silva 5:

> "Como á aquella Latina
> Que apenas nuestra vista determina
> Si fué mujer ó inteligencia pura:
> Docta con hermosura
> Y santa en lo difícil de la corte;
> Mas¿qué no hará quien tiene á Dios por norte?

Lebrija. There seems, however, no warrant for the conjecture, if we except the indication that, notwithstanding her ability, she left on record no literary productions of her own, as did many of her contemporaries.[143]

By far the most remarkable and the best known among these contemporaries of the daughter of Lebrija is the Latin tutor at the Court of Portugal, Luisa Sigea.[144] Luisa was a native of Toledo. Her father, Diego Sigea, was at first preceptor of the Duke of Braganza, and later of the other children of the royal family of Portugal. It was as teacher of the Infanta Maria, daughter of Don Manuel, and of the Spanish Infanta, Dª Leonor, then at the Court of Portugal, that "La Sigea" rendered her greatest services to the cause of humanism. Under her direction and through her inspiration, the court became a center of culture and the rendezvous of enthusiastic students such as were the learned Portuguese ladies who surrounded the Infanta Maria.

As proof of the linguistic talents of this remarkable woman it suffices to refer to the letter which she sent to Pope Paul III, in 1546, written in five languages: Latin, Greek, Hebrew, Arabic, and Syriac.

In this same year she produced a Latin poem, "Sintra," a description of the Portuguese town of that name. It was published in Paris in 1566, under the auspices of the French ambassador to the court of Portugal. The poem consists of one hundred and eight lines, in imitation of Vergil. The following passage is characteristic:

> "Hic philomena canit, turtur gemit atque columba:
> Nidificant volucres, quotquot ad astra volant,
> Silva avium cantu resonat, florentia subtus
> Prata rosas pariunt, liliaque et violas,
> Fragantemque thimon, mentam roremque marinum,
> Narcissum et neptam, basylicumque sacrum:
> Atque alios flores, ramos heroasque virentes,
> Terra creat pinguis vallibus ac nemore;
> Queis passim Dryades capiti cinxere corollas,
> Et Fauni et Nymphae cornigerique Dei."[145]

Two of the poet's epigrams are extant, one of which is the following, with this inscription:

---

[143] Parada, op. cit., 132; Mem. de la Real Acad. de la Hist., Vol. VI, Il. XVI.
[144] Parada, op. cit., 136 ff.
[145] Lines 29–38. Quoted in Parada, op. cit., 143.

"In Aquilam, cui torquem aureum
Maria Infans parabat, Loisiae Sigeae.

Epigramma

"Desine, diva, precor, mirare desine: Quid me
Coelitus huc missam maesta redire vetas?
Quid volueris tentas innectere vincula collo?
In plumis aquilae forsan olor venio."[146]

The other epigram was dedicated to Jerónimo Britonio. Besides
these, another work of poetry is attributed to La Sigea, and a
dialogue on the contrast of country life and city life. As many as
thirty-three of her letters are extant, containing valuable information on her life and labors. Some of these are addressed to Philip
II, others to the Queen of Hungary and others to her brother-in-law,
Alfonso de la Cueva. Parada gives Cerdan y Rico as authority
for the statement that these letters are preserved in the Royal
Library of Madrid.

A very objectionable poem, published under the name of Luisa
Sigea, was circulated in the North, for the sole purpose of dis-
honoring her name and that of Luis Vives which was connected
with that of Sigea in the dialogue. This work, one of many such
libels spread broadcast at that period, has been attributed to different authors, more particularly to one John Westmore, of Holland.
The research undertaken by numerous friends of the injured parties
resulted in a complete vindication of their innocence and established
more firmly than ever the reputation of the learned and virtuous
author of "Sintra." The fact that Vives was one of the Latin
correspondents of La Sigea may have given rise to the libel.

When leaving court, at the age of thirty, Luisa married a gentleman of Burgos, Francisco de Cuevas, who was for some time secretary to Maria, Queen of Hungary and Bohemia. She afterwards
resided in Burgos until her death on the 13th of October, 1560.
Her only daughter, Juana de Cuevas, married Don Rodrigo Ron-
quillo, and was the mother of several children who proudly bore
the honors descending from their illustrious grandmother. Two
of these distinguished themselves in the Philippines; the one, Luis,
as vicar-general of the Augustinians, and the other, Gonzalo, in the
army.

At the time of her death, her husband gave testimony of her
worth in this epitaph:

---

[146] *Ibid.*, 142.

D. O. M.

Loisiae Sigeae foeminae incomparabili cuyus pudicitia cum eruditione linguarum quae in ea ad miraculum usque fuit, ex aequo
certabat, Franciscus Cuevas moerentissimi conjugi B. M. P. valle
[Vale] beata animula conjugi dum vivet perpetuae lachrimae.[147]

Luisa's sister, Angela, shared her labors at the Portuguese court
and was also a poet.   She seems to have left no writings, but was
especially gifted in music.   She married Antonio Mogo de Melo and
lived in Torres Vedras, a small town of Portugal.[148]

Another learned woman at the court of Spain, and one whose
talents place her beside La Sigea and La Latina, is Ana Cervató.[149]
She was of the household of Queen Germana de Foix, and corre
sponded in Latin with Lucio Marineo.   Her knowledge of the
classics was extensive and she proved her love for Latin eloquence
by reciting from memory all of Cicero's orations.

Ana was a Catalan and descended from a noble family of Sardinia.
Her hand was sought by the Duke of Alba, whose suit Marineo
pressed in a letter to her in which he extols her virtues and learning
and the virtues of the Duke.   This letter is a good specimen of the
esteem shown by humanists for women who were at once learned and
virtuous.   It bears the salutation: "L. Marinaeus Siculus Annae
Cervatoniae Virgini Pulcherrimae Sal. Plur. D.," and the date:
"Ex Burgis pridie idus Octobris anno MDXII."

To the very flattering comparison which the writer established
between the gifts of the learned lady and those of the heroines of
ancient history and mythology, she ingeniously replies: "Nos enim
Palladi, Hebe, Veneri, atque Helenae, quas divinis honoribus ipsa
donavit antiquitas, longe cedimus.   Nymphas etiam, clarasque
prisci temporis puellas minime aequamus.   Serenissimae vero
Germanae Reginae domum tantum abest ut illustrare possim, ut
facilius intelligam obscurum sydus, sole pulcherrime radiante, diei
addere posse splendorem."

Referring to the other ladies at the court of Queen Germana she
says: "Reliquae etiam Palatinae virgines tanta forma ac nitore
praestant, ut inter eas ego, qualis nunc inter splendentes sorores
Electra calligat."

These passages also reveal the nature of the style of this Spanish
woman, writing at the dawn of the sixteenth century.[150]

---

[147] Parada, *op. cit.*, 136 ff; Antonio, *op. cit.*, II, 71.
[148] Parada, *op. cit.*, 135.
[149] Or Cervaton.
[150] Antonio, *op. cit.*, II, 344 ff; Parada, *op. cit.*, 130.

Another correspondent of Marineo was Luisa Medrano, a native of Salamanca where she held the chair of humanities.[151]   Like Ana Cervató, Luisa enjoyed the esteem of the historiographer who compared her to the Muses and to the women philosophers in the school of Pythagoras.   But she merited better praise, for in the same letter addressed to her, Marineo salutes her as "Puella doctissima," and says of her, "quae supra viros in litteris et eloquentia caput extulisti."[152]

Another learned woman, Catalina Paz, of Estremadura, was given prizes and ovations in Alcalá and Seville for her Latin poetry. She is highly praised by Matamoros, who extols her above Cornelia and the other Roman ladies of antiquity.   Lamenting her premature death, which occurred in Guadalajara, when she was twenty-seven, he says: "Heu, quae ingenii vena illo die ad summan gloriam eloquentiae florescens exaruit?   Quos poesis fontes subito fortuna prostravit?   Quae non litterae politiores cum illa mortuae, et sepultae fuerunt?[153]   Catalina translated into Latin the work of Hurtado de Mendoza, entitled, "El buen placer trobado en trece discantes de cuarta rima castellana."   The translation was printed in Alcala in 1550.[154]

Ana Osorio, like Catalina Paz, was awarded prizes for her Latin poetry in Alcalá and Seville.   Little is now known of her life, but she is supposed to have been the daughter of D. Diego de Osorio, Lord of Abarca and Governor of Burgos, who was Master of the Drawingroom at the court of the Empress Isabella.   In this case she would be descended through her mother, Isabel de Rojas, from the marquises of Poza.   Matamoros praises, not only her poetic gifts, but her extensive knowledge of theology.[155]

Another woman of the sixteenth century, remarkable for varied accomplishments, was Doña Lorenza Mendez de Zurita.   She was a native of Madrid and wife of D. Tomás Gracian Dantisco who was a writer and a member of the illustrious family of the Gracianes. This noble lady is remembered for her domestic virtues and her solid piety, as well as for her talents.   She spoke Latin fluently and wrote it with ease whether in prose or verse.   Her knowledge of

---

[151] "donde tuvo cátedra de humanidades"—(Parada).
[152] Parada, op. cit., 132; Antonio, op. cit., II, 351.
[153] Matamoros, "De Academiis et doctis viris Hispaniae."   Quoted in, de la Fuente, Hist. de las Universidades, Colegios, etc., II, App. 31, sec. 12, Madrid 1884–89.
[154] Parada—op. cit., 146.
[155] Parada, op. cit., 145; Antonio, op. cit., II, 346.

rhetoric and mathematics and of other branches of study is highly
commended, as well as her skill in music, both in singing and in
playing the harp and other instruments. She composed sacred
hymns but does not seem to have published any of her writings.
Of these, and of her virtues, Lope de Vega says:

> "She wrote sacred hymns
> In verses as divine.
>
> . . . .
>
> Adding to her genius grace of soul—
> Grace of virtue that eternally endures."[156]

This learned woman died in 1599. Her remains were interred in
the Carthusian monastery of Aniago, near Valladolid.[157]

A still more remarkable type of maternal devotedness and love
of wisdom was Doña Cecilia Morillas. She was born in Salamanca
in 1538, a descendant of the family of Enriquez. At an early age
she married D. Antonio Sobrino, a learned Portuguese who then
lived in Valladolid. Of the nine children of this marriage the two
daughters became Carmelite nuns;[158] one son, Francisco, was
Bishop of Valladolid; another, José, was the learned chaplain and
tutor of the Royal Family; a third, Juan, was a celebrated physician; a fourth, Antonio, renounced the honors of a successful
career at law to become a Franciscan Friar in the same monastery
where his brother, Tomás, was a shining light of genius. The remaining two sons, Fr. Diego de San José and Fr. Sebastian de
San Cirilo, were distinguished members of the Order of Mt. Carmel.

Such careers on the part of the children were the result of the
training which they had recived from Doña Cecilia. Having been
invited by Philip II to fill the office of governess and tutor of the
Royal Family, she declined, in order to be able to devote all her
time and talents to the bringing up of her own children, and such
were the breadth of her knowledge and the power of her personality
that all her sons and daughters received from her their youthful
training. Her biographers credit this learned woman with an
education which comprised Latin, Greek, Italian and French, the
humanities and philosophy; theology, cosmography and practical
geography; music, designing and painting. She is said to have
constructed maps and globes, very accurate and very beautiful.

---

[156] *Laurel de Apolo*, silva 1.
[157] Parada, *op. cit.*, 146 ff.; Antonio, *op. cit.*, II, 350.
[158] *Infra*, 71.

This life, full of labors and fruitful in good works was brought to an early close on the 21st of October, 1581, Doña Cecilia being then but forty-three.[159]

That Greek literature was not slow in gaining favor with the Spanish women is evident from the large numbers of students whom we find taking it up in addition to Latin. Like Cecilia Morillas, another matron of the sixteenth century, Angela Mercader Zapata found time for both the classical languages, for philosophy and theology. This woman, whom Vives praises for learning and virtue,[160] was wife of Gerónimo Escribá de Romani, a professor of the humanities in Valentia, and mother of the Jesuit, Francisco de Escribá. The most learned men of her time are said to have consulted her on points of theology, and her home was a center of literary and philosophical reunions, where the professors and students of Valentia held with her scientific discussions. She had collected a large and rich library which she generously opened to her literary friends, and she passed on in like manner her own store of wisdom and information to her gifted son. She left no published works but some authorities suggest that her manuscripts assisted materially the labors of Francisco de Escribá in his famous work "De Novissimis."[161]

Other Greek scholars of the sixteenth century were Geronima Ribot, of Valentia;[162] Catalina de Rivera, who belonged to the family of the dukes of Alcalá;[163] Catalina Trillo, of Antequera, an excellent poet, who married Gonzalo de Ocon, and was mother of Juan Ocon, a professor at Salamanca, and of Bartolome Ocon, an ecclesiastical canon;[164] Maria Urrea, daughter of the Count of Aranda and wife of D. Diego Enriquez de Guzman, fifth count of Alba de Liste.[165]

To Latin and Greek some of the Spanish women of this century added an extensive study of Hebrew. Among these may be mentioned Isabel Vergara, of Toledo, whose brothers were professors of Greek and Hebrew in Alcalá, and who is said to have been "as learned as her brothers." This says much, for they both,

[159] Parada, *op. cit.*, 176.
[160] "De Institutione Christianae Foeminae," *Opera*, Vol. II, Lib. I, p. 655. Basileae, 1555.
[161] Parada, *op. cit.*, 189.
[162] Parada, *op. cit.*, 153; Antonio, *op. cit.*, II, 350.
[163] Parada, *Ibid.*, 154; Antonio, *Ibid*, 348.
[164] Parada, *Ibid.*; Antonio, *Ibid.*, 349.
[165] *Ibid.*, Parada, 155; Antonio, 352.

Juan and Francisco, did good service to Cardinal Ximenes in the work of the Polyglot Bible.[166]

A remarkable instance of the general desire for knowledge among the women of Spain, is that of a poor girl of Seville, "Doña Marcelina." This girl mastered, apparently without assistance, Latin, Greek, Hebrew, Italian and mathematics while living in poverty and obscurity in the parish at St. Vincent of Seville.[167]

Doña Oliva Sabuco de Nantes offers another striking example of the power of intellect exhibited by the women of the Renaissance. She is styled by one of her biographers as "writer, philosopher, and naturalist; honor and pride of Spanish letters, a most wonderful illustration of the aptitude and genius of the mind of woman."[168]

And this estimate is supported by the testimony of numerous other Spanish writers who have made her life and work a subject of study, whether to give her a passing mention or a treatment more or less detailed.[169]

That this woman had schooling cannot be questioned, but what she had been taught of the languages and sciences she effectively applied in individual study and research. Without having actually pursued the study of medicine in the universities, she produced a work on medical science, "Nueva Filosofía." accepted with enthusiasm in Spain, and circulated in foreign parts, where it served as a guide, incognito, to physicians and students alike.[170]

Feijóo y Montenegro interprets the motive of the author, as being, in the words of his translator, "to convince them, that the physics, and medicinal doctrines, which were taught in the schools, went all on erroneous principles."[171] The most important position which Doña Oliva maintains is that of the true relation of the functions of the organism to the functions of thought. From this position she argues that the preservation of health is in no small measure dependent upon brain and nerve stimuli.

If we may judge from the very detailed index, which alone is accessible, and from her own exposition of the work, as well as that

---

[166] Parada, *Ibid.*, 190.
[167] Parada, *op. cit.*, 191.
[168] *Ibid.*, 157 ff.
[169] Cf. Feijóo y Montenegro, *Theatro critico universal.* Translated as "A Defence or Vindication of the Women," in *Three Essays, etc.*, by "A Gentleman," 82, London, 1778; Rada y Delgado, *op. cit.*, II; *Mem. de la Real Acad. de la Hist.*, VI; Antonio, *op. cit.*, II.
[170] Parada, *op. cit.*, 162 ff.
[171] *Ibid.*

given by her biographers, Oliva contributed very substantially to the sciences of biology, psychology, and anthropology, and through these to the sciences of medicine, sociology and agriculture. Her discourses on the nature and functions of the nerves and brain are the most remarkable. From her views on pathological psychology and anthropology she maintains that the study of man's nature is the true foundation for the study of medicine.

The author treats of the emotions and passions from the characteristic point of view of the humanist. There are chapters on such topics as the following: Joy, contentment and gaiety, which form one of the three pillars that sustain human life and health; Expectation of good, one of the columns which sustain the health of man and accomplish all the works of man; Temperance and fortitude, the mistress and governess of the health of man; that friendships and agreeable conversation are necessary in this life; of the evil effects of loneliness; of the beneficial effects of music, which cheers and strengthens the brain and gives health in infirmity.

Rules of everyday hygiene are likewise laid down: Of food, drink and sleep; of strenuous activity of the soul or body after eating; of improvements in nutriments. Under "Ornaments of the Soul," she treats of the virtue of magnanimity, of prudence, the "mother of the virtues;" of wisdom, "the most precious ornament of the soul." She treats questions of politics and sociology under the following heads: Things which improve the world and its republics; Improvements in laws and litigations; Improvements in the condition of the poor and the laboring classes; Improvements in regard to marriages, births and public chastity.

In her treatises on Agriculture she discusses the importance and means of water supply for irrigation and the fisheries; the nature of plants and the propagation of new plant species; the care of vines; the preservation of decadent species of sheep; the destruction of locusts.[172] Her discourses on astronomy and geology have also a direct bearing on the science of farming.

The entire work is divided into seven parts, or treatises, developed in the form of dialogues or colloquies between different philosophers professing divinity or medicine. The first five treatises are written in Castilian, the last two in Latin. The first edition of the work

---

[172] Cf. Anton Ramirez, *Diccionario de Bibliografía Argonómica y de tode clase de escritos relacionados con la agriculturs,* "Sabuco de Nantes Barrera, Doña Oliva," Madrid, 1865.

appears to have been published in Madrid, in 1587. Another edition was published in the same city the next year, 1588, in four volumes. In 1622 there was another edition in Braga, and in 1728 still another in Madrid. This last lacked the matter suppressed by the Inquisition in 1707. These expurgata were slight and unimportant.[173]

The following is the title page of this edition: "Nueva filosofía de la naturaleza del hombre no conocida ni alcanzada de los grandes filósofos antiquos, la cual mejora la vida y la salud humana, con las adiciones de la segunda impresion. Escrita y sacada á luz por Dª Oliva Sabuco de Nantes Barrera, natural de la ciudad de Alcaráz, con la dedicatoria al rey D. Felipe II, de este nombre y la carta al Ilmo. Sr. D. Francisco Zapata, conde de Barajas y presidente de Castilla, etc. Esta nueva impresion va expurgada, segun el expurgatorio publicado por el Santo Oficio de la santa y general Inquisicion el año mil setecientos y siete. Cuarta impresion reconocida y enmendada de muchas erratas que tenian las antecedentes con un elogio del doctor don Martin Martinez á esta obra. Año de 1728. Con licencia," etc.

In her dedication to Philip II, here spoken of, the author states the purpose of the work and estimates its value. She says: "A humble servant and subject speaks from afar, on bended knee, since she is not able to speak boldly near at hand.—The lion, king and lord of animals, through instinctive magnanimity uses clemency towards children and weak women, especially if, prostrate upon the earth, they have strength and courage to speak, as did the captive of Getulia, who, escaping from captivity through a mountain, was shown clemency by all the lions, because she was a woman and because of the words which she had courage to utter with great humility. So I, with the same confidence and courage, venture to present and dedicate this my book to your Catholic Majesty and to beg the favor of the Great Lion, the King and Lord of men, and the protection of these Aquiline wings, beneath which I place this, my child, whom I have engendered. Receive, your Majesty, the service of a woman, which I think, is better in quality than much that has been done by man, subjects and lords who have desired to serve your Majesty. While to the Caesarian and Catholic Majesty have been dedicated many books produced by men, there are at least fewer and rarer that have been produced

[173] Cf. Parada, op. cit., 173.

by women, and none at all treating of this matter. This is as singular and rare as is its author. It examines into the knowledge of self and teaches man this self-knowledge. It teaches him to understand his nature and the natural causes of life, death and infirmity. It gives much and important advice on self-preservation from violent death. It would improve the world in many things. All the knowledge in this book was lacking to Galen, to Plato, and to Hippocrates in their treatises on the nature of man, and to Aristotle when he treated of the soul and of life and death. It was lacking likewise to the naturalists like Pliny, Aelianus and others when they wrote on man.—It belongs especially to kings and great lords, because their health, their wishes, opinions, passions and inclinations are of more far-reaching consequence than are those of others. It belongs to kings, because knowing and understanding the nature and propensities of man, they can better rule and govern their dominions, just as a good pastor better rules and governs his flock when he knows its nature and inclinations.

"From the colloquy on the knowledge of self and the nature of man resulted the dialogue of True Medicine, which was born of that, forgetting that I had never professionally made a study of medicine, but there resulted from it very clearly and evidently, as naturally as light results from the sun, the conclusion that the old science of medicine was in error. This science is read and studied in its fundamental principles, notwithstanding that the old philosophers and physicians did not give attention to the nature of their own beings, which is the foundation and starting point of all medical science. Since my petition is just, let my sect be given a year's trial, as those of Hippocrates and Galen have been given a trial of two thousand years, with such poor results."

That the author did not lack confidence in spite of her humility is here manifest, but the sincerity of her humility is likewise manifest. The entire dedication reveals a character at once strong and modest, another precious Renaissance type of womanhood adorned with virtue and crowned with knowledge. That her confidence did not lack its reward is evident from the number of editions through which the work passed in an age of such careful criticism as was that of the Renaissance, and from the additional editions bearing dates past the middle of the nineteenth century.

Of the life of the author of the "Nueva Filosafía," little that is definite has come down to us. Conjectures of modern students center round her name, as signed by herself in the dedication to Philip II: Oliva Sabuco de Nantes Barrera. Some claim that she was daughter of the physician of Phillip II, named Barrera thus accounting for her medical knowledge;[174] others believe that she was of French origin, from the indication of "De Nantes."[175] but the clearest evidence seems to be that based on her baptismal certificate.[176] This evidence agrees also with the scanty information which she herself gives us in her work. From the baptismal certificate we learn that Oliva was born in Alcaráz in the year 1562, and was baptized in the church of the Holy Trinity on the second of December of the same year. Two of her four sponsors were Barbara Barrera and Bernardina de Nantes, the former being the wife of V. Padilla and the latter the wife of Juan Rodriguez. The names of these two might very naturally be assumed by Oliva later on out of a sentiment of gratitude or for the sake of kinship, or they may have been given her in Baptism. This interpretation of her biographer is supported by the further evidence of the baptismal certificate that her father was Sanchez Sabuco, who bore the title of "Bachelor," and her mother Francisca Cozar. Sanchez Sabuco was governor of Alcaráz in 1581 and again in 1596 and these dates point to the fact that he must have held a long term in that office. At the same time the position and education of the father and of the other relatives present at the baptism throw light on the hidden life and opportunities of Oliva. That her Nueva Filosofía was given to the press in 1587, when she was but twenty-five is proof that her early education must have been a careful one.

According to evidence given by the document concerning her dowry,[177] Oliva was married in 1585 to Acacio de Buedo, who belonged to a distinguished family of Alcaráz, called Cano de Buedo. Her mother was then dead, and the signatures of the brothers and sisters show that there were four of the former and two of the latter, Juana and Catalina. All were older than Oliva, whose name here has another variety, Luisa Oliva Sabuco.

---

[174] Antonio, *op. cit.*, II.
[175] Cf. Feijóo y Montenegro, *op. cit.*
[176] Cf. Parada, *op. cit.*
[177] *Ibid.*

Her place of abode, after leaving Alcaráz is not evident.   Her house was converted, in part, into a municipal building, and in part served to enlarge the convent of the Dominicans.   According to a tradition of this convent, Oliva came to end her days there, taking the monastic habit.   Her portrait was there preserved, thus attired, as it was also preserved in the municipal building in secular dress.   Both these portraits are said to have perished during the wars of the nineteenth century.   The date of her death is uncertain, but the convent tradition accounts for the obscurity of the later years and the documents cited show that her retirement was not owing to her birth, which, says one of her biographers, those have put forward who can account for her scientific knowledge in no other way than that she must have inherited it from the Arabs and come from a Morisco family.[178]

Of the numerous courts of Spanish nobility, distinguished for their learned and virtuous women, there are two others, whose history is especially instructive.   The family of Mendoza and that of Borja produced many noble and saintly women, among whom but a few can be singled out.

The best representative of the Mendozas, although not the best known, is Doña Catalina Mendoza.   She was born in Granada, in 1542, and was the daughter of D. Iñigo Lopez de Mendoza, Marquis of Mondejar.   She was brought up by her grandparents D. Luis Hurtado de Mendoza and Dª Catalina de Mendoza y Pacheco, and with her aunt, Dª Maria Mendoza, known for her great piety and learning as *La Blanca*.   Dª Catalina was lady of honor to Dª Juana of Austria, sister of Philip II, and enjoyed at court the reputation for beauty, wisdom and genius that Ana Cervató enjoyed at the court of Ferdinand.   Like Ana Cervató, Catalina Mendoza had many ardent suitors, and she finally married, by proxy, the Count of Gomera, who resided in Seville, but having discovered an impediment to the marriage, before the arrival of the Count, she asked and obtained of the Pope permission to contract a new marriage or to enter the cloister, which had been her desire.   Her family objecting, she made privately in the hands of the General of the Jesuits, Cláudio Aquaviva, the vows of poverty, chastity and obedience, and lived thus a life of prayer and penance until her death, on the fifteenth of February, 1602.

[178] Cf. Parada, *op. cit.* 157 ff.

This illustrious lady devoted her fortune, as did also her aunt, Dᵃ Maria Mendoza, to the foundation of the Jesuit college of Alcalá. She was herself learned and she favored learning. To an extensive knowledge of Latin and of Sacred Scripture, she added the very unusual combination of great proficiency in arithmetic and calculus joined to the arts of music and embroidery, which last accomplishment was aided by a singular gift of designing, the fruit of her mathematical turn of mind.

Dᵃ Catalina left no published writings, but the Court, through the personal influence received by Dᵃ Juana of Austria, preserved the advantages of learning and wisdom born of her singular gifts.[179]

Dᵃ Maria Pacheco, a sister of *La Blanca*, and aunt of Dᵃ Catalina, shared their opportunities and their talents, but not their happy fortune. Known outside of Spain as the "Widow of Juan Padilla," she has come down to us, with Catarina Sforza, as type of the Renaissance virago. But Dᵃ Maria was gentle as well as learned, and, like Catarina Sforza, she showed her mettle only in the face of very real dangers to her loved ones. However history may have judged of the acts of these women, in causes just or unjust, that they acted their part bravely when "someone had blundered" is noted in terms of highest praise.

Fortunately the Spanish virago (using the term in its pure Italian meaning) has left proof of her character and her motives in the brief letter which she addressed to Padilla on the day of his death. It is sufficiently illuminating, both in tone and in content. She says:

"Do not believe, my own dear Señor, that your letter grieved me more than did the anxiety of mind in which news of your unjust sentence and the suddenness of your execution placed me. Nothing can alleviate my sorrow nor sustain my breaking heart. How has it been able to bear so much and not break? Do hope that it may not prove the end of my life.

"But now there is but one pain which Divine Providence can send me, that you are able to spare me. I beg you, beloved Lord of my soul, prepare yourself for the work before you; fix your eyes on God alone that you may, in expiation, meet as far as possible the demands of His justice, departing assured that I will do whatever you may command me, for you know that you

[179] Parada, *op. cit.*, 187.

were always certain of my obedience, my good will and my love.

"Because I am unable to go hence, I am beside myself with grief and loneliness. She who was ever thine, M. P."[180]

The family of Borja has a number of representative women, but of greatest interest is the "Santa Duquesa," sister of the great St. Francis Borja, of the Society of Jesus. This venerated woman was Dᵃ Luisa de Borja y Aragon, who was born on the 19th of August, 1520. She was daughter of D. Juan Borja, third Duke of Gandía, and Dᵃ Juana de Aragon, the niece of King Ferdinand. In 1540 she was married to D. Martin de Aragon, Count and Duke of Ribagorza and of Villahermosa. In the castle of Pédrola, in the ducal territory of Villahermosa, the Duke and Duchess surrounded themselves with antiques and lived in an atmosphere of culture that recalls the castle of Mantua in the days of the Duchess Isabella.

The castle of Pédrola is believed to be the scene of Don Quixote's adventures in his visit to the duke and duchess, where the faithful Sancho promises solemnly to sew up his mouth or bite his tongue before speaking a word not duly considered and to the purpose.[181] The vigorous Renaissance life here recalled by Cervantes, places before us the Duchess who in the chase, "would have been the foremost [to strike at the boar] if the Duke had not prevented her," and whose valor is commended by her lord in his answer to the frightened squire: "The chase is an image of war . . . you are often exposed to the extremes of cold and heat; idleness and ease are despised; the body acquires health and vigorous activity."

Thus the Santa Duquesa enjoyed her books and her outdoor sports in the company of her husband and her six children, while she found time for prayer and for composing pious works, among which is a paraphrase of the Magnificat. She gave generously of her store of learning and virtue, handing down to her children the rich inheritance which she had received from her noble predecessors. She died on October 5, 1560, at Saragossa, and was interred in Pédrola.[182]

Dᵃ Isabel Borja, known in religion as the Venerable Francisca of Jesus, was aunt of Dᵃ Luisa and St. Francis Borja. Born in Gandía, the fifteenth of January, 1498, she was daughter of D.

---

[180] Parada, *op. cit.*, 188; Cf. *Mem. de la Real Acad. de la Hist.*, Vol. VI, ll. XVI.

[181] "Preface, Madrid Ed., 1854, III, 267." Cited in Parada, *op. cit.*, 184.

[182] Parada, *op. cit.*, 184.

Juan Borja, Duke of Sésaro, and second Duke of Gandía. Her mother was Dª Maria Enriquez de Luna, who belonged to the royal family of Aragon. After the death of her husband, who is said to have been assassinated in Rome by Caesar Borja, Dª Maria entered the convent of Santa Clara of Gandía, where she was known as Sister Maria Gabriela. At the time of her death, she was abbess of the same convent.

Dª Isabel, who was destined to precede her mother to the cloister, experienced on two remarkable occasions the protection of Divine Providence in her regard: When she was but three years of age, her nurse let her fall from a great height from the palace but the child escaped without any injury. Again, to secure her vocation which her parents opposed, it was revealed to Isabel that her only brother, Juan, would have a son who would perpetuate the glorious name of the family and give great honor to the church. When this prophecy was duly recorded in the monastery of Gandía, the parents relented, their only objection having been the risk of bringing up for the world an only child. The prophecy was fulfilled in the birth of St. Francis Borja.

Isabel Borja entered at first the Convent of Discalced Franciscans in Gandía and then passed to that of Madrid, where she was abbess, and where she governed the convent with great mildness and discretion. Such were her gifts for administration, that she was sent as abbess to the Convent of Rioja in 1552 and thence to Valladolid in 1557, where she died on the twenth-eighth of October of the same year.

This holy nun wrote a number of spiritual treatises for the members of her convents, some of which are preserved in manuscript, while others are published by the historian of her order.[183] These writings are collected under two heads: "Spiritual Exhortations," and "Holy Exercises." Many of her letters are also preserved in manuscript and are said to be in the mansion of the Marquis Osera. Of these, some are published by the biographers of St. Francis Borja and of his sister, Dª Luisa, both of whom were her correspondents. The roll of manuscripts has this inscription "In this package are eight letters, the most holy and most consoling possible, of Sister Francisca of Jesus of Santa Clara, of Gandía, to my Señora the Duchess Dª Luisa de Borja, of holy life."[184]

---

[183] Carrillo, "Relacion histórica de la fundacion de las Descalzas de Madrid, IV, 77 ff., Madrid, 1616." Cited in Parada, *op. cit.*, 183.
[184] Parada, *ibid.*

The spiritual exhortations are in tone and subject matter evidence of the sincerity and humility of the abbess and of the happy blending of mildness and firmness with which she is said to have governed the different convents over which she ruled. In one of her exhortations she writes: "Prostrate at the feet of each one of you, I implore, on my knees, that you have union of hearts and preserve peace one with another. It seems to me that what should be able to foster this peace is that each one make at least once a week a sincere examination of the affections of her soul, to see what it loves, what it hates; what it dreads or hopes for; what troubles it and what gives it joy; with what it is carried away; and considering how she has yielded to this and how she has made use of that, she will see the harm done and how vice has mingled with virtue. She will see that that which she believed to be zeal was, perhaps, passion; that what she believed to be discretion vanishes away; that what she thought prudence she finds to be pride; that what she thought to be in order is totally in disorder."[185]

Her biographer affirms that such was the fervor and sanctity of the good abbess that words like these were received as oracles by her devoted nuns, and that her spoken discourses were cherished as precious memories.

Another nun who did good service to her order by her literary labors was Dᵃ Isabel de Alagón. She belonged to the family of the counts of Sástago and was born in Saragossa. In 1545 she was elected prioress of the Royal Monastery of Our Lady of Sixena of the Order of St. John of Jerusalem. She revived the Breviary and the rules of the order, publishing the former in Saragossa, in 1547, under the following title: *Breviarium secundum Ritum Sixenae Monasterii, Ordinis Sancti Joannis Hierosolymitani, sub Regula Sancti Augustini.* It bears the coat of arms of the house of Alagón, and has a preface by the author in which she sets forth her reasons for the revision.

The edition was in use in the order at the time of the decree of Pope Saint Pius V. ordering the universal use of the Roman Breviary.[186]

The abbess who preceded Dᵃ Isabel, Dᵃ Luisa Moncayo, of the family of the counts of Coscojuela, wrote the directory of the

---

[185] *Ibid.*

[186] Latassa y Ortin, *Bib. Nueva de los Escritores Aragoneses*, I, No. 96. Cf. Parada, *op. cit.*, 134.

order. She had a sister, Serena Moncayo, who was also a nun in the same monastery.[187]

A number of other sixteenth century nuns published works, either translations from the Latin, or original productions in Latin or Castilian. Among these was Sister Maria Tellez, a Franciscan of the convent of Tordesillas, who translated the work of Luis Cartusiano, on the Passion of our Lord Jesus Christ, from Latin into Castilian.[188]

Sister Cecilia of the Nativity, who was Cecilia Sobrino, one of the daughters of D[a] Cecilia Morillas,[189] is characterized by her biographer as the "happy image" of her illustrious mother. She was a nun in the Carmelite Convent of Valladolid belonging to the foundations of St. Teresa. Born in 1570, she could enjoy but eleven years of companionship with her noble mother and was deprived of much of the training which fell to the lot of her older brothers and her sister. Still such was her education that besides being an able musician and a very gifted artist, she was a poet and the author of several other works. She was Mistress of Novices and Prioress in the Monastery of Valladolid and at Calahorra, where she directed the founding of the convent. She later founded the convent of Teresans in Madrid.[190]

Her works of art and her writings are preserved in the convents of Valladolid and Madrid. Among the latter are a *Treatise on the Immaculate Conception of the Mother of God*; and *Autobiography*; an account of the merits and virtues of her sister, Maria de San Alberto; and a number of poems.[191]

Sister Maria de San Alberto belonged to the same convent, that of Valladolid. There she spent her days, like her sister, in prayer, study and writing. She, too, was a musician and poet and she left a number of mystical writings. As prioress, she governed the monastery with wisdom and great virtue for a number of years.

Among her literary productions are the following: *Visions of Catalina Evangelista*; *A diary of her own visions*; *Verses on the Nativity*; *A metrical paraphrase of the psalms*; *Various letters.*

---

[187] Parada, *op. cit.*, 193.
[188] Antonio, *op. cit.*, II, 88; Parada, *op. cit.*, 152.
[189] *Supra*, 59.
[190] Cf. Parada y Lautin, "Las Pintoras españolas, In *La Ilustracion Española y Americana*, 1876." Cited in Parada, *op. cit.*, 178.
[191] Parada, *op. cit.*, 178.

Mother San Albertino also arranged and compiled, in part, the letters of Saint Teresa. One of her own letters is published with those of the saint in the collection made by D. Vicente de la Fuente in his life of the great Carmelite.[192]

Many other names of learned women appear in the works of the Spanish historians and biographers. There is Catalina Estrella, of Salamanca, daughter or niece of the chronicler, Don Juan Crisostoma Calvete de Estrella. She was proficient in Latin, French and Italian, and possessed exceptional knowledge of history.[193]

Isabel Coello, of Madrid, daughter of the celebrated artist, Alonso Sanchez Coello, was also an artist and musician. She was born in 1564 and lived until 1612. Vicente Espinel, in his *Casa de la memoria*, has the following lines to her:

> "In her celestial hand the instrument
> Doña Isabel Coello sets atune.
> The sovereign choir attentive hears
> And contemplates the flowing harmony.
> That heavenly grace, that genius all sublime,
> The frozen heart to limpid fountain turns.
> Throat, voice and dexterous fingers all unite,
> One burst of perfect melody to raise."[194]

Another sixteenth century musician, praised by the same poet for her gifts, is Francisca Guzman. Her personal charm and the charm of her voice he thus portrays:

> "Doña Francisca de Guzman, graceful and serene,
> The spell-bound company in fetters held;
> The throng of singing birds she gently hushed
> With sweet alluring notes of sweeter song.
> The air in myriad waves of harmony

---

[192] Vol. II, p. 9. Cited in Parada, *op. cit.*, 179.
[193] Antonio, *op. cit.*, II, 348; Parada, *ibid.*, 190.
[194] *Canto* 2. Quoted in Parada, *op. cit.*, 192:

> "En la divino mano el instrumento
> Doña Isabel Coello tiene y templa;
> Oyelo el soberano coro atento
> Y la disposicion y arte contempla
> La hermosura, el celestial talento
> Que al más helado corzon destempla.
> Garganta, habilidad, voz, consonancia,
> Término, trato, estilo y elegancia."

To heaven mounted, whence it trembling fell
In mellow echoes to the charmèd earth."[195]

Other literary women were Cecilia Arellano, of Saragossa, who knew Latin, Portuguese, French and Italian.[196] Magdalena Bobadilla, noted for her Latin scholarship.[197] Catalina Rizo, author of the work: *Anathema sotericon pro vita Patris servati*, on the index of manuscripts in the National Library and published in *Biblioteca de libros raros*, of Valle y Rayon;[198] and Marion Cardenas, author of another work on the same index: *Noticia de las monjas que introjudo en Roma por las años de* 1525 *llamadas las emparedadas*.[199] Another work in the Royal Library, unedited, *Instrucciones a su hijo D. Luis*, is attributed to Estefanía Requesens, of Catalania.[200]

Besides these minor authors, Antonio [201] mentions eight or ten more of the sixteenth century, whose works were worthy of a place in the nation's archives. Other women, famous for their virtue and learning, wives and mothers of sturdy character, nuns or teachers in the Renaissance schools, receive also more than a passing mention.[202]

This array of cultured womanhood was not a sudden apparition on the fair fields of Spain and Portugal—a mushroom growth fostered in the dewy morn of the Revival, only to catch the blight of its scorching rising sun. In these Renaissance women were preserved and perfected those noble qualities and accomplishments of which the medieval Iberian woman furnishes us the type. Like Dante and Petrarch, Isabel of Castile and her scholarly tutor, La Latina, emerged from the Past endowed with the power which it was hers to bestow and with an ambition, born of that power, which the future alone could satisfy.

---

[195] *Ibid.*, Canto 3; Parada, *Ibid.*, 191:

> "Doña Francisca de Guzman se vió
> Sereno el rostro en movimientos graves
> Tener suspensa aquella compañia
> Con acentos dulcisimos suaves:
> Con la voz y garganta suspendia
> Al escuadron de las cantoras aves;
> El aire rompe y pasa por el fuego
> Al cielo llega y vuelve luego al suelo."

[196] Antonio, *op. cit.*, II, 347; Parada, *Ibid.*, 191.
[197] Antonio, *Ibid.*, 351; Parada, *Ibid.*, 133.
[198] Parada, 134.
[199] *Ibid.*, 193.
[200] *Ibid.*
[201] *Op. cit.*, II, 352 ff.
[202] Cf. Rada y Delgado, *op. cit.*; Feijóo, *op. cit.*; Latassa y Ortin, *op. cit.*

Not to go back for representatives of Iberian culture beyond the Dark Ages to the great heroines of early Christian Spain, nor yet to the Gothic period of darkness itself with its examples of bravery, sanctity, and wisdom, there were the shining lights of the later Middle Ages; Blanche of Castile, mother of St. Louis of France; Beatriz, the gifted daughter of Alfonzo el Sabio, and queen of Portugal; that other queen of Portugal, the Aragonese princess, and canonized saint, Isabel, or Elizabeth, niece of St. Elizabeth of Hungary; and the Portuguese princesses and queens of Castile, Constantia, daughter of the saint, and Maria, queen of Alfonso XI., with Isabel, mother of Isabel the Catholic. From the atmosphere of power and goodness which surrounded the venerated memories of such heroines as these, the Peninsula Renaissance drew inspiration, and guided by Italian tradition, it placed upon the brow of womanhood a lasting crown of knowledge, of wisdom and of honor.[203]

The spirit of the Spanish nation in rejecting the erroneous philosophy and the false religion imported with Eastern emigration, while accepting and appropriating the useful knowledge thus imported, had shielded the Christian maiden from unwholesome influences, and at the same time had given her a share in the advantages to be derived from Arabic culture on the objective side. Her right to participation in scientific studies, however, cannot be attributed to the influence of Arabian custom,[204] but rather to Hebrew and Gospel tradition, reinforced by the direct influences of classical Greece and Rome.

In the library inherited by Isabel of Castile, from her father, Juan II, we are furnished with a very comprehensive history of the traditional form and spirit of literary activity in Christian Spain, previous to the revival of learning. In this collection of two hundred and one[205] manuscripts are numerous translations into Spanish of the Latin classics, of portions of the Bible, and of the Fathers and Doctors of the Church. There are also works of Italian, French and Spanish writers of the Middle Ages, representing the didactic or imaginative branches of literature; as well as valuable manuscripts on history, geography, law, medicine, and the natural sciences.

[203] Cf. Rada y Delgado, *op. cit.*, Vol. II, lib. 2.
[204] Cf. Prescott, *Hist. of the Reigns of Ferdinand and Isabella*, II, 185. Philadelphia, 1882.
[205] *Mem. de la Real Acad. de la Hist.*, Vol. VI, Il. 17.

Among the translations from the classics are Livy, "History of Rome;" A fragment of the same, with the arms of Castile and Leon;[206] Book of Seneca; Tragedies of Seneca; The Aeneid and Aesop in three manuscripts, both the work of the Infante D. Enrique de Aragon, Marquis of Villena;[207] and a Plutarch from the Latin version produced about the same time in Italy.[208]

The Spanish translations from the Bible are catalogued as: Proverbs and Prophecies; Book of Josue; Prophets;[209] Gospels (two copies); and Gospels and Acts.[210] In translations also are: St. Augustine, "De Civitate Dei," eighth and eighteenth books; St. Bernard, "Doctrine," [211] St. Gregory, Pope, "Dialogues and Homilies;" and St. Chrysostom's "Homilies on St. Matthew," sixty-five books, from one of the two Latin manuscripts of St. Chrysostom given in the catalogue.

Here in the original is a copy of Xenophon,[212] the only work in Greek in the catalogue; with Cicero, "De Officiis" (two copies); and Seneca, first and second parts. In the original also is St. Isidore's "Etymologies" with another work of the same author, beginning, "Venerabilis;" and St. Ambrose, "Explanation of Psalm CXVIII." There is a copy of the Apocalypse in Latin. A few minor French poets are represented, and there is a Portuguese version of a poem by Alfonso el Sabio, entitled, "Wonders of our Lady."

Spiritual aids are well provided in manscript copies of missals and breviaries; lives of the Saints in Latin, French and Spanish; sermons in Spanish; moral treatises in the medieval favorite form of mirrors of the Soul, and mirrors of Christian Life, and the like. In the same collection are the Prayer and Rule of St. Francis; the Office of St. James; and a large number of similar works.

The united traditional influences here manifest and of which the history of Spanish literature in general gives evidence, are thus summed up by a modern writer, whose views cannot be interpreted

---

[206] *No.* 121.

[207] Clemencin, in *ibid.*, note to 139–141.

[208] *Ibid.*, note to 117.

[209] Beginning: "Todos los que hablan sobre los razones de Daniel profeta."

[210] *Nos.* 15–20.

[211] Liber de modo bene vivendi ad sororem.

[212] The *Xenophon* is undescribed but there seems to have been no Spanish translation previous to that of Diego Gracian, printed in 1552. Cf. Clemencin, *op. cit.*, note 116.

as resultants of Spanish-Christian sympathies:[213] "Though the Visigoths were not a literary people, and their influence upon Spanish letters was insignificant, yet the Roman-Spaniard, with his exuberant literary talent, and saturated with the later Latin traditions, which his race had largely been instrumental in forming, continued his activity in authorship during the whole of the Gothic dominion."

After showing that the Christian idea seized firm hold of the imagination of Spanish-Latin writers, from the fourth century on, he says of the "Etymologies:" "There is nothing which escapes the pen of St. Isidore, and it is evident from the definitions in the Etymologies that a Christian Bishop had no hesitation whatever in accepting and endorsing to a great extent the views on art, eloquence, music, and literary expression which had been formulated by the writers of Pagan Greece and Rome."

And speaking of St. Isidore's influence through Theodawulf, Bishop of Orleans, the same author remarks: "Possessing all the ancient love of beauty and elegance, all the old admiration for perfect works of art, the Christian Bishop sought to prove in every page of his writings that harmonious beauty in form, color and expression was not necessarily pagan, but that the breath of Christianity would lend to loveliness itself a new life, which should lead the thoughts of men to the Maker of all harmony."[214]

The further evidence given by the manuscripts preserved with the "Etymologies" is in favor of the perpetuated tradition of St. Isidore in regard to the true relation of the laws of religion and morality to those of pagan art.

Here again literature mirrors life and we find in this promiscuous heap of discourses, the pros and cons of the woman question, set forth, as was usual in the Middle Ages, by the other half of the race. On the one hand is the manuscript given as the work of the Archpriest Talavera, Alfonso Martinez, and described as "a book that speaks of women." This production of the Chaplain of Juan II of Castile, afterwards found its way to the press in Burgos (1499) under the title: *Tractate against the women who with little knowledge maliciously meddled, prattling and doing things not pertaining to them.* A second edition of the same, published in Toledo in 1518 was enlarged but not improved, and was popularly called

---

[213] Hume, *The Spanish People*, p. 57 ff. New York, 1901.
[214] *Ibid.*, 59.

"Corvacho," from its resemblance to Boccaccio's drastic satire, the "Corbaccio." [215]

On the other side is the work in Spanish manuscript, entitled: *Tercero tratado del libro de las mugeres*, by Fr. Francisco Jimenez, "of the Order of Preachers." The author is evidently not a Dominican, but a Friar Minor of the same name. [216] The work was dedicated to Dª Sancha Ramirez de Arenos, Countess of Prades. It was afterwards printed in Barcelona, in 1495. Another Friar Minor translated it into Catalan, and published it, with additions under the title: *Carro de las doñas*, in Valladolid, 1542, dedicating, it to Queen Catherine of Portugal. [217] Here, too, is the *Virtuous and Illustrious Women*, of Alvaro de Luna, [218] showing Boccaccian influence on the better side.

By the production of *Celestina* (1480) the realistic dramatist had thrown down the gauntlet and entered the arena.

Thus was Spain prepared for the Renaissance. She had carefully preserved her past history; she had appropriated the world's wisdom, locking it up in her everyday speech, the better to claim its service; and she had raised the tremendous question of the sacredness of womanhood, a question which the revival of pagan culture in her Christian community was to bring forward with peculiar emphasis.

But thinking men and women whose duty it should be to direct aright the moral and intellectual forces of the new social order were not wanting. The difficulties of the new situation were not only anticipated in the Peninsula but forestalled. In the school of Latin-Christian tradition the Iberian ruler and the Italian peda-gogue had together learned the true meaning of culture and the nature of that process by which its blessings can alone be secured to individuals and to nations.

The patronage extended by Queen Isabel to foreign booksellers and to the printer-editors who hastened to set up their presses in her congenial dominions, indicates the tendency of early Renais-sance taste as directed by her. [219] It is not a surprise to find in the printed list of her own private library a *Terence* and *Pliny* closely

[215] *No.* 145. Note by Clemencin.
[216] Cf. *ibid.* Note to No. 51.
[217] *No.* 51, *ibid.*
[218] *No.* 161 and note by Clemencin.
[219] Cf. Altimira y Crevea, *op. cit.*, II, 504 ff.

followed by the *Letters of St. Jerome to St. Paula*, and *St. Thomas on the Ethics and Politics of Aristotle*,[220] with the *Prayer Book of Hernan Perez de Guzman*[221] and the *Morning Star of the Christian Life* of Don Pedro Ximenez de Prejamo.[222]

In keeping with the evidence furnished by the library of Isabel, is the argument in favor of woman's education, as put forth by Vives on foreign soil when the Renaissance had already gained irresistible force in his native land. His great work, *De Institutione Christianae Foeminae* is but the history of his experiences of what had been accomplished in Spain when in his youthful days he learned to admire the virtues of learned Valentian women like Doña Angela Zapata.[223] In his treatise the Spanish humanist thus maintains his position: "I perceive that learned women be suspected of many: as who saith, the subtlety of learning should be a nourishment for the maliciousness of their nature. Verily, I do not allow in a subtle and crafty woman, such learning as should teach her deceit, and teach her no good manners and virtue. . . . But you shall not lightly find an ill woman, except it be such a one. as either knoweth not, or at the least way considereth not what chastity and honesty is worth. . . . And she that hath learned from inborn disposition or from books to consider this and such other things, and hath furnished and fenced her mind with holy counsels shall never find [from them stimulus] to do any villainy. For if she can find in her heart to do naughtily, having so many precepts of virtue to keep her, what should we suppose she should do, having no knowledge of goodness at all? And truly if we would call the old world to remembrance, and rehearse their time, we shall find no learned woman that ever was [ev]ill; where I could bring forth an hundred good."[224]

That the thought here expressed is identical with that of the Italian humanistic theorists is evidence of the inspiration which Italy gave to Spain on the intellectual side as well as of the perfect harmony with which both nations viewed the moral aspect of the new system of education. This unity of purpose is accounted for by the fact that throughout the Middle Ages the two nations had

---

[220] Barcelona, 1478. Cf. Clemencin, notes to Nos. 18–19, *op. cit.*, 475.
[221] Murcia, 1487, *ibid.*, No. 33, p. 479.
[222] Salamanca, 1493. Cf. Clemencin, *ibid.*, No. 34, p. 479.
[223] *Supra*, 60.
[224] *Ibid.* Translated by Hyrde in Watson, *Vives and the Renascence Education of Women*, 48–49. New York and London, 1912.

never ceased the intellectual intercourse begun in the days of the Roman conquest. After the rise of the universities Iberian students flocked to Italy in search of wisdom and returned to enrich with their scholastic treasures the home universities of Salamanca, Palencia, Valladolid and Lisbon. From their own College of St. Clement in Bologna, also, and from Aragonese Naples they came to prepare the way for the Revival by cooperating with the native Italian scholars who chose to labor as teachers at the courts and in the universities of the Peninsula.[225] When, therefore, the Spanish humanist turned to the past greatness of Roman-Spain for examples of proud Antiquity, like his colleagues in the Padua of Petrarch, he sought in the history of the early Church, models of perfect womanhood whose example he might bring forward to reinforce that set by a Corinna or a Cornelia.

Thus Lebrija appeals[226] to the enthusiasm of Queen Isabel: "Then what shall I say of the glory and fame of the men of our nation in whatever field of activity they chose to labor. In proof of this: in an age when Latin letters flourished most our own Spain contributed, if not the best, at least the second best. In heroic verse, Lucan, by common consent, takes lead; and Silius Italicus follows close upon him. In tragedy Seneca is not only first but the one of all the tragedians who merited to come down to us with undiminished fame. In epigram, Martial is the first, if we except those who allow the honor to Catullus. In oratory, if none can equal Cicero in fertility and richness none other can surpass Marcus Fabius Quintilian, to whom next in rank is Seneca. Who of his generation could be more diligent in agriculture than Columella, in cosmography than Pomponius, in history than Trogus?" And following up his train of thought, he exclaims: "O, blessedness of our age in which our Princess and Lady desires to revive, not only the customs and the sanctity of the olden times, but the learning also, in which were so distinguished those holy women Paula, Marcella, Julia, Blessilla, and a multitude of others to whom the holy Doctors of the Church, in their time, dedicated their works."

Reinforcing this thrill of enthusiasm which radiated from Italy through the heart and voice of her ardent students there came from the very dawn of the Revival the sentiment of its great leaders in

---

[225] Marineo, "Address to Charles V." Quoted in *Mem. de la Real Acad. de la Hist.*, Vol. VI, App. XVI.
[226] *Introducciones Latinas*, Dedication, Madrid Ed., 1773.

copies of Latin treatises or Italian verses, many of which were
translated into the vernacular before the movement itself reached
Spain.   Dante and Petrarch had found their way hither.[227]   Their
absence from Isabel's collection is accounted for by the fact that
the libraries in her possession were only a portion of the original
collection possessed by her father.[228]   The catalogue of the manuscripts bestowed by the queen on the convent of San Juan de los
Reyes of Toledo, at the time of its foundation is not accessible.
Many works which are here naturally missed may well be in that
collection.[229]

Boccaccio done into Spanish was in Isabel's possession.   There
were the *Fiammeta* and the *Decameron* with *De casibus illustrium
virorum*, translated into *Caida de principes*.   Another Boccaccio in
Spanish, is undescribed, but the *De Claris Mulieribus* was also in
Spain and translated.   It was printed in Saragossa, in 1494.[230]

Some letters of Pope Pius II are preserved in the private library
of Isabel while his works in general were widely distributed in
Spain, many of them in translations.[231]

Among the manuscripts of the larger collection in her possession,
Isabel had made the acquaintance of another Italian humanist,
who, it cannot be doubted, gave her inspiration in her educational endeavors.   A Latin work is here catalogued as *Leonardo*,
followed by a Spanish translation of the same.   The translator is
not mentioned but the next number points to the conjecture that
Isabel's father may have accomplished the work.   This next
number is given as: *Leonardo de Arecio, Cartas in romance de
Leonardo Arecio Florentino al Señor Rey Don Juan.*[232]

Since Isabel was but three or four years old at the death of her
father,[233] she could not have profited by this correspondence, but
she could read very early the letters in Romance and the other
translated work of D'Arezzo, whatever it may be.   In her own
private library, however, is the indication that she actually possessed the *De studiis et literis*,[234] the description of which seems

---

[227] Cf. Ticknor, *Hist. of Spanish Literature*, I, 297 ff. and 183, note.   Boston,
1891.
[228] Prescott, *op. cit.*, II, 185.
[229] *Ibid.*, II, 184.
[230] *Nos.* 148–151 and *ibid.*
[231] *No.* 47.   Note by Clemencin, p. 481.
[232] *Nos.* 174–176.   Note by Clemencin, *ibid.*
[233] Marineo, *op. cit.*, Lib. XXI.
[234] *Supra,* 29.

sufficiently definite. It reads, "Beginning, *preciosa Señora, of Leonardo aristino.*"[235] This work is in Latin manuscript, and does not seem to have been translated. It is followed by a printed Latin copy of D'Arezzo's commentary on the "Ethics of Aristotle," and the next number is a Latin manuscript entitled, *First part of the Ethics of Aristotle*, by the same author.[236]

The fact that Isabel did not read Latin fluently before the first year of earnest study would not cause a serious delay in her full appreciation of the *De studiis et literis*, since the Renaissance movement in Spain may be said to have received its impulse only after the peace with Portugal, in 1479, and the ordering of the united kingdoms. The indications are, that the year of study spoken of by Marineo, was not with Beatriz Galindo, but earlier, and that the queen read with Beatriz something beyond the De Officiis.

In 1481, six years after the birth of La Latina, Lebrija had published his elementary Latin grammar, *Introducciones Latinas*. In 1485 he gave to the press a second edition of the same work, with parallel columns of Latin and Castilian. This second edition was issued at the express desire of Isabel, as we learn from the dedication, the first edition having been composed at the desire of Cardinal Pedro Gonzalez de Mendoza.

This method of parallel text was suggested by the queen for the benefit of students pressed for time or who lacked the services of a tutor ever at hand. Among these students were the queen herself and a large majority of the women of her realm, who, like her, were thirsting for a share in the knowledge of Latin eloquence, or seeking the key to the treasures contained in the Sacred Scriptures and the Fathers and Doctors of the Church. Isabel would naturally be the first to profit by the new text-book, issued when Beatriz Galindo was but ten years old. The assertion of Marineo in his address to the Emperor Charles V. clearly indicates this: "Quae quidem multis et magnis occupata negotiis, ut aliis exemplum praeberet, a primis grammaticae rudimentis studere coepit."[237] A copy of this edition is among the fifty-two books left in the Queen's cabinet at the time of her death.[238]

The history of the inception of this text-book is instructive,

---

[235] *No.* 13, p. 474.
[236] Clemencin, *ibid.* Note to No. 15, p. 474.
[237] Quoted in *Mem. de la Real Acad. de la Hist.*, Vol. VI, App. XVI.
[238] *No.* 5, and Clemencin, Note to No. 6, p. 472.

throwing light as it does on the solicitude felt by the Queen for the education of all her subjects and on the attitude afterwards assumed by the Spanish Renaissance towards the place to be assigned to the vernacular in the curriculum of liberal studies. In his dedication Lebrija says: "And because I am soon to publish a Latin-Spanish dictionary, by which I shall offend and antagonize all those of ours who have the insignia and profession of letters, I say no more here, except that I prognosticate the denunciations that they desire to make against me with blood and fury, while they provide themselves with arguments against me. I come, rather, my illustrious Queen and Lady, to that which your Highness, in your letters has commanded me, concerning the remedy to be brought to that which is lacking in the Introduction to the Latin Language which I published and which has already been read throughout our possessions; that is, that it be done again in the Castilian language, Latin on one side, Romance on the other.

"I must confess my mistake that in the beginning it did not appeal to me to be practicable (the more credit to your Highness), for our language seemed so impoverished that I feared the possibility of expressing in it all the *finesse* of Latin construction. But since I began to put into execution the command of your Highness I have been so satisfied that already I am urged to publish two phases of one and the same work, in different styles, not having from the beginning hit upon this method. First, for those versed in our language who, with good preceptors may be able to profit much, and equally for all; for those who know and for those who wish to learn; for those who teach and those who study; for those who have forgotten that in which they once excelled and which they wish to learn anew, and for all those who have not the advantage of frequent intercourse with masters.

"To this was added the understood advantage which the Very Reverend Father and Lord, the Bishop of Ávila, made known to me on the part of your Royal Majesty; namely, that for no other cause was I commanded to write this work in Latin and Romance, than that women, and nuns, and virgins consecrated to God, without the assistance of learned men might be enabled to acquire a knowledge of the rudiments of the Latin language."[239]

The dictionary here spoken of was published in 1492 and was

---

[239] Dedication to *Introducciones Latinas,* Madrid, 1773.

possessed by Isabel, together with the less valuable one of Alonso de Paléncia written at her command and printed two years earlier than that of Lebrija.[240] These text-books mark the starting point of the Revival and were speedily to replace the works of Alexander de Villa Dei, three copies of which were in the larger collection in Isabel's possession; of Prician;[241] of Fr. Juan de Balbis of Genoa, whose *Catolicon*, printed by Faust in Mayence 1460, was also there; and the *Mamotreto*, of Fr. Juan Marchesino, also printed in Mayence, 1470, and possessed by Isabel.[242]

The reformed method in Greek found its first home in the University of Salamanca where a Greek grammar was written by Arias Barbosa, the Portuguese who had studied with such success in Florence that he merits the title of Father of Greek Learning in the Peninsula. He was in Salamanca in 1489 and died tutor at the court of Portugal in 1530. Evidence of the date of publication of his grammar is not available, but it is certain that Barbosa was a profound Greek scholar when he returned from Italy.[243] Lebrija later wrote both Greek and Hebrew grammars,[244] and another Greek grammar, sometimes said to be the first produced in Spain, was written by one of the two Vergeras, brothers of Isabel Vergera and professors of Greek and Hebrew in Alcalá.[245] The Spanish humanistic attitude toward the teaching of Greek appears in a treatise on the pronunciation of that language published by Lebrija in the appendix to the Alcalá edition of the "Introducciones Latinas."[246] The fine appreciation of the truly classical here manifest is another evidence that Barbosa had colleagues as well as disciples in his work of hellenizing the Peninsula. Of the services rendered by Lebrija in the teaching of Greek, Bywater says: "But if there was any one man to whom the credit of discovery [of reformed Greek pronunciation] is due, it was assuredly not Aldus or any other Italian, but a Spaniard, the great Spanish humanist, Antonio of Lebrixa, better known outside of Spain as Antonius Nebrissensis."[247]

To a notice of the services of these men in the field of the ancient

---

[240] Clemencin, note to Nos. 7, 8, 9, p. 472–473; Cf. Altimira y Crevea, *op. cit.*, II, 504ff.
[241] *No.* 130.
[242] Clemencin, notes to Nos. 178–183.
[243] Altimira y Crevea, *op. cit.*; Prescott, *op. cit*, II, 197.
[244] McCormick, *Hist. of Education*, 183, Washington, 1915.
[245] Altimira y Crevea, *ibid.*
[246] Cf. Bywater, *The Erasmian Pronunciation of Greek and its Precursors*, sec. 3. London, 1908.
[247] *Ibid.*, 13.

languages must be added those of the great Cardinal Ximenes, in Mosarabic, Greek, Latin and Hebrew; of Hernán Núñez (Pinciano), who bore the title of "Greek Commentator," and of Fr. Pedro Alcalá, author of the Arabic-Castilian dictionary compiled at the request of Fr. Hernando de Zalavera.[248]

The libraries in Isabel's possession, and the rapid multiplication of accessible works imported after the duty exemption law of 1480,[249] furnished abundant texts for study in ancient and Spanish literature, in history, geography, music, ethics and politics, civil and canon law and in medicine.

In the larger collection inherited by Isabel there were, in addition to the classics, numerous Spanish minor works of fiction, as the poems of Alonso de Villasandino; of Juan Alonso de Baena; of Juan de Mena; Ballads of the Archpriest of Hitta; and the "Labors of Hercules," by the Marquis of Villena. There are here also Spanish copies of legends of the Arthurian cycle, entitled: "Merlin"; "Third Part of the Search for the Holy Grail"; "Lancelot."

In six manuscripts the general history of José Rodriguez de Castro was there preserved, the first one described as beginning: *Mui amados amigos.*[250] In two other manuscripts is the *History of Spain*, probably that of Alonso de Paléncia, including the events up to the Moorish invasion.[251] Another chronicle of Spain also in Spanish is believed to be the work later abridged by order of Isabel.[252] Here are the general History and History of Spain of Alfonso el Sabio together with a chronicle of his reign,[253] to which are added chronicles of several other reigns.[254] Following a history of Spain written in Portuguese is a Spanish translation of Guido de Coluna's *History of Troy.*[255] Among several works of its kind is the *Regimiento de principes* of either St. Thomas or Giles of Rome;[256] with a Map of the World,[257] several manuscripts of organ music, and books on methods in music.[258] Law treatises are numerous, among which, besides the *Siete Partidas* of Alfonso el Sabio, are:

---

[248] Altimira y Crevea, *ibid.*
[249] Cf. Altimira y Crevea, *op. cit.*, II, 504.
[250] *Nos.* 9–14 and note by Clemencin, 436–437.
[251] *Nos.* 97–98 and *ibid.*
[252] Cf. *No.* 99 and note:
[253] *Nos.* 100, 100–103 and *ibid.*
[254] *Nos.* 104–107.
[255] Clemencin, note to Nos. 109–110.
[256] Clemencin, note to No. 20, p. 475.
[257] *No.* 25 and note, p. 477.
[258] *Nos.* 43, 44, p. 480.

the *Speculum Juris* of Guillaume Durando, Bishop of Mende, France; the works of Jacobo de Butrigalde, of Bologna, and his disciples, Baldo and Bartulo; of Antonio Butrio, of Bologna also; and many of Spanish authorship. In medicine, Bernardo Gordomio, professor in Montpellier, is represented, with other unknown authors. It must be noted that the Arabic philosophical works not to be had in these private libraries were accessible to research students in the universities, whither they had been relegated by the inquisitors.[260]

To these older sources of ready reference were added the numerous works which the age of the Renaissance itself produced. In his *De Rebus Hispaniae Memorabilibus*, Marineo preserved the intimate history of his generation and Lebrija produced valuable works, not only in grammar and literature but in theology, law, archeology, history, natural science, geography and geology; and in general the literary activity of the fifteenth and sixteenth centuries furnished new works on every phase of human thought.[261]

Living as she did in the age of Columbus and Peter Martyr of Anghiera, the Iberian Renaissance woman had a new source of geographical and historical study in the accounts of discovery and exploration. Peter Martyr's great work, the *De Orbe Novo*, was begun in 1494 and completed in 1526, thus being in reality the "Gazette of the New Discoveries,"[262] while the letters of Columbus supplemented the reports of his personal adventures and those of his followers which were related by word of mouth throughout the Peninsula. To Queen Isabel and her generation these accounts were more than history, they were subjects for devout meditations on the Providence of God and the virtue of His children, as manifested in perilous journeys undertaken for His honor and glory. When the great discoverer wrote of his hardships and of the goodness of God through it all, Isabel could sympathize with both states of feeling, and she might say from afar with the voice of the vision at Veragua: "Of the barriers of the great ocean which were bound up with such mighty chains, He hath given unto thee the keys. . . . What did He more for the people of Israel when he led them forth from Egypt? . . . Many inheritances hath He, and very great. . . . What He promiseth, that He fulfilleth, and yet

---

[260] Cf. Prescott, *op. cti.* II, 413.
[261] Cf. Altimira y Crevea, *op. cit.*, II, 504ff.
[262] Cf. Mariéjol, *Pierre Martyr D'Anghera*, Chap. 12, Paris, 1887.

more.   And doth the world thus? . . . Fear not; be of good
cheer; all these thy griefs are written in marble; and not without
cause."[263]

But most significant of all the Spanish Renaissance studies
auxiliary to those of the classical languages and literature is that
of the vernacular. Lebrija completed his Castilian grammar and
printed it in Salamanca in 1492, the same year that he published
the Latin-Spanish dictionary. The Spanish-Latin dictionary
followed this and in 1517 the *Rules of Orthography in the Castilian
Language.*[264]

In his dedication to the Castilian grammar[265] the great humanist reminds the Queen that the history of the past teaches beyond
question that language is ever the companion of empire, in proof
of which he reviews the history of the Jewish people and of Greece
and Rome, concluding that what is true of these nations is more
forcibly true of Spain whose language had its cradle in the reigns
of the great kings of Castile and Leon, showing its power under
Alfonso el Sabio, when he wrote the Siete Partidas and the General History, and translated many works of Arabic and Latin into
Castilian.   This prestige extended to Aragon, Navarre, and Italy
with the extended rule of the Infantes.

Then he reminds the Queen that the nation is at peace, through
the bounty of Divine Providence and the diligence and hard labor
of her Majesty, and that uniformity should be sought for in the
nation's language.   He admits that time is needed for such results
but he recalls the other work in grammar, where by the aid of the
vernacular one can learn "Latin grammar not in a few months but
in a few days," and much more than up to now "could be learned
in many years."

In stating the divisions of his subject, Lebrija makes it clear that
his purpose is to elevate the Castilian to the dignity of classical
expression as he had before proposed to render it acceptable as the
universal language of the nation.   In pursuance of the plan hinted
at in the dedication to the *Introducciones Latinas* he divides the
work into two parts.   The first part, composed of the first four
books, is intended for the first two classes of students; namely,

---

[263] "Letter of Columbus to Ferdinand and Isabella, July 7, 1503."   Quoted
in Ticknor, *op. cit.*, I, 221, 222 and note.
[264] Walberg, in Preface to *Gramatica Castellana, Reproduction phototypique
de l'edition princeps* (1492).   Ed. by Niemeyer, Halle, 1909.
[265] *Ibid.*

those wishing to make a scientific study of the language, which they have used from childhood; and those who wish to use the vernacular as an aid in studying Latin. The fifth book is for the third class of students; that is, those to whom the Castilian is a foreign language. Among these, he says, are the infidels to whom the Queen desires to carry the light of the Gospel.

In the Prologue to the Fifth Book, Lebrija discusses the subject matter of each division and the reason for the choice made by him: "Moreover, as says Quintilian, children beginning to learn the constructions of language, by the declining of nouns and the conjugating of verbs, suffer fatigue and in their meagre, confused knowledge of letters, syllables, parts of speech, put together nouns and verbs because they resemble others for which they have learned the rule. We have examples of this in those who write but the merest rudiments of Greek and Latin grammar."

The first four books, therefore, contain a very complete treatment of the science of grammar beginning with a treatise in Philology under the headings: Origin of terms (Greek); The invention of letters and history of their introduction into Spain; History of the characters used and their values; Of the letters and pronunciation of the Latin language; Of the letters and pronunciation of the Castilian language; Of the corrections to be made in order to speak pure Castilian; Of the kinship and relation of letters among themselves.

Under Orthography he treats of accents, of special rules for vowels and consonants and general rules for Castilian Spelling. Under Prosody he discusses especially the iambic foot, the functions of vowels and consonants, and gives a special chapter to Adonic verse. The third book is devoted to a detailed study of Etymology and Diction with a chapter on the "Order of the parts of a discourse." The fifth book, for the study of foreign students who need grammar as an aid to understanding the language, is brief and to the point. There are eleven chapters, the first of which treats of letters, syllables and words; the second, of nouns; the third, of pronouns; the fourth, of the conjugation of verbs; the next six, of the formation of verbs in general and of each mode in particular; and the eleventh chapter, of the "gerundive participle" and the "infinitive noun."

The pedagogical works of Lebrija reveal the source of his daughter's scholarship and the power of the home influences that produced so many of the earlier types of Renaissance womanhood in the Peninsula. Like Francisca Lebrija, numerous other daughters of savants enjoyed the privilege of parental tutorage and many of them shared the enthusiasm of fraternal devotion to the new learning. The number of women trained under humanism who followed the profession of private tutor, indicates, too, a fruitful source of domestic classical culture.

The universities were from the first important centers of learning for women students. Like the Italian universities, those of the Peninsula were ever open to both sexes on equal footing, and while the number of women present in any one of the universities at a given time seems not to have been great it is clear that at no time was their presence an anomaly. The position held by Luisa Medrano in the early years of the Renaissance period was one to which she rose through training received, if not within the walls of the University of Salamanca, at least within the shadow of those walls. And the presence of so many learned women, who, like her, claim Salamanca for their birthplace, seems to warrant that she counted among her auditors not a few of her own sex. Queen Isabel herself is said to have attended the lectures at this university, not only to encourage the professors and students, but for her own profit as well, even taking part in the disputations and other exercises.[266] Whether La Latina acquired her classical Latin in the University of Salamanca is uncertain. Some of her biographers assert that her teacher was an ecclesiastic, one of her kinsmen.[267] Women continued to frequent Salamanca, and in 1546 we find matriculated there Doña Alvara de Alva, a student of Greek, rhetoric and grammar.[268]

Alcalá had been patterned after the Italian universities by the great Ximenes and here, too, the lectures of a woman were entirely acceptable to both sexes, and evidently not only because the fair instructor was the daughter of the greatest humanist in all Spain.

Of the institutions below the university, established for the education of girls, the Palace School at the Royal Court is first both in order of time and of importance. Here the Infantas had their own tutors, apart from the Infante Juan and the ten noble youths, five older and five younger, whom the queen had chosen

---

[266] Cf. Reynier, *La Vie Universitaire dans l'ancienne Espagne*, Chap. IV, p. 138 ff.   Paris and Toulouse, 1902; Parada, *op. cit.*, 108 ff.

[267] Cf. Parada, *ibid.*, 127 ff.

[268] De la Fuente, *op. cit.*, II, Chap. LXV, p. 230.

to be educated with him. D. Fr. Diego de Deza, who was afterwards Archbishop of Seville, was the Infante's first tutor and Juan de Zapata was later on rector of the School of the Princes.[269]

The Infanta Isabel, eldest daughter of Ferdinand and Isabel, was 8 years old at the birth of Juan. She was thus 18 in 1488, in which year occurred the death of her tutor, Antonio Geraldino, the Italian who was engaged expressly for her service. Isabel's literary training under this Latin scholar was of the best Italian type, judged from his character and learning, as manifest in the poems which he dedicated to Don Alonso de Aragon, Archbishop of Saragossa, some of which were printed in Salamanca in 1505.[270] The years of close companionship with her illustrious mother rounded out the education of Isabel to a degree of perfection which won the unstinted praise of her contemporaries, among whom was the author of the *Carro de las doñas*. The queen fondly styled this beloved daughter "My mother-in-law," from her resemblance to Doña Juana, mother of Ferdinand.[271] Being the eldest, Isabel shared the queen's confidence and maternal training even more completely than did her three gifted sisters.

During the early years of quiet the Infanta learned to imitate her mother's dexterity in sewing and weaving and her skill with the tapestry needle as well as her piety in furnishing and adorning the altars and churches with the fruits of her diligent labor. But those years were followed by years of lessons in virile courage, blended so happily with womanly tenderness. Isabel and her sisters cannot have been absent from the band of virgins in the Queen's company before Granada there to learn the secret of that magnetic power wielded by the Royal Leader both on the field of battle and in the quiet study.

"She [Isabel] appeared," says Peter Martyr, "surrounded by a cortege of virgins, apparelled as if to celebrate the marriage of one of her children. She found our men dejected by watches and fatigue, by cold and hunger; she strengthened them and roused their courage anew."[272]

Here, too, the Princesses could learn from the great Queen's example the practical lessons in charity which drew from foreign writers such commendations as that made by Henry Clifford in his

---

[269] Cf. Clemencin in *Mem. de la Real Acad. de la Hist.*, Vol. VI, Il. XIV.
[270] Cf. Clemencin, *ibid.*, Il. XVI.
[271] *Ibid.*, Il. XIV.
[272] Ep. 73. Quoted in Mariéjol, *op. cit.*, Chap. II.

life of Jane Dormer, Duchess of Feria: "And it is very ordinary among the great ladies in Spain to visit hospitals and to give the sick and diseased to eat with their own hand, to serve them, to wipe their sores, to clean their wounds, to feed and cherish them with such alacrity and humble diligence as evidently showeth that it proceedeth from true fervor of Christian devotion and piety, which is really to wash the feet of saints.[273]

Of the material assistance thus procured for her soldiers by Isabel, Peter Martyr writes: "She has caused to be erected four hospital tents, wishing in her charitable foresight to relieve and care for, not only the wounded, but all those suffering from any infirmity. Such is the number of physicians, pharmacists, surgeons, and their attendants, such is their diligence and such the supply of remedies, that neither our House of the Holy Spirit in the suburbs nor the other hospitals in Milan can come up to this in comparison.[274]

The Queen had engaged as tutor to the younger Infantas, Alessandro Geraldino, brother of Antonio. He had fought on the side of Castile in the Portuguese war and was afterwards ordained to the priesthood. He died Bishop of San Domingo, in 1525.[275] Juana was 9 years old at the death of the elder brother, Antonio, and may have shared his instructions with Isabel. Maria was at this time 6, and Catherine only 3.

On the foundations of these domestic classes the Palace School was built up, a revival of that of Alfonso el Sabio, where large numbers of nobles were educated in humanistic studies and whence the movement spread to the other courts of Spain and Portugal. Here the Infantas continued to grow in wisdom and knowledge until they "were well learned all," and so virtuous and wise, says Vives, that "there were no queens by any man's remembrance more chaste of body, none better of name, none better loved of their subjects, nor more favored, nor better loved their husbands: none that more lawly did obey them, nor that kept both them and all theirs better without spot of villainy; there did none more hate filthiness and wantonness; none that ever did more perfectly fulfill all the points of a good woman."[276]

---

[273] *Life of Jane Dormer*, by Henry Clifford, 173. London, 1887.
[274] *Ibid*.
[275] Clemencin, *op. cit.*, Il. XVI.
[276] "De Institutione Christianae Foeminae," Lib. I. Translated by Hyrde, in Watson, *op. cit.*, 53.

The court of Emmanuel the Great of Portugal partook of the fruits of the prudent and powerful education given to the two sisters, Isabel and Maria, who each in turn exercised there the queenly rule, while Juana and Catherine bore the treasure to the Netherlands and England.

From 1492 to 1501, Peter Martyr taught in the Palace School and was at the same time Chaplain and *contino*. After his return from the political mission into Egypt the Queen made him Master of the Cavaliers in the Liberal Arts. Marineo succeeded Peter Martyr in the work of the classroom and as chaplain, and from his account it seems certain that both boys and girls, other than those of the Royal Family, partook of the instructions given in the Palace School. In his address to the Emperor Charles V[277] he says: "Ut enim in Italia, Rex Alphonsus quem supra memoravimus, sic in Hispania Rex Ferdinandus et Isabella Regina, catholici principes, dormientes Musas excitarunt, et bonis ingeniis hominibusque studiosis favere prudentissime liberalissimeque coeperunt, Isabella praesertim Regina magnanima virtutum omnium maxima cultrix. Quae . . . omnes suae domus adolescentes utriusque sexus nobilium liberos, praeceptoribus liberaliter et honorifice conductis erudiendos commendabat. Regnantibus itaque catholicis principibus, Hispania litteris latinis et bonis moribus excoli coepta est."

Since it was the custom for students to attend lectures with their tutors, who afterwards assisted them in their work, it would be a simple matter for all to profit by the teaching of Marineo and Peter Martyr.[278]

D'Arezzo's plan for the education of girls was doubtless appreciated by Isabel and followed out at court. In the accounts of their work given by Marineo and Peter Martyr we have also a hint that the spirit of Vittorino thrilled in their veins and informed the work of their classrooms. Marineo tells the Queen that he has compiled for his pupils a brief grammar to replace the ponderous tomes of the "grammarians," and that he then turns them quickly to the application, in pleasant reading. And Peter Martyr writes to the son of the Duke of Alba: "Since your father has withdrawn you from here, your companions are abundantly nourishing themselves with the De Officiis of Cicero, and certainly they have not

---

[277] *Op. cit., ibid.*
[278] Cf. Watson, *op. cit.,* 6.

disdained the Orations. We have almost finished the second book of the new Rhetoric. . . . I intend to reserve this year for Latin prose, since we have spent the last two years in riddling the mysteries of poetry."[279]

Vives is in this respect again rather the historian than the prophet of the Spanish Renaissance. When his work was translated into Castilian by Juan Justiniano it was widely circulated, but less as a book of instruction than as a subject of national interest because of the fame of the author and of his exposition of theories supported by the experience of practice.[280]

In the Palace School the studies auxiliary to the study of the classics were not neglected. The success of Lebrija's plan for teaching the vernacular is evident from the style employed by Isabel and her daughters in their familiar correspondence,[281] and from the fact that the Queen's Castilian has been pronounced as standard by the Spanish Royal Academy.[282] Here, too, "the history of the Church was studied with care," as the letters of Peter Martyr show,[283] and his biographer gives testimony of his power over the moral side of his work in the significant phrase: "Lui aussi enseigna à la fois les lettres latines et les bonnes moeurs."[284]

Marineo also draws a pleasing picture of the purity and simplicity of the Queen's household, where her maids of honor shared her solicitude as though she had been their mother abbess,[285] and in Isabel's library are still to be seen the beautiful illuminated Books of Hours from which she and Ferdinand said their daily office.[286]

While separate humanistic schools for boys gradually rose upon all sides in Spanish and Portuguese territory, directed either by individual humanists or by the religious orders, especially by the Jesuits, similar schools for girls were established throughout the Peninsula and in the colonies. The domestic education for girls as well as for boys was thus rapidly supplemented by

[279] Mariéjol, op. cit., Chap. IV, p. 39 ff.

[280] Libro llamado Instruccion de la Muger Cristiana. Printed in Valentia, 1528; Alcalá, 1529; Seville, 1535; Saragossa, 1539, with other editions. Cf. Watson, op. cit., p. xiii, No. 1.

[281] Cf. Parada, op. cit.; Clemencin, op. cit.

[282] Catholic Encyclopedia, Isabella I.

[283] Ep. 476 and 722. Cited in Mariéjol, op. cit., Chap. IV, p. 40.

[284] Ibid., 38.

[285] De Rebus Hispaniae Memorabilibus. Lib. XXI, f. 122.

[286] Ibid., Nos. 30–31, p. 478.

institutions endowed for the benefit of all classes of students. Such was the impetus given to the movement by Queen Isabel and her humanistic colleagues that, from the time of her death (1504) until the new order was firmly established throughout the Spanish and Portuguese dominions, girls' schools continued to multiply until before the end of the sixteenth century provision had been made for the higher education of every class of society, whether noble or poor.

The schools founded under the direct influence of the Court and of the Palace School were for the most part in favor of poor students. Thus, La Latina, after her years of honorable service as companion to Isabel, found means of extending the sphere of her usefulness after the Queen's death, by founding and directing a school for poor young ladies in Madrid, [287] and similarly Philip II later founded two colleges in the same city for orphan girls and the daughters of the attachés of the court. The first of these, completed in 1581, called Loretto, was situated in Atocha Street at the entrance to Anton Martin Square. It was demolished in 1583, with the church, where a precious statue of the Blessed Virgin sent to the king by Pope Saint Pius V was venerated. The second college, founded in 1592, was called St. Isabel and was built near the site of the first establishment. Its direction was confided to a community of Augustinian nuns and a beautiful church was provided for it. Both these colleges received boarders and day students. [288]

Among the other private endowments in favor of the poor was that of a boarding college for poor orphan girls belonging to the nobility, founded in Salamanca, in 1518, by Rodriguez Varillas. This college was provided with an income of 4,000 ducats and it was stipulated that 400 ducats should be bestowed on each student as a marriage or convent dowry. [289]

In Toledo, Cardinal Ximenes founded a college for young ladies, which his secretary, the Bishop of Ávila, Fr. Francisco Ruiz, extended and enlarged and in which he was interred. The Cardinal gave this college into the charge of the Franciscan Sisters. [290] A large college for young ladies of the nobility was also founded in the same city by Cardinal Silíceo. [291]

[287] *Supra*, 53.
[288] de la Fuente, *op. cit.*, II, 512.
[289] *Ibid.*, 118.
[290] *Ibid.*, 78.
[291] *Ibid.*, 511.

Similar in its organization to the work begun by Beatriz Galindo was the College of the Virgins, in Saragossa. This institution was founded by Mosén Juan Gonzalez de Villasimplez, Secretary of King Ferdinand, and was approved by a bull of Pope Clement VII, in 1531. Some difficulties in the internal management having arisen, the founder made over the buildings and rents to St. Ignatius and the Fathers of the Company of Jesus. But two of his daughters were students in the college and a third was dean. The students acquiesced, but the dean, "more Aragonese than her father," says the historian, disputed the claim. Her father held her in detention but she escaped with her papers to Rome, where from afar she pleaded her cause with him and was victorious. The incident led to the drawing up of a petition signed by many of the nobles of Saragossa, the Archbishop and Viceroy, D. Fernando de Aragon, uncle of Philip II, and the Deputation of the Realm, in response to which Pope Pius IV took the college under his patronage and favor.

The students of this college wore a uniform made of kersey, and the faculty was evidently composed of lay women under ecclesiastical direction. The Archbishop, D. Tomás de Borja, brother of St. Francis Borja, enlarged the church and was there interred. Some modern propagandist has perpetuated the memory of the holy man's benefactions to the women students of his time by defacing his monument with a lampoon in which the Archbishop is characterized as a hypocrite and the inmates of the college as crazy.[292]

The solicitude of Ferdinand and Isabel and of Emmanuel the Great of Portugal for the moral and intellectual improvement of the natives in the new territories was not overshadowed by anxiety for the personal needs of the settlers, and whenever a Spanish or Portuguese flag was raised, there was planted beside it the symbol of Redemption and of Christian Brotherhood, announcing the nature of the conqueror's mission. In these colonies education for girls kept pace with that for boys. Not only did the great Franciscan, Fr. Pedro de Gante, a relative of the Emperor, shelter in his Mexican convent the first elementary school in America, but as early as 1531 a college for girls was established under Cortes and was directed by his wife, the Marchioness of Valle.[293]

---

[292] de la Fuente, *op. cit.*, II, 512 ff.
[293] *Ibid.*, Chapt. LXXXV; Arrangoiz, "Historia de México, tome 3, App. VIII, p. 66 ff." Cited in *Ibid.*, 492.

The Queen had not been less concerned for the education of the religious whose duty it would necessarily become to perpetuate the institutions founded for the intellectual needs of her subjects. When Cardinal Ximenes began the work of founding the University of Alcalá, he heartily sympathized with the zeal of his Royal Penitent, and soon after the opening of the university, in 1508, he hastened to gather around it the various religious orders of the realm that they might profit by the advantages offered through the services of the foreign savants who came at his invitation to augment the number of native professors.[294] Among the colleges here established was one founded and endowed by the Cardinal himself for the training of nuns.   It was in charge of the Franciscan Sisters and was called San Juan de la Penetencia.   The date of the foundation is not clearly evident but the work seems to have been well established before the death of Ximenes, in 1517. Philip II afterwards increased the endowment which the Cardinal had bestowed in favor of students without dowry.[295]

In addition to their training schools for candidates to the cloister, the different sisterhoods, Augustinians, Benedictines, Franciscans, Dominicans, Tertians, and Carmelites, all had schools, in some places for the nobility, in others for the poor, and many of these schools either developed into colleges or were colleges by establishment.[296]   Among these latter, in addition to those already mentioned, were that of the Discalced Carmelites in Guadlajara, founded in 1591 by the Archbishop of Toledo, D. Gracia Girón de Loaisa,[297] and other similar foundations in Santiago, Seville and Cordova.[298]

The Augustinian Convent of Santa Maria de Gracia, in Ávila, where St. Teresa spent a year and a half of study after she was something past 14, was founded in 1509, and in her time there were forty nuns "of great virtue, piety and prudence," who taught "seculars."   Among these nuns was Sor Maria Briceño, whom her fond disciple described as "very discreet and holy."[299]

Precisely where many of the Iberian Renaissance women acquired their perfect Castilian and their fluent Latin seems to be a

---

[294] Catholic Encyclopedia, *Ximenes.*
[295] de la Fuente *op. cit.*, II, 78, 386.
[296] *Ibid.*, Chap. LXXXIX.
[297] *Ibid.*, 511.
[298] *Ibid.*, 512.
[299] *Ibid.*, 511 ff.; Cf. Catholic Encylcopedia, *Teresa of Jesus.*

mystery concealed behind convent walls or hidden beneath ruined palaces, but the mode of acquisition is written in their lives and labors as well as in the lives and labors of the theorists and practical educators of their day. The literary merit of the great St. Teresa is not altogether uncommon.[300] The Seraphic Saint was but one of that vast army of nuns, powerful in intellect and in soul, with whom the Peninsula Renaissance peopled the convents whence their virtue and wisdom reacted upon Iberian society to purify and enlighten it. Among these nuns were her own spiritual daughters, like Sor Cecilia of the Nativity and Sor Maria de San Alberto, and the great Franciscan abbess, Isabel Borja, the Venerable Francisca of Jesus.[301] Of such as these and of their foster children might an angelic Crashaw also sing:

> "Thy bright
> Life brought them first to kiss the light
> That kindled them to stars."[302]

To these convent women and to their unassuming devotion to the New Learning Spain and Portugal owed much. Under the direction of zealous and learned ecclesiastics like Cardinal Ximenes and his worthy successors, the nuns labored to steady the current of the Revival, after the monastic Court of Isabel of Castile had passed away; and because of the multitude of strong women moulded here after the pattern formed by Christian humanism there was brought into the gayer life of the later Iberian Renaissance the spiritualizing and refining influences of Religion and Art powerfully to counteract Self-Culture and Vanity, the baneful elements of radical humanism and the false Renaissance.

---

[300] Cf. Fitzmaurice-Kelly, *History of Spanish Literature*, 193 ff., New York, 1898.
[301] *Supra*, 68ff.
[302] "Hymn to the Name and Honor of the Admirable Saint Teresa."

CHAPTER III

The English Educational Renaissance may be described as the confluence of three streams of thought, originating in a common source but more or less modified by the nature of their differentiating channels.

While the education of boys was affected most by the branch taking its course direct from the center of the Italian Revival,[303] the education of girls in general seems not to have felt the influence of this current of thought; it aroused interest in the question of woman's classical education without widely transforming that interest into action. In the Chaucer of the *Legende of Goode Wimmen* the pure and sensible woman found a champion against the Chaucer of the *Romaunt of the Rose*, just as in the Boccaccio of the *De Claris Mulieribus* she had a defender against the Boccaccio of the *Decameron* and the *Corbaccio*. Further than this, early Italian influence apparently did not go.

The cause of the tardy acceptation of the complete ideal on the part of Englishmen must be sought rather in political history than in the history of pedagogy. When Marguerite of Anjou came to the Court of England as the Queen of Henry VI, the time was ripe for the diffusion of classical culture among the wives and daughters and sisters of the numerous native students already being trained in the schools of humanism, whether at home or abroad. But civil strife had prepared for the Princess of Sorrow the yet more bitter rôle of the "Queen of Tears," the while that the Wars of the Roses strewed a hundred English battlefields with the remnants of that feudalism which here as elsewhere was the destined Maecenas of the Revival. Back to the court of France the broken-hearted Marguerite was to bear the solacing memory of those sad yet peaceful days when in classical Naples she stored her mind with knowledge and girded her heart with wisdom against her future destiny. To England she had given proof of her zeal for learning and of what that zeal would have accomplished, when she founded in her own name Queen's College at Cambridge and as "the better

---

[303] Cf. McCormick, *op. cit.*, 204; Sandys, *Hist. of Classical Scholarship*, II. Cambridge, 1906.

97

man of the two" shared in promoting Henry's munificence in his educational benefactions.[304]

The new order of nobility that rose at the beck of Henry VII had a fostering mother in the mother of that monarch, Margaret, Countess of Richmond and Derby, type of the medieval learned woman of England. This Margaret helped to prepare the way for woman's participation in the new learning by her benefactions to the universities, whence their tutors were later on to issue, and by the example of her own devotion to serious study.[305]

With the peace established by Henry VII and the accession of Henry VIII the time was once more propitious and again the movement advanced, this time in the two indirect currents, by way of Spain on the one hand, and of Geneva on the other. Through the spirit of Catherine of Aragon and of her countryman Juan Luis Vives, the Spanish-Italian influence was to predominate in the education of girls, in this particular modifying the earlier views of Erasmus and intensifying those held by such men as Blessed Thomas More and the youthful Henry VIII. Had Henry wedded a native princess or even a princess of any other European nation there seems no doubt that in his court the girl would receive her full share of participation in the New Learning, but the coming of Catherine of Aragon determined the nature of her training apart from the acquisition of classical knowledge, while it incidentally influenced the mode of such acquisition itself.

The earliest influence of Queen Catherine and through her of the Spanish Renaissance, is manifest in the domestic school of Blessed Thomas More. When Catherine came to England as the bride of Prince Arthur, More made Latin verses in her honor and was rewarded with her lasting appreciation and friendship.[306] When the future chancellor established his own household (1505) the coming of his three daughters strengthened more and more his desire to see reflected in the women of England the perfections of their noble Queen, and so wisely and lovingly did he educate Margaret and Cecilia and Elizabeth, with their kinswoman, Margaret Giggs, that the mere mention of their names could serve the

---

[304] Cf. Hookham, *The Life and Times of Margaret of Anjou*, I, London, 1872; Drane, *op. cit.*, II, 261 ff.; Strickland, *Lives of the Queens of England*, III. London, 1842.

[305] Watson, *op. cit.*, 2 ff.

[306] Cf. Watson, *op. cit.*, 16 ff.

English humanists as a powerful argument in favor of the Renaissance ideal of woman's education.[307]

In Blessed Thomas More is exemplified the humanistic theorist trained under Italian masters and the pedagogue inspired by Spanish-Italian practice. With all the Christian humanists he supports the thesis of man's duties in the matter of the girl's complete and full training in liberal studies and in the exercise of virtues. His views are clearly expressed in the letters which he addressed to his children and to their several tutors. To Gunnell, one of these tutors, he writes:[308] "Neither is there anie difference in harvest time, whether it was man or woman, that sowed first the corne; for both of them beare name of a reasonable creature equally whose nature reason only doth distinguish from bruite beastes, and therefore I do not see why learning in like manner may not equally agree with both sexes; for by it, reason is cultivated, and (as a fielde) sowed with wholesome precepts, it bringeth forth excellent fruit. But if the soyle of womans braine be of its owne nature bad, and apter to beare fearne then corne (by which saying manie doe terrifye women from learning) I am of opinion therefore that a woman's witt is the more diligently by good instructions and learning to be manured, to the ende, the defect of nature may be redressed by industrie. Of which minde were also manie wise and holie ancient Fathers, as, to omitt others, S. Hierome and S. Augustine, who not only exhorted manie noble matrones and honourable virgins to the getting of learning, but also to further them therein, they diligently expounded unto them manie hard places of Scriptures; yea, wrote manie letters unto tender maydes, full of so greate learning, that scarcely our olde and greatest Professours of Divinitie can well reade them, much lesse be able to understande them perfectly; which holie Saints workes you will endeavour, my learned Gunnell, of your courtesie, that my daughters may learne, whereby they may chiefly knowe, what ende they ought to have in their learning, to place the fruits of their labours in God, & a true Conscience; by which it will be easily brought to passe, that being at peace within themselves, they shall neither be moved with praise of flatterers nor the nipping follies of unlearned scoffers."

As a practical outcome of his theories there was established in the chancellor's manor at Chelsea the ideal Renaissance academy,

---

[307] *Ibid.*
[308] More, *Life of Sir Thomas More*, 128 ff. London, 1726.

praised by Erasmus as "a school, or university, of Christian religion,"[309] so [310] "that the schoole of Sir Thomas More's children was famous over the whole world; for that their witts were rare, their diligence extraordinarie, and their maisters most excellent men, as above the rest Doctour *Clement* an excellent Grecian and physician, who was after reader of the phisicke-lecture in Oxford, and set out manie bookes of learning. After him one *William Gunnel* who read after with greate praise in *Cambridge*, and beside these one *Drue*, one *Nicolas*, and after all one *Richard Hart*."[311]

The humanistic spirit of joyous enthusiasm pervading this most perfect of domestic schools breathes from every page of the epistles. In one of these the fond father writes:[312]

"Thomas More to his whole schoole sendeth greetinge: Behold how I have found out a compendious way to salute you all, and make spare of time and paper, which I must needes have wasted in saluting everie one of you particularly by your names; which would be verie superfluous, because you are all so deare unto me, some in one respect, some in another, that I can omitt none of you unsaluted. Yet I know not, whether there can be any better motive, why I should love you, then because you are schollars, learning seeming to binde me more straytely unto you, then the nearenesse of bloud. . . . If I loved you not exceedingly, I should envie this your so great happinesse, to have had so manie great schollars for your maisters."

And in another he says:[313] "Thomas More to his best beloved Children, and Margarett Gigs, whome he numbereth amongst his owne, sendeth greeting: The marchant of Bristow brought unto me your letters, the next day after he had receaved them of you, with the which I was exceedingly delighted. For there can come nothing, yea though it were never so rude, never so meanely polished, from this your shoppe, but it procureth me more delight then anie other mens workes, be they never so eloquent; your writing doth so stirre up my affection towards you; but excluding these your letters may also very well please me for their owne worth, being full of fine witt and of pure Latin phrase. . . . And how can you want matter of writing unto me, who am delighted to

---

[309] Watson, *op. cit.*, 175.
[310] More, *op. cit.*, 124.
[311] Richard Hyrde, cf. Watson, *ibid.*, 15.
[312] More, *ibid.*, 131.
[313] *Ibid.*, 132 ff.

heare eyther of your studies, or of your play; whome you may
even then please exceedingly, when having nothing to write of, you
write as largely as you can of that nothing, then which nothing is
more easie for you to doe, especially being women, and therefore
pratlers by nature and amongst whome daily a great storie riseth
of nothing."

Passing then from light jest to serious earnest the letter continues: "But this I admonish you to doe, that whether you write
of serious matters, or of trifles, you write with diligence and consideration, premeditating of it before; neither will it be amiss, if
you first indite it in English, for then it may more easily be translated into Latine, whilst the mind free from inventing is attentive
to finde apt and eloquent wordes. And although I put this to
your choice, whether you will do so or no; yet I enjoyne you by
all meanes, that you diligently examine what you have written
before you write it over fayre againe; first considering attentively
the whole sentence, and after examine everie parte thereof, by which
meanes you may easily finde out, if anie solecismes have escaped
you; which being putt out, and your letter written fayre, yet then
let it not also trouble you to examine it over againe; for sometimes
the same faultes creepe in at the second writing, which you before
had blotted out. By this your diligence you will procure, that
those your trifles will seeme serious matters. For as nothing is so
pleasing but may be made unsavorie by prating garrulitie, so
nothing is by nature so unpleasant, that by industrie may not be
made full of grace and pleasantnesse."

The proficiency attained by these English Renaissance girls
indicates their ready response to the interest taken in them by
their noble father. One of his biographers says:[314] "His children
used to often translate out of English into Latine, and out of
Latine into English; and Dr. Stapleton testifieth that he hath
seene an Apologie of Sir Thomas More's to the universitie of Oxford
in defense of learning, turned into Latine by one of his daughters,
and translated againe into English by another."

Of evidence of Margaret's learning much more information is
available than of that of her sisters, her position as eldest giving
her precedence in her father's confidence. Of her, Cresacre More
says:[315] "This daughter was likest her father as well in favour as

---

[314] *Ibid.*, 93.
[315] *Op. cit.*, 139.

witt, and proved a most rare woman for learning, sanctitie, and
secrecie, and therefore he trusted her with all his secretts. She
wrote two Declamations in English which her father and she
turned into Latine so elegantly, as one could hardly judge which
was the best. She made also a treatise of the Foure Last things;
which her father sincerrely protested that it was better than his,
and therefore, it may be, never finished his. She corrected by her
witt a place in S. Cyprian, corrupted, as Pamelian and John Coster
testifye, in steede of *nisi vos sinceritatis*, rectoring *nervos sinceritatis*."[316]

Her father relates a conversation held between him and the
Bishop of Exeter over Margaret's literary productions, in which
the Bishop describes one of her letters to More as of "so pure a
Stile, so good Latine, so eloquent, so full of sweete affections," and
praises an "Oration" of hers and "many of her verses," sending her
in recognition a "portegue." She also made an oration, the biographers say, defending the rich man whom Quintilian accuses of
poisoning the poor man's bees, "so eloquent and wittie that it may
strive with his," and she translated "Eusebius out of Greek,"
which never was printed because "Christopherson of that time
had done it exactly before."[317] Margaret also translated into
English Erasmus' "Treatise on the Lord's Prayer."[318]

Alluding to a doubt expressed by Cardinal Pole as to the genuineness of Margaret's writings,[319] More tells her that he has
informed the Cardinal that she has no master in her house and no
man but needs her help.[320]

The education provided for these daughters of Sir Thomas More
was far from the narrow classical type developed by the later
school of humanists. In all respects it conformed to the best
principles laid down in Italy and Spain for the careful training of
the whole woman. Instances of this care are abundant in the
history of the Chelsea household. Recommendations on the
study of the natural sciences and of logic are to be found in the
letters of More to his daughters, and here also are commendations
on their progress. In one of these he expresses his gratitude to
"Mr. Nicolas our deare friend (a most expert man in astronomie)"

[316] Cf. Watson, *op. cit.*, 188, note.
[317] *Ibid.*, 141, 143.
[318] Watson, *op. cit.*, 159.
[319] More, *op. cit.*, 68.
[320] *Ibid.*, 140.

for his good lessons in "philosophie," and he commends Margaret for diligently studying "phisicke and holie Scriptures," adding, "And whereas I am wont alwaies to counsell you to give place to your husband, now on the other side, I give you license to strive to maister him in the knowledge of the sphere."[321]

Of his daughters' application to logic in company with Margaret Giggs, he says:[322] "I cannot sufficiently expresse, my best beloved wenches, how your eloquent letters have exceedingly pleased me; and this not the least cause, that I understande by them, you have not in your journeys, though you change places often, omitted anie thing of your custome of exercising yourselves, either in making of Declamations, composing of verses, or in your Logike exercises; by this I perswade my selfe, that you dearely love me, because I see you have so great a care to please me by your diligence."

The care exercised by this holy man for the training of his daughters in virtue and in religious knowledge is everywhere apparent in his correspondence. In another letter, after jesting pleasantly of the study of astronomy he adds a characteristic admonition:[323] "Goo forward therefore with this your new and admirable skill, by which you do thus climbe up to the starres, which whilst you daily admire, in the meane while I admonish you also to thinke of this holie fast of Lent, and lett that excellent and pious song of Boethius sound in your eares, whereby you are taught also with your mindes to penetrate heaven, least when the bodie is lifted up on high, the soul be driven downe to the earth with the brute beasts. Farewell."

In a letter to Gunnell, More discourses at length on the nature of virtue and knowledge, exhorting him to be diligent in seconding his efforts and those of his wife to foster solid virtue in his children. The following passages are characteristic:[324] "For as I esteeme learning, which is joyned with vertue more then all the threasures of kings; so what doth the fame of being a great schollar bring us, if it be severed from vertue other than a notorious and famous infamie, especially in a woman, whome men will be readie the more willingly to assayle for their learning, because it is a rare matter, and argueth a reproche to the sluggishness of a man, who will not stick to lay the fault of their naturall malice upon the

---

[321] *Ibid.*, 143 ff.
[322] *Ibid.*, 135 ff.
[323] *Ibid.*, 132.
[324] *Ibid.*, 124 ff.

qualitie of learning supposing all their owne unskillfullness by comparing it with the vices of those that are learned, shal be accounted for vertue: but if anie woman on the contrarie parte (as I hope and wish by your instruction and teaching all mine will doe) shall joyne manie vertues of the minde with a little skill of learning, I shall accounte this more happinesse, then if they were able to attaine to Craesus's wealth joyned with the beautie of fayre Helene; . . . that avoyding all the gulphes and downe-falls of pride, they walke through the pleasant meadowes of modestie, that they never be enamoured of the glistering hue of golde and silver, nor lament for the want thereof, which by errour they admire in others, that they thinke no better of themselves for all their costlie trimmings, nor anie meaner for the want of them; not to lessen their beautie by neglecting it, which they have by nature, not to make it anie more by unseemely art, to thinke vertue their chiefe happinesse, learning and good qualities the next, of which those are especially to be learned, which will avayle them most, that is to say, pietie towards Gods [God], Charitie towards all men, modestie, and Christian humilitie in themselves, by which they shall reape from God the rewarde of an innocent life, by certaine confidence thereof they shall not neede to feare death. . . . Nothing is more avayleable, then to reade unto them the holesome precepts of the Fathers,whome they knowe, not to be angrie with them, and they must needs be vehemently moved with their authorities, because they are venerable for their sanctitie."

What the father here taught by precept he confirmed by example. His own penitential spirit did not even suggest itself behind its outward expression of perfect self-control and seemingly spontaneous affability. But his daughters knew and felt the secret of that power and were drawn on to filial imitation. To Margaret was confided the sacred task of cleansing the hair shirt whose roughness was concealed beneath the silken folds of the chancellor's robe and whose sting prompted the smile of the devoted friend and genial courtier. In like manner the corded scourge with which the father disciplined his own flesh became to his daughters the symbol of that Christian self-denial to which they had so often been exhorted.[325]

But in the More household Morality was the daughter of

---

[325] Roper, op. cit., 26.

Religion, the study of Seneca and Cato only confirming by reason what the Ten Commandments had taught through faith. William Roper, for long years a member of the inner circle as husband of Margaret More, says of the family devotions:[326] "As Sir Thomas More's custom was daily (if he were at home), besides his private prayers with his children, to say the Seven Psalms, the Litany, and the Suffrages following, so was his guise nightly before he went to bed, with his wife, children and household, to go to his chapel, and there on his knees ordinarily to say certain psalms and collects with them."

Accompanying the devotional exercises were careful instructions in religious matters given by the devoted father both orally and in his correspondence. In one of these exhortations, Roper quotes his father-in-law as saying:[327] "It is now no mastery for you children to go to heaven, for every body giveth you good counsel, every body giveth you good example. You see virtue rewarded and vice punished, so that you are carried up to heaven even by the chins. But if you live in the time that no man will give you good counsel, no man will give you good example, when you shall see virtue punished and vice rewarded, if you will then stand fast and firmly stick to God upon pain of life, though you be but half good, God will allow you for whole good."

On very substantial questions the learned father directed his daughters and led them to heroism, as we learn from the incident in the Tower where Margaret reasoned with the prisoner over the legality of the Act of Supremacy, reminding him that many bishops, doctors and learned men had supported it; that he being only a layman might not put his judgment before theirs, and that he did wrong to bring suffering upon himself and his children without sufficient cause. His reply brought conviction and peace, and reconciled his daughter to the heroic act of separation. He patiently instructed her that for seven years he had studied all the Greek and Latin Fathers on the subject of the Pope's supremacy and they all agreed in supporting it; that some prelates did deny it while many more in other parts condemned their act; that if a general council decided the question he would acquiesce,

---

[326] Roper, *The Mirrour of Vertue in Worldly Greatness or the Life of Sir Thomas More, Knight*, 13, London, 1902.
[327] *Ibid.*, 14.

but not to the decision of the council of one realm; and that therefore it was against his conscience to sign the act.[328]

The after history of Blessed Thomas More's children must be
read in the annals of the masses, but concerning one of Margaret's
daughters, very probably the "wench better than three boys;"[329]
Ascham gives us an interesting bit of information in his letters.
Writing from London, January 12, 1554, to Lady Clarke, then
at the Court of Queen Mary, he says:[330] "Your remarkable love
of virtue and zeal for learning, most illustrious lady, joined with
such talents and perseverance, are worthy of great praise in
themselves, and greater still because you are a woman, but greatest
of all because you are a lady of the court; where there are many
other occupations for ladies besides learning, and many other
pleasures besides the practice of the virtues.   This double praise
is further enhanced by the two patterns that you have proposed
to yourself to follow, the one furnished you by the court, the
other by your family.   I mean our illustrious queen Mary, and
your noble grandfather, Thomas Moore—a man whose virtues go
to raise England above all other nations. . . .

"It was I who was invited some years ago from the University
of Cambridge by your mother, Margaret Roper—a lady worthy
of her great father, and of you her daughter—to the house of your
kinsman, Lord Giles Alington, to teach you and her other children
the Greek and Latin tongues; but at that time no offers could induce
me to leave the University.   It is sweet to me to bear in mind this
request of your mother's, and I now not only remind you thereof,
but would offer you, now that I am at court, if not to fulfill her
wishes, yet to do my best to fulfill them, were it not that you have
so much learning in yourself, and also the aid of those two learned
men, Cole and Christopherson, so that you need no help from me,
unless in their absence you make use of my assistance, and if you
like, abuse it."

In Richard Hyrde's strong support of woman's educational
rights is clearly manifest the influence of Blessed Thomas More,
and of his success in educating his daughters.   This inmate of
Chelsea and sometime tutor to the More children has left on the
subject two noteworthy expressions of his views, the one in the

---

[328] More, *op. cit.*, 228–231.
[329] *Ibid.*, 141.
[330] *The Whole Works of Roger Ascham.*   Ed. by Giles, Vol. I, Pt. I, p.
lxxxiv.   Letter CLXVI.   London, 1865.

dedication to his translation of Vives' *De Institutione Christianae Foeminae*, and the other in his preface to Margaret More's translation of Erasmus' *Treatise on the Lord's Prayer*. In the former he says: "For what is more fruitful than the good education and order of women, the one half of all mankind, and that half also whose good behaviour or evil tatches giveth or bereaveth the other half, almost all the whole pleasure and commodity of this present life, beside the furtherance or hindrance further growing thereupon concerning the life to come? And surely for the planting and nursing of good virtues in every kind of women, virgins, wives and widows, I verily believe there was never any treatise made, either furnished with more goodly counsels, or set out with more effectual reasons, or garnished with more substantial authorities, or stored more plenteously of convenient examples nor all these things together more goodly treated and handled than Master Vives hath done in his book. Which book when I read, I wished in my mind that either in every country women were learned in the Latin tongue, or the book out of Latin translated into every tongue. And much I marveled, as I often do, of the unreasonable oversight of men, which never ceased to complain of women's conditions. And yet having the education and order of them in their own hands, not only do little diligence to teach them and bring them up better, but also purposely withdraw them from learning, by which they might have occasions to wax better by themselves."[331]

In Hyrde's preface to Margaret More's translation the thought common to the entire school of Christian humanists is thus expressed: "I have heard many men put great doubt whether it should be expedient and requisite or not, a woman to have learning in books of Latin and Greek. And some utterly affirm that it is not only nother [neither] necessary nor profitable, but also very noisome and jeopardous. But these men that so say, do in my judgment, either regard but little what they speak in this matter, or else, as they be for the more part unlearned they envy it and take it sore to he[a]rt, that others should have the precious jewell, which they nother have themselfe nor can find in their hearts to take the pain to get. For first, where they reckon such instability and mutable nature in women, they say therein their pleasure of a contentious mind, for the maintenance of their mat[t]er, for if they would look thereon with an even eye and consider the matter

---

[331] Watson, *op. cit.*, 30.

equally, they should find and well perceive, that women be not onely of no less constancy and discretion than men, but also more steadfast and sure to trust unto than they."[332]

And following up Vives' argument, he continues: "And where they find fau[l]t with learning, because they say it engendreth wit and craft, then they reprehend it, for that that it is most worthy to be commended for, and the which is one singular cause wherefore learning ought to be desired, for he that had leaver have his wife a fool than a wise woman, I hold him worse than twice frantic. Also reading and studying of books so occupieth the mind, that it can have no leisure to muse or delight in other fantasies, where in all handiworks that men say be more meet for a woman, the body may be busy in one place, and the mind walking in another; and while they sit sewing and spinning with their fingers, may cast and compass many peevish fancies in their minds, which must needs be occupied either with good or bad, so long as they be waking. And those that be evil disposed will find the means to be nought, though they can [know] never a letter in the book, and she that will be good, learning shall cause her to be much the better.   For it sheweth the image and way of good living, even right as a mirror sheweth the similitude and proportion of the body.   And doubtless the daily experience proveth that such as are nought are those that never knew what learning meant.   For I never heard tell, nor read of any woman well learned that ever was (as plenteous as evil tongues be) spotted or infamed as vicious.   But on the other side, many by their learning take, such increase of goodness that many may bear them witness of their virtue, of which sort I could rehearse a great number both of old time and of late."[333]

In the Royal Court itself the classics found favor from the beginning of the reign of Henry and Catherine, but with the birth of the Princess Mary (1516) came definite educational plans, in which the needs of the girl were alone considered.   A humanistic father, like Henry, whose domestic virtues were as yet untainted by germs of social vice, could share his sympathies with the Renaissance mother so perfectly fitted for the rôle of guardian to her daughter and governess of a school of princesses.   The education of Mary was begun, therefore, from the cradle and, according to the pedagogical ideas handed down from her illus-

---

[332] *Ibid.*, 162, 163.
[333] *Ibid.*, 166, 167.

trious grandmother, Queen Isabel, she had as companions in work and in play a few noble maidens chosen with care. Among these were her first cousin, Frances Brandon, daughter of Mary Tudor and mother of Lady Jane Grey;[334] and the Lady Elizabeth, daughter of Gerald Fitzgerald, the Earl of Kildare. The latter, the "Geraldine" of the Earl of Surrey's poems, was a kinswoman of the subject of Leonardo da Vinci's "La Gioconda," or "Mona Lisa," both being descendants of Geraldini brothers, Guelf exiles from Florence, the family of "Mona Lisa" having retired to Naples, while that of "Geraldine" emigrated to England where "Geraldo" became "Gerald" with the added distinction "Fitz-gerald" as Earl of Kildare.[335]

The soul of this little school was the Queen Mother, whose character in this capacity is drawn by Vives in his dedication to the "De Institutione Christianae Foeminae" and in the chapters of the same work in which he treats of the virtues and duties of motherhood and the early training of the child. He makes clear the allusion when he says:[336] "And this work (most excellent and gracious Queen) I offer unto you in like manner, as if a painter would bring unto you your own visage and image, most cunningly painted. For like as in that portraiture you might see your bodily similitude; so in these books shall you see the resemblance of your mind and goodness; because that you have been both maid, wife and widow, and so you have been handled yourself in all the order and course of your life, that whatsoever you did might be an example unto other to live after. But you had leaver the virtues to be praised, than yourself; howbeit no man can praise the virtues of women, but he must needs comprehend you in the same praise, howbeit your mind ought to be obeyed. Therefore you shall understand, that many like unto you be praised here by name expressly: but yourself spoken of continually, though you be not named. For virtues can never be praised, but they must needs be praised withal, that be excellent in them, though their name be not spoken of. . . . Therefore all other women shall have an example of your life and deeds: and by these books that I have dedicated unto your name, they shall have rules and precepts to live by; and so shall they be bounden unto your goodness both for

[334] Cf. Watson, op. cit., 160.
[335] Vasari, op. cit., Vol. III, Pt. 3, p. 14 ff.; Staley, Famous Women of Florence, Chapt. VI. London, 1909. Cf. Watson, op. cit., 70.
[336] Preface. Translated by Hyrde, in Watson, op. cit., 37.

that which itself hath done in giving example: and that it hath
been the occasion of my writing."

As governess little Mary had the Countess of Salisbury, niece
of Edward IV and mother of Cardinal Pole, the "Blessed Margaret
Pole," later martyred in the cause of Papal supremacy.[337]   The
Princess' physician was Thomas Linacre, who also directed her
first studies and wrote for her the *Rudimenta Grammatices*.[338]
Vives was at the English court from 1523 to 1528 and, while it is
doubtful whether he actually taught the princesses, his share in
directing the work of their tutors was not inconsiderable.   In 1523,
the year of his arrival in England, the Queen requested him to
draw up a plan of studies for the Princess.   In response he produced the *De Ratione Studii Puerilis* (for a girl), concerning which
he says: "You have ordered me to write a brief plan of study
according to which thy daughter Mary may be educated by her
tutor.   Gladly have I obeyed thee, as I would in far greater
matters, were I able.   And since thou hast chosen as her teacher,
a man above all learned and honest, as was fit, I was content to
point out details, as with a finger.   He will explain the rest of
the matters.   Those questions which I thought either obscurely
treated or omitted by writers on the art of grammar I have noted
somewhat copiously.   I pray Christ that this plan of teaching
may effectively help thy daughter to her erudition and virtue."[339]
At the conclusion of the work the author says: "This is only, in
my view, a rough sketch of studies.   Time will admonish her as
to more exact details, and thy singular wisdom will discover for
her what they should be."[340]

But what Vives does here suggest is neither little nor slight.   As
a "heuristic Latinist" he proves himself the colleague of D'Arezzo,
indorsing all the views of the Italian humanist on methods for
language and literature, and supplying further directions in forcible
passages on drill in both Latin and Greek classical pronunciation,
on colloquial matter for conversation exercises, on the detailed use
of the note book, and on the exercise of memory.   The suggestions
here given for written exercises from the vernacular into Latin on
short themes of courtesy or morality were widely adopted by his

---

[337] Cf. Catholic Encyclopedia, *Margaret Pole (Blessed)*.
[338] Cf. Watson, *op. cit.*, **14**.
[339] Watson, *op. cit.*, **137**.
[340] *Ibid.*, **147**.

successors both in England and elsewhere. With all the practical educators of his school, Vives places more stress on the moral content of the works to be read than does his predecessor, D'Arezzo. For the girl's reading he highly recommends the Christian Latin poets and among heathen poets he prefers Lucan, Seneca, and Horace. His devotion to the Ancients does not forbid him to include also among the books worthy of study the Paraphrases of Erasmus and the Utopia of Sir Thomas More. Among works of piety and religion the New Testament was to be read both morning and evening under the tutor's direction. Vives here prefers prayers said in the vernacular, or, lacking this, a thorough understanding of the Latin prayers used, by means of oral translations.

The practical part taken by the Queen in Mary's schooling is suggested by a letter which she addressed to the Princess, apparently after they had been separated by reason of the divorce negotiations. In an undated letter from "Oborne" she says: "Doughter—I pray you thinke not that any forgetfulnes hathe caused me to kepe Charles so long here, and answered not to you good Letter, in the whiche I perceyve ye wold knowe howe I doo. I am in that caas that the long absence of the King and you troublethe me. My helthe is metely good; and I trust in God, he that sent me the last dothe it to the best, and woll shortly torne it to the fyrst to come to good effecte. And in the meane tyme I am veray glad to hear from You, pecially when they shewe me that ye be well amended. I pray God to contynue it to hys pleasour. As for your writing in Lattine I am glad that ye shall chaunge frome me to Maister Federston,[341] for that shall doo you moche good, to lerne by him to write right. But yet some tymes I would be glad when you doo write to Maister Federston of your owne editing when he hathe rede it that I may see it. For it shalbe a grete comfort to me to see You kepe your Latten and fayer writing and all. And soo I pray You to recommaunde me to my Lady of Salisbury. At Oborne this Friday night. Your loving mother— Katherine, the Quwene."[342]

In the "Privy Purse Expenses" of this Princess is given a glimpse of her physical exercises and of her further accomplishments in

---

[341] John Fetherstone. Cf. Madden in Preface to *Privy Purse Expenses of the Princess Mary*, p. cxxix. London, 1831.

[342] *Original Letters, illustrative of Eng. Hist.* Edited by Ellis, II, 19. London, 1825. Cf. Madden, *ibid.*

music and needlework. Here are items of outlay as follows:[343]
"To Christopher that keepeth my lady graces grey hounds.[344]
For mending of my lade graces virgynall.[345]   To Paston saynt
marke Daye techyng her on the vyrgynalles.[346]   To Chambre the
same day for techyng her on the lute.[347]   For gold to embroyder a
qwyssion.[348] For Silver to embraudre a Boxe for my lady Elizabeth
grace."[349]

To the lessons in practical morality hourly given Mary by her
mother and governess, were added moral precepts from the *Satellitium sive Symbola* which Vives composed for her,[350] saying in his
dedicatory epistle:[351] "It has been customary that a satellitium
(escort, guard) should be attached to princes, to keep constant
watch over the safety of their life and body . . . but I for my
part, often requested by your mother, an illustrious and holy
woman, will set around thy soul a guard, which will preserve thee
more securely and safely than any spearmen or bowmen whatever.
For a body-guard has been known to desert its Emperor, for
reward, or for fear, or for sport. . . . But this body-guard of
mine once assimilated by thee in good faith, for thy safety, will
block the way against all attacks and assaults on thy breast.   For
there is greater danger to the soul from the forces and cunning of
vices than to the body from either external or internal contests.
And as each one's soul ought to be so much dearer to him than his
body, so the more crafty and hidden snares of vices and their
tyranny are more grievous, and their destruction of the soul is
more violent and horrible.

"You will receive, therefore, from me two hundred guards, or a
few more, whom you will get to know familiarly, so that neither by
night nor by day, neither at home nor in public, will you permit
yourself to depart a finger's breadth from them."

Vives closes the epistle with these words: "May the Lord Jesus
impart to thee His spirit, that thou mayest live most happily, as
long as ever may be, and that thou mayst prefer goodness before

[343] *Privy Purse Expenses of the Princess Mary.*   Edited by Frederick
Madden.   London, 1831.
[344] *Ibid.*, 22.
[345] *Ibid.*, 15, 21.
[346] *Ibid.*, 26.
[347] *Ibid.*
[348] *Ibid.*, 50.
[349] *Ibid.*
[350] Watson, *op. cit.*, 151 ff.
[351] *Ibid.*

all fortune." It is dated from Bruges the Calends of July, 1524. Among the "body-guards" are maxims like the following: *Generositas virtus, non sanguis.*[352] *Magnum satellitium, amor.*[353] *Princeps, multis consulendo.*[354] Each symbol is accompanied by an exposition of its meaning, the entire work being in Latin.

The influence which Catherine of Aragon exercised in the moral training of Mary is manifest in the letters that passed between them. In one of these the Queen writes: "I will send you two Books in Latin, one shall be, *de Vita Christi*, with the Declaration of the Gospels; and the other, the Epistles of St. Hierome, that he did write always to Paula and Eustochium, and in them trust you shall see good things. And sometimes, for your Recreation, use your Virginals, or Lute, if you have any. But one thing specially I desire you, for the love that you owe unto God and unto me, to keep your Heart with a chaste Mind, and your Body from all ill and wanton Company."[355]

Henry's early proclamations, concerning the government of the Church as he found it, are enlightening as to the religious instruction which he had given to the princess in better days. Those, for instance, concerning rites and ceremonies, among which are such articles as the following: "On Candlemas Daye it shall be declared, that the bearynge of Candles is done in the memorie of Christe, the spirituall lyghte, of whom Simeon dyd prophecye, as it is redde in the churche that daye."—"On Ashewenisday it shall be declared, that these ashes be gyven, to put every christen man in remembraunce of penaunce at the begynnynge of Lent, and that he is but erthe and asshes."—"On Palmesonday it shall be declared that bearynge of palmes renueth the memorie of the receivynge of Christe, in lyke maner into Jerusalem before his deathe."—"On Good Friday it shall be declared, howe crepynge of the crosse, sygnyfieth and humblynge of oure selfe to Christe, before the crosse, and the kyssynge of it a memorie of our redemption, made upon the crosse." "And at foure tymes in the yere at the leste, to declare the sygnification of the other ceremonyes."[356]

These proclamations are evidence that the practical religious

---

[352] *No. 53.*
[353] *No. 65.*
[354] *No. 121.*
[355] "Two Important State Papers," in *Historical Reprints*, XV, p. 6. Edinburgh, 1886.
[356] *Tudor Proclamations*, 30 *Henry VIII*. Edited by Garnett. Oxford, 1897.

instructions given to the Princess Mary were not inspired by super-
stition.   On the entire subject of Mary's struggles to preserve her
faith and of her attitude towards heretics when Queen of England,
evidence is not wanting in favor of her natural spirit of uprightness
and clemency.   Her motives in adopting the political methods
common to both Catholic and Protestant rulers in her time when
dealing with public movements of this nature, are clear from historical records.[357]

With the coming of Catherine Parr serious study and sober living
were held in honor at the Court as in the days of Catherine of
Aragon, with the difference in religious influence brought about
by the Queen's Puritan leanings and her outward adherence to the
King's rights of supremacy in Church and State.   Catherine Parr's
early education had been in all respects like that of the Princess
Mary.   Her knowledge of the classics, her skill in music and in
artistic needlework, all recall the exercises of the princesses at the
Royal Court.   Born about 1513, Catherine was three years Mary's
senior.   In her early teens she learned well the duties of a devoted
stepmother, as wife of Edward, Lord Gainsborough, and guardian
of his grown-up children.   When married to the widower John
Neville, Lord Latimer, she was still under twenty, and only at his
death did she change her religious beliefs, "When," says the
Protestant biographer, "unbiased by the influence of that zealous
supporter of the ancient system, she found herself at liberty to
listen to the impassioned eloquence of the apostles of the Protestant
faith."[358]

Because of her Puritan sympathies Catherine Parr was the "joy
of the University of Cambridge," and, it may be said, the foster
mother of the Renaissance movement which set in through Geneva.
The part which Catherine had to play, however, as Queen of Henry
VIII and stepmother to the royal children, revealed her diplomatic
tendencies and rendered null her Puritan influence in the education
of the English woman.   In her "Lamentations of a Sinner" is
portrayed the duplicity of character which enabled her to manage
so cleverly her dangerous husband while taking the liberty secretly
to differ from him in matters of religion.   Here she styles the
"Godly and learned King" the Moses who has taken away the veils

---

[357] Cf. *Tudor Proclamations* 1 *Mary I, Ibid.*; Catholic Encyclopedia, *Mary Tudor*; Stone, *History of Mary I, Queen of England*, London, 1901; Vacandard, *The Inquisition.*   Translated by Conway, New York, 1908.
[358] Strickland, *Lives of the Queens of England*, V, 1–28.   London, 1842.

and mists of error and subdued Pharaoh, the Pope of Rome; while
she levels against the "gospelers" of her own sect and of Cambridge
the shafts of would-be indignation. In the passages addressed to
women she is again the practical Puritan. Here she says: "If
they be women married, they learn of St. Paul to be obedient to
their husbands, and to keep silence in the congregation and to
learn of their husbands at home. Also, that they wear such
apparel as becometh holiness and comely usage, with soberness,
not being accusers or detractors, not given to much eating and
delicate meats and drinking of wine, but that they teach honest
things; to make the young women sober-minded, to love their
husbands, to love the children, to be discreet, housewifely, and
good, that the word of God may not be evil spoken of."[359]

To Catherine Parr's views as here expressed and to the resulting
rigor in the matter of Elizabeth's *toilette* has often been attributed
the reacting excesses in freedom of dress manifested later on by
that Princess. Whatever may be said as to Elizabeth's proficiency
in the classics it is generally admitted that the fuller and richer side
of Renaissance training failed to leave its impress upon her mind
and character. To the child of Anne Boleyn the essential influences were wanting, and lacking these influences the weaker side
of her nature asserted itself when Machiavellian policy took possession of her judgment and petty vanity claimed her heart. Nothing
can be farther from the humanistic ideal than the fitful woman,
elated with flattery and driven to desperation by indifference or a
show of neglect. And nothing so surely indicates the absence of
the genuine humanistic spirit as the bombastic element of literary
style.[359a] But if Catherine Parr failed to seize the whole meaning
of the possibilities of her task her supervision of the Princess
Elizabeth's studies was nevertheless characterized by motherly
devotion and earnest zeal. Richard Coxe at first taught both
Prince Edward and Elizabeth, instructing them in the rudiments of
Latin grammar from Linacre, and exercising them in the subject
matter of Vives' *Satellitium sive Symbola*.[360] In 1544, when Elizabeth was nine years old, Grindal, a pupil of Roger Ascham, was
engaged as her tutor,[361] and in 1548 Ascham himself assumed the

[359] Strickland, *ibid.*, 44.
[359a] Cf. Madden in Preface to *Privy Purse Expenses of the Princess Mary*,
London, 1831.
[360] Cf. Watson, *op. cit.*, 1.
[361] Cf. *The Whole Works of Roger Ascham*. Edited by Giles, Pt. I, Vol. I,
pp. xlvii and lvi.

charge, holding it for two years.   Writing to Sir John Cheke on
the twelfth of February, 1548, he says of the invitation of Elizabeth:
"That illustrious lady is thinking of having me in the place of
Grindal. . . . She told me how, the Queen and the Lord Admiral
had labored in favor of Goldsmith; and I advised her to comply.
I praised Goldsmith. . . . I prayed her not to think of any good
to be got by me, but to let nothing stand in the way of her bringing
to perfection that singular learning of which Grindal had sown the
seeds.   It cannot be believed, most accomplished Sir, to what a
knowledge of the Latin and Greek tongues she will arrive, if she
goes on as she has begun under Grindal. . . ."[362]

As Latin secretary to Queen Mary and afterwards to Queen
Elizabeth, Ascham did good service to the cause of humanism, by
his classical culture influencing the Court circle and seconding the
efforts of the Royal Ladies, whose taste for the New Learning he
could appreciate.   From his letters it appears that during these
earlier years at Court his feelings were not embittered by religious
controversy.   The man who later on could boast that he thanked
God he had visited Italy but once and that his stay there had been
but nine days,[363] did not learn to belittle and libel the Catholic
clergy because of unfriendly behavior on the part of their adherents.
His attitude towards Queen Mary is always that of the devoted
servant and subject, grateful for her friendship and for that of her
ministers.   Besides the evidence of this mutual good will given in
the letter addressed to Lady Clarke there are other letters which
reveal the same spirit.   Thus in 1554 he writes to the Bishop of
Winchester:[364] "No time since I was born so sticketh in my
memory as that when I, unfriended and unknown, came first to
your lordship with my Book of Shooting, and what since that
time you have done for me, both with King Henry, King Edward,
and Queen Mary, I never shall forget, nor hitherto have hidden,
either in England or abroad. . . ."

Again in a letter to Sturm, dated September 14, 1555, he says:[365]
"All that the former kings, Henry and Edward, bestowed upon me,
has been restored and doubled.   I have been made secretary for
the Latin tongue to the king[366] and queen; and I would not change

---

[362] *Ibid.*, p. lvi.   Letter LXXXV.
[363] "The Scholemaster," in *Whole Works*, III, 163.
[364] *Ibid.*, Vol. I, Pt. II, p. 418.
[365] *Ibid.*, Vol. I, Pt. I, p. lxxxvi.   Letter CXCI.
[366] Philip.

it, so help me Christ, for any other way of life that could be offered me. Stephen, Bishop of Winchester, Lord High Chancellor of England, has patronized me with the greatest kindness and favour, so that I cannot easily determine whether Paget was more ready to recommend me, or Winchester to protect and exhalt me. There have not been wanting some who have endeavoured to hinder the flow of his benevolence towards me on account of my religion, but they have not succeeded. I owe much therefore to the kindness of Winchester and I willingly owe it. . . . I have often been meditating to speak to him of your great analytical work. I know he favours literary study, and I promise myself much from his bounty. . . ."

Through this spirit of union, despite conflicting beliefs, the Court could profit from Ascham's practical ideas on the teaching of the classics. These ideas he embodied in his method of double translation, doubtless testing out this method in teaching Elizabeth. In "The Scholemaster," he later left to his successors the results of his experience.[367] Vives' plan of composing bits of useful and interesting matter in the vernacular and requiring the pupils to put it into Latin[368] is also recommended by Ascham. On this point he says[369]: "Write you in English some letter, as it were from him to his father, or to some other friend, naturally, according to the disposition of the child: or some tale, or fable, or plain narration, according as Aphthonius beginneth his Exercises of Learning; and let him translate it into Latin again, abiding in such place where no other scholar may prompt him. But yet, use you yourself such discretion for the choice therein, as the matter may be within the compass, both for words and sentences, of his former learning and reading."

Among the ladies who shared with Lady Clarke the benefits of Ascham's learning were the sisters of the unfortunate Lady Jane Grey, Lady Katherine and Lady Mary Grey, with Lady Margaret Seymour and her sister, Lady Jane Seymour, daughters of the Earl of Somerset.[370] From the eulogy bestowed by Ascham on Cole and Christopherson,[371] it is evident that humanistic tutors were well provided here.

[367] *Whole Works*, III, 177.
[368] "De Ratione Studi Puerilis." Translated by Watson, *op. cit.*, 144.
[369] "The Scholemaster," Book II. In *Whole Works, etc.*, III, 171.
[370] Strickland, *Lives of the Tudor Princesses*, 191.
[271] Letter to Lady Clarke (*supra*).

The work accomplished by Catherine of Aragon and Catherine Parr thus bore its best fruit in the Court of Queen Mary. The perfect understanding that existed between the Puritan Queen and her Catholic stepdaughter is everywhere manifest in the history of their domestic relations,[372] but perhaps the best evidence of their friendship is that found in Udall's dedication to Queen Catherine Parr of the translation of Erasmus' "Paraphrases." Of Mary's translation of the Paraphrase of St. John's Gospel he here says:[373] "It [England] may never be able enough to praise her Grace for taking such great study, pain and travail in translating this Paraphrase of Erasmus upon the Gospel of St. John, at your Highness' special contemplation, as a number of right learned men would have made courtesy at, and also would have brought to worse fame in the doing."

Udall's eulogy of the Princess, appended to the dedication, may be said to have been the swan song of the English humanistic theorists in the cause of the higher education of women:[374] "O how greatly may we all glory in such a peerless flower of virginity as her Grace is! who in the midst of courtly delights, and amidst the enticements of worldly vanities, hath by her own choice and election, so virtuously and so fruitfully passed her tender youth, that to the public comfort and gladful rejoicing, which at her birth she brought to all England, she doth now also confer unto the same the inestimable benefit of furthering, both us and our posterity, in the knowledge of God's Word, and to the more clear understanding of Christ's gospel. O royal exercise indeed of virginly education! O inestimable and precious fruit of maidenly studies. O noble success of princely spending the time, especially in a woman."[375]

The third phase of the English Renaissance, originating with John Calvin and finally centering in Geneva, took also an important part here in the humanistic training of girls. At the Royal Court the spirit of the Spanish-Italian phase of the movement prevailed, on the intellectual side, and on the moral and religious side either Catholic or Anglican influence, as political events

[372] Cf. Madden, Preface to *Privy Purse Expenses of the Princess Mary*, p. cxxxv ff.   London, 1831.
[373] Watson, *op. cit.*, 148.
[374] *Ibid.*
[375] For further evidence of the solid literary accomplishments of the Princess Mary, see Madden, Preface to *Privy Purse Expenses*.

determined. Catherine Parr's humanistic education had been Catholic, and she had brought to the Court only a suggestion of the Puritan Revival, while the University of Cambridge, where this current of thought was especially acceptable, still failed to impress the household of Henry and his successors. But at the minor courts the Genevan influence was particularly felt and it is to these courts that the Puritan ideals of woman's education appealed.

The education of Lady Jane Grey is typical of this phase of the English Renaissance. In the Lady Jane are embodied all the characteristics of the classical culture that looked to the ancient languages as to a means above all of Scripture study, and which emphasized a moral and religious training rigorously opposed to social enjoyment and to the cultivation of every form of beauty, whether in life or in the fine arts. Even at her father's court, under the tutelage of Eylmer, the Lady Jane manifested signs of aversion from the outdoor pastimes in the enjoyment of which her mother had been bred in company with the Princess Mary. In Ascham's account of his visit to Bradgate is given in this respect a foreshadowing of the future Puritan maiden, while his report of her impatience under the exactions of conventional forms and the restraints of serious application to other duties than book lessons reveals the spirited nature of the child and the heroic courage needed to gain that perfect self-control with which she was later on to meet the demands of justice. According to Ascham[376] the Lady Jane pitied those "good folk," her parents, for believing hunting a pastime and for disdaining the reading of Latin and Greek. From this passage it cannot be inferred that Jane's mother lacked either taste for the classics or the knowledge of them.[377] The humanist is here setting forth the plea of his school in favor of mildness in discipline, a feature of the system abundantly exemplified in the spirit of that phase of the Renaissance under which the Lady Jane's training was commenced.

When the Marquis of Dorset gave over his daughter to the care of her guardian, the Lord-Admiral Thomas Seymour, she first came under the influence of Calvinistic teaching, and began under Bucer[378] the course of training which distinguished her after

---

[376] "The Scholemaster," Book I. In *Whole Works, etc.*, III, 118.
[377] *Supra*, 109.
[378] Bucer and Peter Martyr Vermigli were both in England in 1549.

career.[379] Her correspondence with Bullinger reveals the history of this phase of her education.   In one of her letters addressed to him she writes:[380] "On many accounts I feel myself indebted to God, the greatest and best of beings, but especially for having, after I was bereaved of the pious Bucer, that most learned man and holy father, who night and day, and to the utmost of his ability, supplied me with all necessary instructions and directions, and by his advice promoted and encouraged my progress in probity, piety, and learning; for having, I say, granted me in his place, a man so worthy to be revered as yourself, who, I hope, will continue as you have begun, to spur me on, when I loiter, or am inclined to delay.   No better fortune can, indeed, await me, than to be thought worthy of the wise and salutary admonitions of men so renowned, whose virtues, who shall sufficiently eulogize? and to experience the happiness enjoyed by Blesilla, Paula, and Eustachia, to whom the divine Jeronymus imparted instruction, and who were brought by his discourses to a knowledge of sacred truths—or the happiness of the aged lady, to whom the divine John addressed an exhortatory and truly evangelical epistle—or lastly, the happiness of the mother of Severus who profited by the lessons of Origen and was obedient to his precepts. . . .

"I now come to that part of your letter which contains a panegyric on myself. Your praises, as I cannot claim, so also I ought not to allow.   Such of my acts as bear the characteristics of virtue, I must ascribe solely to that great Being who is the author of all my natural endowments. . . .

"To conclude, as I am now beginning to study Hebrew, if you can point out the way in which I may proceed in this pursuit to the greatest advantage, you will confer on me a great obligation. . . ."[381]

Among the many testimonials of sincerity left in the writings of Lady Jane the most significant is the letter addressed to her sister Katherine on the eve of her execution.   It is written on the blank leaves of her Greek Testament:[382]

"I have sent you, good sister Katherine, a book, which, though it be not outwardly trimmed with gold, yet inwardly it is of more

[379] Strickland, *Lives of the Tudor Princesses*, 109.
[380] Nicolas, *Memoirs and Literary Remains of Lady Jane Grey*, 6 ff.   London, 1832.
[381] This letter is dated 1552.
[382] Strickland, *op. cit.*, 187 ff.

worth than precious stones.   It is the book, dear sister, of the laws of the Lord; it is His Testament and last Will, which He bequeathed to us poor wretches, which shall lead us to the path of eternal joy; and if you, with good mind and an earnest desire, follow it, it will bring you to immortal and everlasting life.   It will teach you to live—it will teach you to die—it will win you more than you would have gained by possession of your woeful father's lands."

While the spirit of this phase of the English Renaissance was favorable to the cause of woman's classical education, its influence was practically annulled by the failure of its leaders in the political struggle that followed Henry's assumption of autocratic power.   On the other hand, the impression made upon England by the translation and publication of Vives' *De Institutione Christianae Foeminae* was effaced by the action of the monarch in banishing its author[383] and consummating the downfall of the Queen.   By these two concerting acts the cause of woman's education in England lost at one stroke the services of a great humanist and the influence of a powerful patroness, and in consequence the Spanish-Italian current of the New Learning was seriously checked.   The movement still struggled on but so feebly that it spent itself within the precincts of the Tudor courts.

For preserving to the girl the fruits of Renaissance culture in either phase of its development, England failed to provide.   The democratic ideals in pedagogy everywhere fostered by humanism were here hopelessly shattered against the stony breast of Tudor Policy.   In vain did the banished Vives address to the once "noble King Henry" one more appeal in favor of womankind.   The earnest warning of the *De Officio Mariti* [384] fell upon deafened ears.   Equally in vain did the author of *The Governour*, Sir Thomas Elyot, hasten to voice the sentiments of his school in a brave *Defense of Good Women*.[385]   Henry's initiative autocratic acts did promise well for the cause of humanism but the early subsequent events of his reign left no doubt as to his intention.   In the acts of visitation of monasteries and nunneries, for instance, the instructions to visitors included directions as to enquiries to be made into the provisions for training the novices in "holy learning."[386]   It might be pre-

---

[383] McCormick, *Hist. of Education*, 198.   Washington, 1905.
[384] *Opera*. II, 395 ff.
[385] Cf. Watson, *op. cit.*, 211.
[386] "Instructions of King Henry VIII, etc."   In *Historical Reprints, XIII*, Edinburg, 1886.

sumed that under a humanistic sovereign a liberal patronage would be extended to the existing convents of women. Granting that these institutions were to die out for want of candidates to the conventual life when the transformation of belief would have been accomplished, the buildings and rents of these privately endowed schools would naturally be devoted to the girl's training and to that of her teachers in institutions reverting to the State. But the subsequent Acts of Suppression[387] and the gifts of convent property thus made to the Tudor nobles, shut up these free schools that were prepared to accept the humanistic ideals and removed from the daughters of the Commons the possibility of a classical education. The few grammar schools that were later established under Henry and Edward to replace the numerous monastic schools that had been suppressed were preparatory to the universities and did not contemplate the needs of the girl. With the change in the Church government came also a gradual decline of the Guilds which removed the possibility of repairing the loss caused by the sudden breaking-off of their power in educational matters.[388] To these acts of government policy were added the wanton destruction of libraries in the vandalism that tore down the works of art preserved in the churches and monasteries.[389]

The reaction under Queen Mary was vigorous but short-lived. Her restoration of the Crown possessions belonging to the Church laid the foundation of a new system of institutions, but time was needed to bring about a like manifestation of justice on the part of the nobles.[390] The confirmation by the Pope of the grants of abbey lands made to the nobles by Henry, while it had the desired effect of facilitating their return to the faith,[391] did not prompt them to hasten their benefactions to their benefactors. Before a fair adjustment could be effected the final blow was dealt by the Laws of Elizabeth. During this reign, not only was a liberal education in England impossible to non-conformists, but even

---

[387] *Statutes of the Realm, III, 27 Henry VIII, cap. 28; 31 Henry VIII, cap. 13.* Quoted in Bewscher, *The Reformation and the Renaissance,* 64, 79. London, 1913.

[388] Cf. Catholic Encyclopedia, *Guilds*; Guggenberger, "Medieval Guilds," *General History of the Christian Era,* Vol. II, p. 140.

[389] Cf. *The Loseley Manuscripts, etc.* Edited by Kempe, London, 1836. Among "Curious Old Parochial Accounts," p. 162, is the following with similar items for sales of Church plate, etc.: "It'm solde by ther tyme to Thomas Kendall, all ower lattyn bokys of parchment, for the som'e of xs."

[390] Cf. Stone, *The Hist. of Mary I,* Appendix.

[391] Catholic Encyclopedia, *Mary Tudor.*

such non-conformists as had means found it sufficient risk to smuggle into foreign parts for their schooling those of their sons who seemed destined to the ministry, without attempting the risk for the less urgent needs of their daughters.[392]

The pedagogical theory in the cause of womanhood that had found expression in the work of the Chelsea Circle—of More, Hyrde, Erasmus, Vives and Elyot, was thus in England destined to work out its influence in the world of reality but for a few short years, then to find its embodiment on the Elizabethan stage in the seeming creations of a poet's fancy. After generations might conclude that earth must needs be too sordid and human society too man-ridden to serve as the milieu for the prototype of Shakespearian womanhood. The Puritan maiden of the Renaissance was to remain a memory in the world of reality but only as an awe-inspiring example of the chilling effects of "other-worldliness" as over-emphasized in the Genevan phase of the English Revival. The narrow classicism of this phase opened the way for the realistic reaction, and this reaction must have followed in England as elsewhere had the movement there gained ascendency.

---

[392] Cf. 27 *Elizabeth, cap. II, sec. 5.* In *Select Statutes and Other Constitutional Documents.* Edited by Prothero, p. 85, Oxford, 1898.

CHAPTER IV

FRANCE

So far as Renaissance ideals are concerned the question of woman's education in France divides itself into two distinct phases corresponding to the two opposing forces at work in the social life of the nation during the period covered by the closing years of the fifteenth century and practically all of the sixteenth century. At the close of this period the attitude of representative Frenchmen toward existing conditions is one of dissatisfaction. This dissatisfaction Fénelon expresses in terms of sincere regret, while Molière is no less sincerely endeavoring to remedy matters by means of dramatic ridicule.[393] The one deplores the lack of useful knowledge,[394] while the other satirizes the empty show of learning.

The two forces are represented on the seventeenth century stage by the coxcomb leaders of the *précieuses ridicules* and their amiable opponent, the *femme sans esprit*. The keynote of the struggle is sounded when Vadius and Trissotin are endeavoring to secure the admiration of the ladies with the characteristic: "Ma plume t'apprendra quel homme je puis être." "Et la mienne saura te faire voir ton maître." "Je te défie en vers, prose, grec, et latin." "Hé bien! nous nous verrons seul à seul chez Barbin." And Henriette replies to her patronizing mother:

"C'est prendre un soin pour moi qui n'est pas nécessaire;
Les doctes entretiens ne sont point mon affaire:
J'aime à vivre aisément; et, dans tout ce qu'on dit,
Il faut se trop peiner pour avoir de l'esprit;"[395]

In Armande's speech, addressed to her earthly-fettered sister, the purpose of the dramatist is again put forward by means of a strong contrast:

"Que vous jouez au monde un petit personnage,
De vous claquemurer aux choses du ménage,
Et de n'entrevoir point de plaisirs plus touchants
Qu'une idole d'époux et des marmots d'enfants!

   .   .   .   .

---

[393] Cf. *Hist. de la Langue et de la Litt. française.* Edited by L. Petit de Julleville, Vols. IV and V. Paris, 1896–1899.
[394] Cf. Fénelon, *De l'Education des Filles.*
[395] Molière, *Les Femmes Savantes*, Act III, scenes 5, 6.

> Vous avez notre mère en exemple à vos yeux,
> Que du nom de savante on honore en tous lieux;
> Tâchez ainsi que moi, de vous montrer sa fille;
> Aspirez aux clartés qui sont dans la famille."[396]

And finally in the person of Clitandre, Molière clearly states his whole purpose:

> "Je consens qu'une femme ait des clartés de tout;
> Mais je ne lui veux point la passion choquante
> De se rendre savante afin d'être savante:
> Et j'aime que souvent, aux questions qu'on fait,
> Elle sache ignorer les choses qu'elle sait;
> De son étude enfin je veux qu'elle se cache,
> Et qu'elle ait du savoir sans vouloir qu'on le sache,
> Sans citer les auteurs, sans dire de grands mots,
> Et clouer de l'esprit a ses moindres propos.
>
> .   .   .   .
>
> Son monsieur Trissotin me chagrine, m' assomme;
> Et j'enrage de voir qu'elle estime un tel homme,
> Qu'elle nous mette au rang des grands et beaux esprits
> Un benêt dont par-tout on siffle les écrits."[397]

In life these two elements of social activity were represented by the *salon*, such as the Hôtel de Rambouillet, and by the imitators of the *salon*, the coteries of the *précieuses ridicules*. Molière draws the distinction when in the preface to the *Précieuses Ridicules* he says: "The true *précieuses* would do wrong to be offended when one laughs at the expense of the *ridicules* who badly imitate them." The true object of his satire he further designates: "The atmosphere of the *precieux* has not only infected Paris, it has also diffused itself throughout the provinces and our *donzelles ridicules* have imbibed their good share of it. In one word, they are playing the double rôle of *précieuse* and *coquette*."[398] The nature of the reception given to the Bourgeois dramatist by the real *précieuse* makes it clear that they were far from misunderstanding him.[399]

From this vantage point of the Age of Louis XIV the history of the French Renaissance can best be reviewed, and its mission to womankind best understood.

The struggle between classical culture on the one side, and ped-

[396] *Ibid.*, Act I, scene 1.
[397] *Ibid.*, Act I, scene 3.
[398] *Précieuse Ridicules*, Act I, scene 1.
[399] Cf. Bourciez. In *Hist. de la Langue et de la Litt. française*, IV, 132.

antry, allied to immorality, on the other, had been a long one in
the social life of France.   In no country outside of Italy did the
Renaissance era open under more favorable auspices than here.
The University of Paris had sheltered Petrarch and Dante and
very early in the movement Italian scholars were established in
Paris and Avignon.   At the Royal Court humanism was active
from the time of John II when Oresme there taught the princes
and translated the classics.   Under Charles V the work continued
to advance and it is at this court that we meet with the first
representative woman of the French Renaissance, the Italian,
Christine de Pisan.   In the life and labors of this remarkable
woman are found blended the medieval and Renaissance characteristics as they were blended in all the early patrons of the
Revival.   As poet, Christine is of the Middle Ages, but as the
brave champion of womanhood at the dawn of the classical re-
birth, she ranks with the Chelsea School of humanists and their
predecessors in Italy and Spain.

Christine was but five years of age (1368) when her father,
Tomaso Pisano, was invited from Venice by Charles V to fill the
office of astrologer at the Court of France.   Under the protection
of her cultured parents Christine here imbibed the spirit of the
early Renaissance.   Her numerous literary productions are composed in French and give little positive proof of her classical
training, but the spirit of these works and the teachings embodied
therein are significant evidence of the nature of woman's position
in the courts of the earlier Valois Kings.

After the wise monarch and his honored queen, Jeanne de
Bourbon, had passed away and Christine had been bereaved of
father and husband in sad succession, she slipped into obscurity
at the age of twenty-five in the company of her mother and her
three little children, to contemplate the new order of things and
busily to employ her pen with the double purpose of gaining a live-
lihood and of checking the growing frivolity of the Court which had
so coldly rejected her father's widowed child.[400]

Christine's tender reminiscences of former days are precious as
pictures of the ideal conditions which the Revival met at the
court of Charles the Wise.   Among her accounts of the great

---

[400] Roy. Int. to *Oeuvres Poétiques de Christine de Pisan.* Société des Anciens
Textes Français, Vol. I, p. i–iv.   Paris, 1886–96.   Laigle, *Le Livre des Trois
Vertus de Christine de Pisan etc.,* IV, 25.   Paris, 1912.

king's patronage of all that was beautiful and good are descriptions of the scenes of his constant companionship with his wise and virtuous queen, and the rigorous supervision which he exercised over the courtiers, even hanging without mercy, to a tree in the forest, the culprit who dared to offend against the strict virtue of his exemplary court.[401]

During the lifetime of Christine de Pisan the question of woman's right to respect and honor arose among the Paris literati in the form of a vigorous debate over de Meun's portion of the *Roman de la Rose*. Her energetic entrance into the discussion on the side of Gerson, then Chancellor of the University of Paris, and his colleagues, won for her a place among the great theorists on the moral side of Renaissance education, while her subsequent works of the same nature deserve more prominence in the catalogues of pedagogical writings than time has allowed them.

In the famous debate over the *Roman de la Rose*, Christine condemns the part of the work written by de Meun, and so injudiciously praised by some of the Paris humanists, among others Jean de Montreuil, Gontier Col, Secretary to the King, and Pierre Col. In her attitude toward this phase of the Revival, Christine ranks with Dominici and Vives. She reiterates again and again her condemnation of vicious poetry in forcible passages of her later works.

The history of Christine's zealous campaign begins with this debate seemingly provoked by Jean de Montreuil, with whom she held a literary correspondence, and who, it appears, took exception to her attitude toward de Meun in her poem *L'Epître au dieu d'Amours*.[402] Christine appeals to the authority of her colleague, Gerson,[403] and to that of "tous iustes preudhommes, théologiens et vrays catholiques, et gens de honneste et soluable vie." After exhausting her arguments, apparently in vain, she ends the matter with a firm and confident reassertion addressed to Pierre Col: "I do not know why we debate this question, for I believe that neither you nor I have power to change each other's opinions. I don't care if it is good! When you with your accomplices have so well contended by your subtle reasoning as to establish that bad is good,

---

[401] "Hist. de Charles V, Roi de France." In Kéralio, *Collection des meilleurs ouvrages composés par des femmes*, Paris, 1787, II, 177 ff.

[402] Cf. Roy, *op. cit.* Int. II, iv.

[403] Cf. Ward, *Epistles on the Romance of the Rose and Other Documents in the Debate*, 17 ff. Chicago, 1911.

I will believe that the *Roman de la Rose* is good.   As that great good man says:[404] 'May it please God that such a rose never be planted in the garden of Christianity!' "

Then she concludes: "I end my speech in this debate without indignation, as I began and continued it without ill-will towards any one.   I beg the Blessed Trinity, the Perfect and Eternal Wisdom to deign to enlighten with the light of truth both you and all those who love science and the nobility of a good life and to conduct you to the Heavenly Kingdom.   Written and finished by me, Christine de Pizan, the eleventh day of October, 1402. Your well wishing friend of science, Christine."[405]

In the poems Christine invites attention to her argument over and over again.

In the work entitled *Les enseignemens moraux*, or *Les enseignemens que je Cristine donne a Jehan de Castel, mon filz*, she says:

> "Se bien veulx et chastement vivre,
> De la Rose ne lis le livre
> Ne Ovide de l'Art d'amer,
> Dont l'exemple fait a blasmer."[406]

The importance of the efforts here made by Christine de Pisan can best be estimated from the results of her influence on her own time.   A remarkably long list of works in vindication of woman appeared after the middle of the fifteenth century, among them *Le Chevalier aux Dames*; *Le Miroir des Dames*, of Bouton; and *La Déduction du Procès de Honneur Féminin ou L'Advocat des Dames*, by Pierre Michaut.[407]

Christine was equally successful in enlisting the support of influential men and women in opposing the spirit of the poem by means of societies founded in honor of pure womanhood.   One of these, called *L'écu verd à la dame blanche*, was founded on Palm Sunday, 1399, by the Maréchal Boucicaut.[408]   The *Cour amoureuse* was organized in the palace of the Duke of Burgundy, on the fourteenth of February, 1400.   This society had no fewer than 600 members, and significantly enough, among them were Gontier Col and Pierre Col, two of Christine's former opponents.   *L'Ordre*

---

[404] Gerson.
[405] Ward, *op. cit.*, 107, III.
[406] No. LXXVII, *op. cit.*, 39.
[407] Cf. Roy, Introduction to *Oeuvres Poétiques de Christine de Pisan*, p. viii. Société des Anciens Textes Français, II.
[408] *Ibid.*, p. iv.

de la Rose, founded by Christine, grew out of the spirit of these two societies.[409]

In the works following the debate she endeavored to build up sentiment and arouse to action in support of the domestic and social virtues.   In *La Cité des Dames* are to be found her earliest and strongest theories regarding the social position of woman.[410]

She begins by feigning surprise and perplexity at the attitude of Matheolus,[411] whose book she had taken up eagerly, since it treated of the subject of womanhood.   She muses that if he is right, then God must have made a very wicked and vile creature when He created woman, and she wonders how so good a Workman could produce so bad a piece of work.   As she meditates, plunged into grief and dismay, she gently reproaches God for not having made her a man that she might be by nature inclined to serve Him worthily.   She is afflicted by the delineation of woman's character drawn by Matheolus and others, but she is more sorely grieved by their gross and licentious expressions.   While she thus muses and weeps, three crowned ladies of dazzling splendor appear before her. Assuming an attitude of dread, lest they have come to her as things of evil, she makes the sign of the cross.   But the apparition proves to be the impersonation of the three virtues, *Raison*, *Droiture*, and *Justice*.   The first smiles and sweetly inquires whether Christine takes all the sayings of the philosophers and poets for articles of faith.   She advises her to despise Matheolus as a "*menteur*," and perhaps knowingly so.   She speaks too of the *Roman de la Rose*, in which the more faith is placed that the author is a man of some reputation.

Raison then counsels Christine to build a city where the good and wise women of past ages and of the present may have an asylum against the assaults of their enemies: to surround the city with a strong wall; and that this defended city will prove a lasting protection to womankind.   Her two companions, she assures Christine, will assist her in the building, and she counsels her to seek out the noble women in history, sacred, ancient and modern, in the writings of the Fathers, in the memoirs of illustrious ladies and in the poets.   This founding on history, she says, will insure the endurance of the City.

---

[409] Cf., *Ibid.*, p. x ff.

[410] MS. 1395, Bibliothéque du Roy.   Cited in Kéralio, *Collection des meilleurs ouvrages composés par des femmes*, III, 22.   Paris, 1787.

[411] Mahieu, *Lamenta*.   Cf. Ward, *op. cit.*, 4.

There then follows the account of a long list of heroines as in all the other works of the kind.   When the City is built ladies worthy to dwell there are invited, beginning with the Blessed Virgin, the martyrs who were virgins, and the women who merited canonization by their chaste, pure and pious lives.   Only the good may enter, and Christine gives them advice similar to that found in the work which follows this, *Le Livre des Trois Vertus.*[412]

This work was printed in 1536, under the erroneous title of *La Cité des Dames*, which has never been printed in full.[413]   It was probably composed about 1405, and is really a continuation of the *Cité des Dames*, the three virtues being the same, with the mission to instruct the inhabitants of the city in virtue.

After Christine promises them to do their bidding they say to her: "Take your pen and write: Blessed shall be those who inhabit our city to augment the number of the companions of the Virtues. To all the college of womankind and to their religious sentiment let the exhortation of Wisdom be addressed; and first to queens and princesses and to all ladies of high rank.   Then from degree to degree let us chant our doctrine, that the discipline of our school may extend to all womankind."

Calling upon every class to listen to the instructions to be given, Christine then says: "Come, then, to the school of Wisdom, all ye ladies of high degree, and do not blush to descend and to humble yourselves to listen to our lessons, because according to God's word, he who humbles himself shall be exalted.   What is there in the world more pleasing and agreeable to those who desire earthly riches than gold and precious stones; but there is no comparison between the ornamentation of the body which they afford and that resulting from the practice of virtue and a good life."   Then taking up the private, social and domestic virtues one by one, the author gives counsel on each to all classes of women, high and low, good and bad, from the princess to the servant, and from the nun to the "femme de mauvaise vie."   She emphasizes the duty of properly educating children, and she reminds the princess that she should educate the orphan and be a mother to him.   She insists upon the duty of good example on the part of those in high places, and exhorts the princess to so live as to be a pattern of virtue to all. After advising her to learn to manage her own finances she suggests

[412] MS. 7395.   Imperial Library.   Cf. Kéralio, *op. cit.*, II, 416.
[413] *Ibid.*

a division of her revenues into five portions: the first to be bestowed in alms; the second to be devoted to household expenses; the third for the salaries of her officers and servants; the fourth for personal gratifications; the fifth for the entertainment of her guests. On each of these points she gives special counsel and direction.

In 1403, previous to the production of the *Livre des Trois Vertus*, Christine had composed *Le Chemin de Longue Etude*,[414] in which her personal literary tastes appear and her interest in the intellectual pursuits of other women. This work, with the two given above suggests something like a general pansophic idea—a "Solomon's House"[415]—for the education of women. It was dedicated to Charles VI, and contains a description of the ideal ruler, one endowed with virtue, a philosopher and poet, wise, learned and brave. At a parliament presided over by *Raison*, the evils of the world are discussed and the remedies, through a wise government, suggested. *Sagesse, Noblesse, Chevalerie, and Richesse*, each in turn gives her opinion and cites the authority of the philosophers and the Fathers of the Church. The personal virtues of Charles VI are also complimented, as well as the wisdom of his predecessors.

This work is allegorical, like all the prose writings of Christine, and begins with a vision following upon the reading of Boethius. A lady appears, described by the author as "that ancient goddess, whom Ovid called Pallas." The vision speaks of the high honor in which she was formerly held in Rome and of the disturbances in the modern world that diminish her influence. She exhorts Christine to leave the troublesome earth and to follow her into a world "more pleasant and agreeable" where she will find beautiful and profitable things. The thought in this work recalls Dante's *Il Convito*, and the plan suggests a conscious imitation of the *Divina Commedia*. The goddess conducts Christine through the *chemin de longue étude*, pointing out to her the wonders of nature, visiting historical scenes, journeying through the regions of antiquity where the philosophers and poets dwell in the company of the Muses; making a long and interesting tour of the heavens, and finally pausing at the gates of the supernatural, the secrets of which, the goddess reminds Christine, she may not yet venture to learn.

In *La Vision*,[416] the author represents Chaos as appearing in

[414] *Ibid.*, II, 297 ff.
[415] Bacon, *New Atlantis*.
[416] MS. 7394, Bibliothèque du Roi. Kéralio, *op. cit.*, III, 1 ff.

human form and from the complaints made by Earth, Christine takes occasion to draw lessons as before. Here she visits Paris, the second Athens, and listens to the disputations in the schools. She is perplexed by the utterances of Dame Opinion, whose Shadow colors all the assertions of the savants. In her doubts she exclaims: "Behold me fallen into an abyss of darkness, where I am plunged into a chaos of confused ideas from which I cannot extricate myself; I escape from one error only to fall into another; I am reduced to nothingness before the marvels of nature, by reason of my weakness and my incapacity; I am sensible of nothing but my disappointed and sorrowful heart . . . O Philosophy! you have deceived me. The human mind is too weak to suffice for itself, and after the soul has suffered, the heart can find nothing with which to fill its aching void."

Philosophy then appears and chides Christine, enabling her to define the mission of true wisdom as humanism defined it. She recalls the blessings she enjoys in her daughter, who has become a Dominican nun at Poissy, and in the son still left to her. She is conscious of new strength which she draws from the pages of the true poets and philosophers, from the Fathers of the Church, and from religion, the remembrance and esteem of which bring her comfort and peace.

The works of Christine de Pisan were widely circulated in France through the multiplied manuscript copies sold among the nobles, particularly at the courts of Burgundy and Berry, where the author was honored and favored.

Jean de Castel, the only surviving son of Christine de Pisan and of Etienne de Castel, was at the court of Philip of Burgundy, and after the death of Philip he became secretary to the Dauphin (Charles). A letter of Louis XI, published by Quicherat, in his *Procès de Jeanne d'Arc*, speaks of "Jean Castel, notary and secretary to our late very dear Lord and Father." At the Dauphin's flight (1418) Jean followed him, and Christine returned to the convent of Poissy for protection, where she ended her days near her daughter, in 1432, the year of the execution of Blessed Jeanne d'Arc.[417]

Like Christine de Pisan in her spirit and in her teachings was Ann of France, or of Beaujeu, daughter of Louis XI and regent for Charles VIII. Her court was a school of virtue and of knowledge,

---

[417] Laigle, *op. cit.*, Chap. IV, p. 25. Cf. Hentsch, *op. cit.*, 154.

where learning was esteemed and learned men honored, as in her
father's time and during the reign of Charles the Wise.   Brantôme's
account of this princess is in keeping with the testimony of history.
Of her he says:[418] "She was very skillful in managing her household,
my grandmother says, and among her ladies and the daughters of
the nobility, there was not one who had not received her lessons.
The House of Bourbon was then one of the greatest and most
brilliant in all Christendom; and she helped to make it so; for to
the opulence of wealth and her personal magnificence there was
added during her regency the reputation of her wisdom in governing.   Being splendid and munificent by nature, she would preserve
these early endowments.   She was full of goodness toward her
friends and toward all those to whom she extended her patronage.
In a word, this Ann of France was very wise and very good."

The training given by Ann of Beaujeu to the ladies of her
household is embodied in a treatise written for her daughter
Susanne, who later became the wife of the famous Constable de
Bourbon.   In this work, *Les enseignements d'Anne de France à sa
fille Suzanne*,[419] we have but another exposition of the general
principles held by all the Catholic moralists of the time.

After setting down the usual moral and religious counsels for
personal guidance, and touching upon the training of children in
these particulars, Ann gives detailed advice on conduct toward the
neighbor: "In your home be loyal and frank toward all, procuring
for each what is rightly due, and giving counsel when it is asked.
Visit your neighbors or your relatives when they are ill, and if
possible send them a little offering of fresh fruit or flowers. . . .
Honor the stranger. . . .   Honor the learned and the wise and
do nor withdraw from them your support suddenly or without
good reason; invite them to your table and propose a toast in their
honor, for they will then praise you in their works, and men of
worth are rare."[420]

The Courts of Charles VIII and Louis XII, while presided over
by Ann of Brittany, present a like spectacle of magnificence joined
to sober living.   Brantôme[421] characterizes this queen as "the
most worthy and most honorable since Queen Blanche, mother of
St. Louis, the King."   Surrounded by her retinue of noble ladies,

---

[418] Discours VI, Art. III.   *Oeuvres Complètes*, V, 205 ff.
[419] Cf. Hentsch, *op. cit.*, 199.
[420] *Ibid.*
[421] *Op. cit.*, Vol. V, Discourse I.

and brilliant guards, Ann of Brittany appears in true Renaissance splendor, and while her court was one of "poetry and ladies" it was, as Brantôme says, "a very beautiful school" for them, for she trained them well and wisely and all were patterned after their queen.[422]   The title of "Kingdom of Womanhood" seems a more just one for the court of Ann of Brittany, who loved science and poetry, and the classics, and was at one and the same time "grave, severe, elegant and good."[423]

The patronage extended by this queen to the poets of her time, and particularly to Jean Marot, recalls the advice given by Ann of Beaujeu to Susanne, and the return of appreciation on Marot's part has helped to immortalize her fame.[424]

While Ann of Brittany encouraged all forms of true learning and of art, still her influence seems not to have extended to definite classical training either of her own daughters or of other women of her household.   The traditions here, and backward to the time of Charles the Wise, seem to be rather those of the later Middle Ages in general than of the Renaissance.   Both Charles VIII and Louis XII were in close touch with Italy, but rather as leaders of military campaigns into an enemy's country than as patrons of the literary and pedagogical arts propagated by the Revival.   To the disputes between the two nations during these reigns and to the attitude of Louis XII towards the Church, resulting from the strained political relations between that monarch and the Pope, must be attributed the failure of the French Court to recognize the possibilities to womankind of the overflow of classical ideas from the courts of Renaissance Italy.   Only with the reign of Francis I did the high Renaissance burst forth at the Court of France, and only now was woman invited to full participation in the Revival. But unfortunately for her, the leaders of the movement at this court were of the school of Poggio and Filelfo, rather than of Vittorino da Feltre.   While the College of France had its stanch supporters of the principles of Christian humanism, it had too its share of coxcomb humanists, whose empty vanity perfectly harmonized with the spirit of Louise of Savoy and that of her yet weaker daughter, Marguerite of Navarre.   As the leader of ideas at her brother's court, and as Queen of the French Renaissance in

[422] *Ibid.*
[423] Cf. d'Héricault, *Oeuvres de Clément Marot,* I, 1 ff.   Paris, 1867.
[424] Cf. *Les Oeuvres de Jean Marot,* 5 ff.   Paris, 1723.

her own household, Marguerite gave a turn to the movement in favor of pagan ideals and set the pace for the company of *Femmes Savantes* led by such men as Postel[425] and Clément Marot.[426]

Marguerite's education on the intellectual side was brilliant rather than profound. She studied Latin and had the Venetian Jew, Paul Paradis (Canossa), for tutor in Greek and Hebrew.[427] She wrote Italian and French verses and French prose but seems never to have attained to any skill in Greek and Latin composition. Her biographers have sometimes been mistaken in her real identity, attributing to her the literary accomplishments, now of her niece Marguerite, daughter of Francis I, now of her grandniece, Marguerite, daughter of Catherine de'Medici. The history of the moral side of Marguerite's education is mirrored in her masterpiece, the *Heptameron*. To understand her motives in the production of these tales is to understand one phase of the French Renaissance; hence the importance attached to this work by modern critics. To some of these critics, Marguerite of Navarre is a sixteenth century sex-hygienist, a social reformer, devoutly striving to uplift her sisters by means of minutely detailed, intensely realistic stage-pictures of vice;[428] to others she is the utter extreme of all this, the flagrant defier of all law, human and Divine, who dares to entertain an enlightened Renaissance society with "those charming tales of love."[429]

The former view is unjustified by French tradition and by Renaissance tradition up to the time of the *Heptameron*. The admirers of Boccaccio's "hundred fables" had never been either learned or devout, and were never so regarded. Vives' sentiment in this particular was the sentiment of his school: "Which books but idle men wrote unlearned, and set all upon filth and viciousness in whom I wonder what should delight men but that vice pleaseth them so much."[430] The humanist's opinion of such methods for the teaching of virtue appears also in the same work. In forecasting

[425] Author of the "Feminine Messiah." Cf. Thompson, *Saint Ignatius Loyola.* Edited by Pollen, 232. London, 1913; Lefranc, *Hist. du Collège de France*, 188, 381, Paris, 1893.
[426] d'Héricault, Int. to *Oeuvres de Clément Marot.*
[427] Lefranc, *op. cit.*, 179.
[428] Cf. Saint-Amand, *Women of the Valois Court.* Translated by Elizabeth Martin. New York, 1898.
[429] Wormley, Katherine Prescott, Int. to translation of Brantôme, *Illustrious Dames at the Court of the Valois Kings*, 7. New York, 1912.
[430] "De Inst. Christ. Foem." Translated by Hyrde. Watson, *op. cit.*, 59.

his subject matter Vives here says:[431] "For I had leaver as S. Jerome counselleth, adventure my shamefastness a little while, than jeopard my matter; so yet that I would not fall into any un-cleanliness, which were the greatest shame that can be for him that should be a teacher of chastity."

On the side of French tradition, Kéralio[432] draws a very just comparison between the romances of the times of Charles VI, Charles VII and Louis XI, and those of the Queen of Navarre. She ends her exposition thus: "Love is not there represented under such colors as to cause innocence to blush. . . . The lovers are respectful, the women modest." And of the *Heptameron* she says: "It is to be regretted that this beautiful and intelligent princess assumed a part so little becoming in any woman of rank, whose conduct not only should be irreproachable, but whose discourses should give proof of her integrity."

On the other hand, it cannot be admitted that Marguerite of Navarre had thoroughly steeped herself in the paganism of the *Roman de la Rose,* once more revived at her court by Clément Marot, a sign that the spirit of Christine de Pisan had there passed away. She appears to have wavered between Christianity in the Calvinistic form, and the daring freedom of Pagan philosophy. Her open renunciation of the Catholic faith was followed by a period of doubt and unbelief while she harbored the reformers and adapted to their tastes the forms of worship and religious discipline at her brother's court and her own. "She had embraced that form of philosophy," says Father Stevenson,[433] "which begins in speculative doubts and ends in practical unbelief. Her residence at Nerac became the shelter for those rebellious spirits who found in it a place of refuge from the laws by which otherwise they would have been punished. In the Court of Paris itself, even under the eyes of the sovereign, heretical opinions were fostered by the Duchess d'Etampes, one of the royal mistresses. She and the Queen of Navarre caused an amended edition of the Missal to be issued, by which we may ascertain the changes which they wished to introduce into the national religion. It forbade private Masses: it ruled that both the Elevation and Adoration of the Eucharist should be suppressed, and that Communion in both kinds should be everywhere considered imperative. Ordinary household bread

---

[431] *Ibid.,* 36.
[432] *Op. cit.,* III, 322 ff.
[433] *Mary Stuart,* 157. Edinburgh, 1886.

alone was to be used at the altar. No mention was to be made of our Blessed Lady, or of the Saints, during Mass. Priests were no longer to be debarred from marriage."[434]

This breaking down of stable principles of Christian morality began in the rejection by Marguerite's mother, of the ministrations of the Catholic clergy and the consequent indifference in religious opinions and practice. In December, 1532, Louise of Savoy noted this item in her diary:[435] "My son and I, by the grace of the Holy Spirit, begin to know the hypocrites, white, black, grey, smoke-color and all colors, from which may God, by His clemency and infinite goodness, preserve and defend us; for, if Jesus Christ is not a deceiver, there is not a more dangerous generation in all human nature."

The paradoxical phenomenon presented by the alliance of Marguerite's morning hymns with her evening Boccaccian tales, is explained by the story of her various experiences as she passed through each successive stage of transition from Catholicism through Calvinism and unbelief and Calvinism again, back to the faith of her fathers in which she devoutly died.[436] By her free interpretation of the Scriptures and by her gross retaliating attacks on the monks and the clergy in her private theatricals after the condemnation by the Sorbonne of her *Miroir de l'âme pécheresse*, Marguerite kept alive the flames of contempt for religious authority enkindled by her mother, thereby influencing her courtiers and weakening their moral stamina.[437]

On the literary side she patronized such humanists as Eustache Deschamps, author of *Le Miroir de Mariage*, and Jean le Fèvre, who translated into French the *Lamenta* of Matheolus. Although Clément Marot was not a classicist, yet he won the favor of the "Muse of the Renaissance," by his French translation of the Psalms, by his amorous verses, and by the flattery of his platonic friendship. While not a pedant, the younger Marot was incapable of directing Renaissance taste among the devotees whom he found in Marguerite's court, and in Lyons, where he, later on,

---

[434] Cf. also Le Vicomte de Meaux, *Les Luttes Religieuses en France.* Paris, 1876.

[435] "Journal de Louise de Savoye." In *Nouvelle Collection de Mémoires pour servir à l' Histoire de France.* Edited by Michaud and Poujaulet, V, 93; Le Vicomte de Meaux, *op. cit.*, 18.

[436] Cf. Le Vicomte de Meaux, *op. cit.*, 9.

[437] *Ibid.*, 6 ff.

all but turned the heads of the cultured Belle Cordière, Louise Labé, and her literary friends.[438]   Having failed to solve the mysteries of Latin and Greek grammar in the universities,[439] Marot had nothing left but a vernacular still unstandardized and so incapable of serving as the medium of classical expression.

To this sterilizing literary influence must be added the effects of that social element injected into the French Renaissance by this school of translators, and developed in the *Heptameron*.   Speaking of the training here received by Ann Boleyn, d'Héricault says: "It is at the court of Marguerite, between Clément Marot and Louis de Berquin, at that famous school of love and of heresy, that Ann Boleyn learned the hatred of the Roman Church and that science of coquetry which the redoubtable Henry VIII could not resist."[440]   And his conclusion seems to be just: "Southern impetuosity and Norman pedantry both reached their climax in this woman [Marguerite] who had the double heart of a *grande coquette* and a *précieuse ridicule*."

The spirit of Louise of Savoy still predominated at the court of Francis I when the fourteen-year-old Catherine de' Medici entered it as the bride of the Duke of Orleans, afterwards Henry II. Catherine's childhood had been spent in tribulation and turmoil, first as an orphan in the care of her grandmother, and when bereaved of that guardian, in successive convents of Florence, either as ward or as hostage, according as the friends or the enemies of her family had her in custody.   The short time of security and happiness spent with her uncle, Pope Clement VII, before her betrothal was not of sufficient duration to make a lasting impression on her nature.[441]

The correspondence which Catherine held with the nuns of Florence is evidence of the strong attachment which she felt for her former teachers, and of the influences which she there received even under circumstances so unfavorable to solid training.[442]   But the young girl seems to have been easily led into the by-paths of indifference when she reached France, freely chanting Marot's psalms and listening to the discourses of the reformers, if not

[438] Cf. Colonia, *Hist. Litt. de la Ville de Lyon*, III, 542 ff.; Kéralio, *op. cit.*, IV, 1 ff.
[439] Cf. d'Héricault, *op. cit.*, p. xix ff.
[440] *Ibid.*, p. xliii.
[441] Cf. de la Ferrière.   Int. to *Lettres de Catherine de Medicis*, I.   Paris, 1880–1909.
[442] *Ibid.*, I, 49 ff.

practicing the reading of French from Calvin's *L'Institution chrétienne*, which the author dedicated to her father-in-law when Catherine was in her sixteenth year (1535).[443]

All impartial historians of the regency of Catherine de'Medici agree in their estimates of her services to the cause of the Renaissance at the Court of France. It is plain that she was "Dictatorial, unscrupulous, calculating and crafty," and that, "The subtlety of her policy harassed all parties concerned,"[444] but the indications are that she was not immoral in the sense that she encouraged feminine dishonesty, openly or otherwise. In spite of the differences of politico-religious policies which divided the hearts of the courtiers and duplicated that of the Queen, the struggle that checked literary progress throughout the kingdom for nearly a century had apparently as little effect on the private life of the Court as the ducal wars of Italy had on the Palace Schools of Italian humanism.

Here the political ambition of the Guise party, materially helped to promote the interest of woman's education, after the death of Francis I, through the interest taken in Mary Stuart by her guardian, Cardinal Lorraine (Guise). This Cardinal was connected with the College of France, and was one of the greatest humanists of his time.[445] Under his guidance and that of the Medician Queen, a new phase of Renaissance life arose at the Royal Court, closely corresponding to the Florentine Revival in its artistic features, and in its literary features rather Spanish-Italian than Italian-French. From the results obtained on the moral and religious side, it may be inferred that the Cardinal's influence considerably outbalanced that of the Queen.

In Mary Stuart's theme-book is preserved the history of this phase of the movement, while in the story of her life and that of her companion students there is evidence of the efficacy of humanistic training in the face of difficulties such as those arising from the adverse circumstances attendant upon politico-religious differences. Both the form and content of this little book furnish a good specimen of the method employed by the humanists at the Court of England, under the direction of Vives and Ascham. Noting this fact the editor calls attention to the similarity between

---

[443] Le Vicomte de Meaux, *op. cit.*, 13.
[444] Catholic Encyclopedia, *Catherine de' Medici*; Ibid., *Saint Bartholomew's Day*.
[445] Cf. Lefranc, *op. cit.*

Mary's notebook and the one kept by Prince Edward,[446] concluding therefrom that her tutor may have come with her from England. The influence of Italy, however, at the Court of France during this time was strong and it is an established fact that all the humanists of the Italian school employed methods based upon a unified system of pedagogy, while in practice they drew inspiration from their colleagues. Publications of Vives' pedagogical works were also widely circulated at this time and not unknown at the Court of France.[447]

Whether consciously or unconsciously Mary's tutor followed Vives, exercising her in the letter-forms on themes of "morality and courtesy," and only a very superficial reading of the text could lead to the conclusion drawn by the editor of the only printed edition,[448] when he says: "As to the turn and form of this education, it was naturally, in accordance with the character of the time, rather profane than sacred.   The first letter is an invocation to the sacred muses, and the gods are as frequently cited as God."[449]

The first two letters, written as all the others, in French on the left hand page and in Latin on the right, run thus:

"Puis que les Muses (comme toutes autres choses) prennent leur commencement de Dieu: il est raisonnable, que pour bien faire l'oeuvre que je commance, mon entrée soit de par lui, et que du tout mon entendement implore son aide et sa grace très saincte. A Reims.

.   .   .   .

"Quum musae (ut caetera omnia) principium a Deo accipiunt, aequum est, ut bene faciam in ea re quam aggredior, meus primus aditus. . . .

.   .   .   .

"Ce n'est pas assés au commancement de tes estudes, ma seur très aimée, de demander l'aide de Dieu: mais il veut que de toutes tes forces tu travailles.   Car, ma mie, les anciains ont dit que les Dieus ne donnent leurs biens aus oisifs, mais les vendent par les labeurs.   Adieu, et m'aime autant que je t'aime.   A Reims.

.   .   .   .

"Non est satis in principio tuorum studiorum a Deo petere auxilium.   Sed ipse vult ut totis viribus labores.   Nam, amica

---

[446] Harleian MSS. 5087.
[447] Cf. Watson, *op. cit.*, xiv.
[448] *Latin Themes of Mary Stuart, Queen of Scots.*   Edited by Montaiglon. Warton Club, No. 3.   London, 1855.
[449] *Ibid.*, Int. p. x.

summa mea et soror, antiqui dixerunt Deos non dare bona sua otiosis, sed ea vendere laboribus. Bene vale, et me, ut amo te, ama."

This thought, "God helps those who help themselves," is worked out in lessons in diligence and thoroughness throughout a number of the remaining themes. On the moral side, the exercises are evidently intended to give the Princess a high and sacred idea of her future duties as a ruler, and to implant in her heart the germs of all the virtues. Some of the letters are directed to Elizabeth, daughter of Catherine de'Medici, one of Mary's companions in study. To this Princess, as to a younger sister, are addressed the counsels which the tutor evidently intended for Mary herself. Among these are such exercises as the following: "I wrote you yesterday, my sister, that virtue follows upon the study of good literature, and for this reason is more necessary to us princesses than to others. For since a prince surpasses his subjects in riches, in power, and in authority, so should he excel in prudence, in counsel, in benevolence, in affability, and in all kinds of virtue. For this reason the Egyptians painted an eye on the sceptre of their kings and said that no virtue is so becoming to a prince as prudence."[450]

Other letters relate the subject matter of her reading, and draw the lessons intended to be conveyed by the text. Some are from Aesop's fables, from Erasmus' dialogues, from Cato, Cicero and Plutarch. The practical turn given to these lessons also appears. In one addressed to Elizabeth and to her sister Claude, there is the following advice: "It was but just, my very dear sisters, that the Queen commanded us yesterday to do as our governesses say. For Cicero says, in the beginning of the second book of the *Laws*, that he who knows how to command well, has first well obeyed, and that he who obeys modestly, is worthy to command in the future. Plutarch, an author worthy to be believed, says that the virtues are learned by precepts as are the arts, and makes use of this argument: Men learn to sing and to dance, to read, to till the ground, to manage a horse, to put on their shoes, to dress themselves, to cook. And do we think that to overcome our affections, to command in a republic (of all things most difficult), to well conduct an army, to lead a good life, do we think, says he, that all this comes by chance? Let us not think it, but let us

---

[450] *Op. cit.*, No. 3.

learn to obey now, that we may know how to command when we shall be of age."[451]

The next letter is addressed to a boy, Claude, either to a real companion, or probably to her cousin Claude, with the gender form changed to give practice in grammar. The salutation is: Ma. Sa. Regina Claudio Quarlocoio condiscipulo, S.P.D. Here the recipient is advised to beware of flattery and to distrust praise. It begins: "Quibuscumque virtutibus, sapientia, eruditione, et aliis gratiis praeditus sis, ne gloriare, sed potius da gloriam Deo qui solus caussa [causa] est tanti boni."

Other thoughts developed are: The true grandeur and excellence of a prince is not in dignity or gold or purple or jewels or other empty pomp but in prudence, virtue, wisdom and knowledge: A prince should not boast of the glory of noble birth but of the virtue of his ancestors.

Speaking of the idea of Plato, that a prince should be the watch-dog of the flock, St. Paul and Solomon are quoted and then: "Let us learn the virtues now, then, my sister, that we may become the faithful watchdogs of our flocks and not wolves, nor bears, nor lions." And in the next letter the thought continues: "If in our youth we study to be virtuous, the people will not call us wolves or bears or lions, but honor and love us as children love their parents. 'He hates who fears.' "[452]

That theory was aided by practice is again apparent in a theme written shortly after these (Aug. 25, 1554): "When yesterday evening, my master asked you to reprove your sister, because she wanted to get a drink, wishing to go to bed; you answered him that you wanted a drink yourself as well. See then, sister, what we ought to be, since we are the people's example. And how shall we dare to reprove others if we are not ourselves without fault? A good prince should live in such a manner that little and great may take example from him. . . ."[453]

Another letter addressed to Elizabeth has the following passage: "I have heard, sister, that yesterday at your lesson you were self-opinionated. You have promised to be so no more. I beg of you to abandon that habit. And think that when the princess takes up

---

[451] *Ibid.*, No. 9.
[452] *Ibid.*, Nos. XIV–XVII.
[453] *Ibid.*, No. 29.

her book, she should take it not only to amuse herself but to return from her lesson bettered by it."[454]

Of the virtue of liberality, for which the Queen of Scots was renowned, there are reflections in the exercises. In one of the letters to Elizabeth is recounted the incident of the request made to Alexander by Anaxarchus for one hundred talents with which to erect a "college," and the desired effect of Alexander's example of generosity on the prince. The letter ends: "Seeing this king acquire so great renown for liberality, I am sorry that I have not wherewith to prove my good will."[455] And the next exercise ends with: "Let us learn, sister, that it is more honorable to give than to take, and let us think that God has not given us riches to be stored away, but to be dispensed to those in need."

One of the letters addressed to Mary's uncle, probably the Cardinal, is as follows: "M. Sc. R. Avunculo a Lotheringia S. P. D.— Carueades said that the children of kings learn nothing better than to spur a horse, because in everything else people flatter them. But a horse, because it does not know whether its rider is a rich man or a poor man, a prince or a private citizen, throws him when he manages him badly. And we still often witness the truth of this: for not only the nurses and the companions and servants of princes flatter them but even the governors and preceptors, not considering what will make them better but what will increase their riches. O wretched condition! what makes the poor suffer so much is that princes are not well educated. This makes me beg you, uncle, to recommend me always to those who possess virtue rather than riches."[456]

The letters addressed to the Dauphin are interesting indications of the spirit which directed the education of the parties to the political marriages of the time. The lack of the romantic element is conspicuous, such topics as the following forming the theme: "M. Dei Gratia Scotorum Regina Francisco Delphino S. P. D.— When I read of Alexander's great exploits, the greatest deeds in arms ever accomplished, I have noted, My Lord, that he loved nothing so much as letters. For when they brought him a little casket, so beautiful that there was nothing else like it among the riches of Darius, and when they asked him to what use it should be put, one saying one thing, another, another; 'It shall protect

[454] *No. 25.*
[455] *Ibid.*, No. 49.
[456] *Ibid.*, No. 23.

Homer,' he said, by which he would say that there was no treasure
like him. . . . Love letters, then, My Lord, which not only will
increase your virtues but which will render your great deeds
immortal."[457]

In the next letter the Dauphin is exhorted to converse only with
good and wise people and to love his preceptor, after the example
of Alexander.

The religious influences back of these moral precepts appear in
several of the letters, notably in one addressed to Calvin: "Socrates
says there are two ways by which the spirit leaves the body.
Those who have kept themselves chaste and whole, and who in
the human body have led the life of the gods, return easily to them,
while those who are all stained with vices, are on the road that is
turned away from counsel and from the presence of the gods.
The spirits of such as have been the servants of voluptuousness are
a long time groping upon earth before entering the heavenly abode.
You see then that Socrates, Plato and several other moral philosophers had a knowledge of Purgatory, which you, living under the
Law of Grace, miserably and to your perdition, deny.   May Jesus
Christ, the Son of God, recall you, Calvin."[458]

In another, addressed to Mary's uncle, there occurs the following
passage: "The reason why so many men err these days in Holy
Scripture is because they do not approach it with a pure and clean
heart.   For God does not impart His hidden secrets but to the
innocent and good.   And it is not easy for all to understand the
things of God, which you know better than I.   I have read that
Simonides, being asked by Hiero what God was, and what were
His attributes, he demanded a day in which to reply; and when
asked the answer the second day, desired another two days; but
always doubling the time, and Hiero questioning him as to the
cause of this, 'Because,' replied Simonides, 'the more I think, the
more obscure the matter appears.' "[459]

With the twenty-sixth exercise, begins a series of letters on the
learning of women, in which the usual humanistic arguments are
brought forward and a long list of examples of learned women given.
Besides a number of famous Greek and Roman women, mention
is made of "Elizabeth, the German Abbess, who wrote many

---

[457] *Ibid.*, No. 53.
[458] *Ibid.*, No. 18.
[459] *Ibid.*, No. 24.

beautiful prayers for the sisters of her convent, and a work on the
way to go to God." A list of Italian Renaissance women also
appears: Cassandra Fidele, with mention of the epistles of
Poliziano; Battista di Montefeltro; Isotta Nogarola; Constantia
Sforza, and her daughter Battista. The first exercise begins:
"In order to answer those gentlemen who said yesterday that it is
proper for women to be ignorant."

When Mary Stuart was 14 years old she delivered a Latin
address in the presence of the Court on this subject.[460] The study
required to put into passably good Latin such exercises as these
apparently rendered it possible to the student to compose of herself
such an address, rather than to recite by rote a composition of
her tutor's, as the editor concludes.[461] His testimony that the
Latin themes are written in Mary's own handwriting, of which he
gives specimens, and in different ink, apparently at various times,
while the French version is composed in the same ink and apparently all at one time,[462] seems good evidence that the method of
Vives was here employed.

The proficiency attained by Mary Stuart and her companions
under this training, points to the fact that the practical humanists
who assisted Cardinal Lorraine by superintending the princesses'
daily studies, partook of his spirit and shared his zeal. There is
no positive evidence available as to the precise identity of these
tutors, except the passing mention of their names. In the household accounts of the Queen of Scots,[463] from 1548, the year of her
arrival in France, to 1553, there appears (1550) the name of
Claude Millot, "*Maistre d'école à 200 livres de gage,*" while among
the accounts of the household of the Dauphin and the other sons of
Henry II are the following items:[464] "*Précepteurs à 500 livres de
gages.— Pierre Danès, maistre d'escolle et précepteur de M. le
dauphin, hors en 1559. Jacques de Corneillan, év. de Lavaur,
précepteur et aumonier de M. le dauphin, en 1557. Jacques Amyot,
abbé de Bellosanne, précepteur et aulmonier [aumonier] de M. M. les
ducs d'Orléans et d'Angoulême, en 1547.*" Henri le Maignan, is
mentioned as tutor to Marguerite, the youngest daughter of

---

[460] Brontôme, *op. cit.*, Vol. V, Dis. III, p. 83 ff.
[461] Montaiglon, *op. cit.*, p. xvii.
[462] *Ibid.*, pp. iv and viii.
[463] Ruble, *La Première Jeunesse de Marie Stuart*, 281 ff. Paris, 1891.
[464] *Ibid.*, 267 ff.

Henry II and of Catherine de'Medici.[465]   Ronsard and Du Bellay were both at Court at this time.

Among the Italian courtiers that followed Catherine de'Medici to France were the poet Louis Alamanni; the four Strozzi brothers, sons of Clarisse de'Medici; the Count of Mirandola, and his two sisters.[466]   Further wholesome companionship, if not in study, at least in the other exercises of the day, was furnished Mary by the presence of the noble ladies who accompanied her from Scotland. Among these were Ann and Mary Flemming (*de Flamyn*); Mary Seton; Mary Livingston (*Livington*) and Mary Beaton.[467]

The usual accomplishments of Renaissance girlhood are here exemplified, such as proficiency in music, in the modern languages, in physical exercises, especially the classical dance, in embroidery and all kinds of needle work.[468]   Among Mary's personal accounts are items of outlay for these such as: (1551) *"Pour deux livres laine torse pour servir à la royne d'Ecosse à apprendre à faire ouvrage—32 sol."*[469]

Brantôme testifies that besides her proficiency in Latin, Mary Stuart was remarkably facile in speaking and writing French and that even the "barbarous" language of Scotland fell in harmonious accents from her tongue.   He also testifies that all during her stay in France she reserved two hours each day for study and reading: "She loved poetry and poets," he continues, "and above all M. de Ronsard, M. du Bellay, and M. de Maison Fleur, who wrote beautiful poems and elegies for her. . . .   She herself composed beautiful and graceful poems, and quickly, as I often saw her do, retiring into her chamber and returning immediately to show them to the company of honest people there assembled."[470]   Of the verses claimed by her enemies to be criminally addressed to Bothwell, Brantôme asserts positively that both he and Ronsard examined them and that the latter declared them to be entirely foreign to her style and to her habits.[471]

In connection with the controversy over Mary Stuart's relations with Bothwell and the above mentioned verses, is a work produced

---

[465] Ruble, *op. cit.,* 141.
[466] Cf. de la Ferrière, *op. cit.*   Int. to I, p. xxxiii.
[467] Ruble, *op. cit.,* 281.
[468] Cf. Brantôme, *op. cit.,* Vol. V, Dis. III.
[469] Ruble, *op. cit.,* 305.
[470] *Op. cit.,* V, 84.
[471] *Ibid.*

by "Simon Goulart,"[472] which offers a striking example of the length to which party spirit carried men in these troubled times. This author quotes specimens of verses, in support of his assertions as to the depraved character of the Queen of Scots, but in none of these verses does the name of the alleged recipient appear, nor any direct allusion to him. A very curious conclusion drawn by the author of these *Mémoires* is that of the utter wickedness of a life that could prompt such bitter acts of contrition in the last hours.[473]

If Mary Stuart's after career proved her lacking in shrewdness and even in consummate virtue, as the unascertained facts of the Bothwell case still leave open to question,[474] the history of her tremendous trials, whether public or private, and of her conduct through them, is the history of the Renaissance heroine, crowned with honor in her moral victories and with pity in her sad misfortunes. "During the whole of Mary's residence in France," says Father Stevenson, "not one single censorious voice (as far as I know) was ever raised to the disparagement of her conduct as a maiden, a wife or a widow."[475] The testimony of this student of the early years of Mary Stuart's life is borne out by the estimates of such witnesses as her guardian, Cardinal Lorraine, and her mother-in-law, Catherine de'Medici. Among the letters of the former informing Mary's mother of the state of her daughter's health and speaking of her officers and income are such passages as the following:[476] "I can well assure you that no one could be more beautiful or more modest than the Queen, your daughter, and she is very devout. She rules the King and the Queen." This letter is dated April 8, 1556.

Similarly, nowhere among Catherine de'Medici's correspondence is to be found the expression of sentiments contrary to those manifested in the letters addressed to Mary's mother toward the end of the first year at the Court of France (1548). In one of these she says: "The Queen, your daughter, is exceedingly beautiful, and wise and virtuous, even beyond her years. . . .

---

[472] Evidently, "Goulard," 1543–1628. Protestant Theologian and writer, Geneva. Cf. Goulart, *Mémoires de l'estat de France sous le règne de Charles IX*, I, 142–226. Meidelbourg (*Geneva*), 1578.

[473] *Ibid.*, 224–228.

[474] Cf. Catholic Encyclopedia, *Mary, Queen of Scots*.

[475] *Op. cit.* Preface XVI.

[476] *Recueil des Lettres de Marie Stuart, Reine d'Ecosse.* Edited by Prince Labanoff. I, 36. Londres, 1844.

I assure you that the King is as pleased with her as you could possibly desire, and for myself I can only say the same."[477]

At this Court in the days of Mary Stuart are to be found some of the most remarkable examples of humanistic culture, such as Marguerite, daughter of Francis I and sister-in-law of Catherine de'Medici; Catherine's own daughters: Claude, afterwards Duchess of Lorraine; Elizabeth, the second wife of Philip II of Spain; and Marguerite, whose life as the forced wife of Henry of Navarre was so filled with sorrow and tears.

The description of the Queen's own personal habits and of her private occupations as given by Brantôme, is a pleasing contrast to the accounts of her public deeds as recorded on the pages of history. Brantôme speaks of Catherine de'Medici with his usual flow of superlatives, but his statements are corroborated by her graver biographers of later times.[478] In spite of her Machiavellian policies which directed her political schemes, the Florentine love of art gained an ascendency over her tastes, guiding her in educational matters and in the patronage which she extended to painters and architects. Her cordiality was manifest when, with her ladies and the King, her husband, she took part in the chase and in all "honorable exercises," being then "great good company." She loved the dance, in which, says Brantôme, she exhibited "wonderful grace and majesty." At her Court theatrical spectacles found favor as in Mantua and Ferrara in the days of ducal splendor. Like all the Renaissance queens, she spent each day some hours after dinner with her ladies, employed in the skilful needlework for which those times are famous.

Of her literary occupations Brantôme says: "She loved to read. . . . I once saw her, being embarked at Blaye to go to take dinner at Bourg, reading a parchment, a *procès verbal*, all the way, like a clerk or lawyer. . . . I saw her once, after dinner, write with her own hand twenty duplicate copies of letters, very long. She spoke and conversed in very good French, although she was Italian."[479]

Catherine must have studied the classics in Italy, but her lack of systematic education there could not have very marked results

---

[477] *Lettres de Catherine de Medicis.* Edited by Le Comte de la Ferrière. In "Collections de Documents Inédits sur l'histoire de France," I, 555. Paris, 1880.
[478] Cf. de la Ferrière, *Ibid.*, p. xxxiv ff.
[479] *Op. cit.*, Vol. V, Dis. II, pp. 34, 62.

on the literary side. Her long years of companionship with Marguerite, daughter of Francis I, afterwards wife of Philibert of
Savoy, must have told on her lierary tastes. This princess, the
"Minerva of France," was thoroughly accomplished in Latin and
Greek and in all Renaissance learning. Brantôme's remarks on
the patronage which Marguerite extended to the savants of her
time, and the honor which they paid her in turn, furnish one of the
sources whence the biographers of her aunt, Marguerite of Navarre,
have drawn misinformation. The relations of this Marguerite,
Duchess of Savoy, with the men of the Huguenot party was friendly
but literary, and apparently free from pedantry.[480]

There is no doubt that the history of the third Marguerite of
Valois, the daughter of Catherine de'Medici, has contributed
even more to the confusion of ideas concerning the Queen of
Navarre. This Marguerite is the author of the *Mémoires*,[481] and
of various poetical works, some of which have at times been attributed to the eldest Marguerite. Of the accomplishments of this
Marguerite, Brantôme makes the following estimate, wrongly
quoted by Kéralio as being his article on her great-aunt, Marguerite
of Navarre:[482] "This is enough to say of the beauty of her person,
although the subject merits ten pages. But another time I hope
to speak of that more at length. Something must now be said of
her beautiful soul, which has so fitting a habitation. From her
birth she took care to preserve its beauty. In her youth as well
as in her more advanced years she loved literature and reading.
Thus we may say of her that she is of all princesses the best conver-
sationalist, the most eloquent and most graceful speaker of all.
When the Poles, as I have said before, would greet her, it was the
Bishop of Cracow, the chief ambassador, who delivered the address,
and in Latin, being a learned and clever prelate. The Queen
responded so fittingly and so eloquently, without the assistance of
an interpreter, having very well understood his discourse, that all
present were in great admiration of her, calling her a second
Minerva or a goddess of eloquence.

"But if she was grave and majestic and eloquent in her sublime
and serious discourses, she was also very affable and very pleasant
in familiar conversation. . . . Moreover, if she knew so well

---

[480] Cf. *Ibid.*, Dis. VI, Art. VIII.
[481] *Les Mémoires de la Roine Marguerite.* Edited by de Mauleon, Paris, 1628.
[482] *Collection des meilleurs ouvrages, etc.*, III, 275.

how to speak, she knew equally well how to write. . . . This Queen took great pleasure in dancing grave dances, which called for modesty and majesty, rather than other dances. . . . She wished to keep the commandments of God, Whom she always loved, feared, and devoutly served. As the world abandoned her and made war against her, she took sole refuge in God. . . . Never did she miss assisting at Mass; she often received the Sacraments and read the Sacred Scriptures much, there finding her rest and her consolation. . . . She was very anxious to procure all the books that were new or beautiful, as well on spiritual as on human topics. . . . She composed very beautiful verses, which she sang herself and desired others to sing. She had a beautiful voice and accompanied herself very gracefully on the lute. Thus did she pass her time and spend her unfortunate days without offending any one, leading a quiet life which she had chosen for the better part."[483]

When Brantôme does speak of the Queen of Navarre it is in the tone of criminal pleasantry which betrays the author of the *Dames Galantes*,[484] rather than the reverential chronicler of the deeds of the *Dames Illustres*.

The popular opinion concerning this Marguerite of Valois in her character and motives appears to be founded on the assertions of unscrupulous historians in whose hands the printing press was an instrument of propaganda at the expense of their political enemies. Nothing in the writings of this princess can serve as a pretext to condemn either her deeds or her intentions, and nothing in the testimony of reliable historians condemns her. The *Mémoires* are self-defensive but modest and chaste, and of her conduct concerning the marriage with Henry of Navarre, the last word might have been considered as said when Rome decided that there had never been any such marriage, for the double reason that the needed dispensation because of consanguinity was not obtained and that the ceremony was performed without the consent of the bride.[485]

Marguerite's account of her sufferings for her convictions before the time of the forced marriage, reveals her motives in the stand she afterwards took. She says in the *Mémoires*:[486] "I also made

---

[483] Brantôme, *op. cit.*, V, 158 ff.
[484] *Ibid.*, 227.
[485] Cf. Hurault, in *Nouvelle Collection des Mémoires pour servir à l'Histoire de France*. Edited by Michaud and Ponjoulat, Vol. X, p. 587 ff.; Guggenberger, *op. cit.*, II, 246, 247.
[486] p. 9.

resistance to preserve my religion at the time of the Conference of Poissy, where all the Court was infected with heresy, and against the imperious persuasions of several ladies and gentlemen of the Court, and even of my Brother Anjou, since King of France, whose youth had not been able to resist the impressions of the unhappy Huguenotism. He urged me incessantly to change my religion, often throwing my office book into the fire and giving me instead the Huguenot psalms and prayers, obliging me to keep them; but as soon as I had them I ran to Madame de Curton, my governess, whom God had granted me the grace to preserve a Catholic, and she sent me at once to the good man Cardinal Tournon, who gave me advice and strengthened me to suffer everything to keep my religion, giving me other office books and beads in place of those which my Brother Anjou had burned."

Apart from the religious motives which the Duke of Anjou might put forward in thus persecuting his sister, there remains the more evident motive arising from the contrast of their characters. It was to this Prince that Brantôme dared to dedicate his infamous book, the *Dames Galantes*. Marguerite of Valois was but one of the victims of that long and bloody struggle which marked the political crisis of the sixteenth century in France, where, in the midst of sedition and murder, of intrigue and rebellion, civil strife accomplished its work of destruction.[487]

The movement begun at the Royal Court lacked sufficient patronage to secure its development, and such girls' schools as escaped the inroads of fanaticism, continued, as in the century before, their work of noble service in elementary education,[488] without receiving the strong impulse of the Revival in the direction of higher classical training. Those who refused to patronize these convent schools were to a great extent deprived of the means of literary culture. The exponents of the movement developed in the College of Guyenne, present in their writings theories indifferent to woman's education, if not adverse thereto. Thus Cordier would have the child withdrawn from the society of his mother, except for an hour or two a day, that her ignorance of the classical languages might not be a stumbling block to his progress under the

---

[487] Cf. Le Vicomte de Meaux, *op. cit.*

[488] Cf. Allain. *L'instruction primaire en France avant la Révolution*, Paris, 1881.

guidance of his learned servants,[489] and Montaigne says on the
subject of woman's learning: "A sword is a dangerous weapon
and very likely to wound its master, if put into an awkward and
unskilful hand. . . . And, this, perhaps, is the reason why
neither we nor divinity (la Theologie) require much learning in
women."[490]   The result of such methods for rescuing from pedantry
the French girl of Montaigne's acquaintance, seems rather to have
led her into a willing acceptation of his further proposal: "The
learning that cannot penetrate the mind, hangs upon the tongue.
. . . It is a great folly to put out their own light and shine by
borrowed lustre. . . . It is because they do not sufficiently
know themselves or do themselves justice. . . . The world has
nothing fairer than they. . . . What need have they of anything
but to live, beloved and honored?   But, if, nevertheless, it angers
them to give precedence to us in anything, and if they will insist
upon having their share in books, poetry is a diversion proper for
them.   It is a lively, subtle, underhanded and prating art—all
show and pleasure like themselves. . . . They may also get
something from history.   From the moral part of philosophy
they may select such teachings as will help them to lengthen the
pleasures of life and gently to bear the inconstancy of a lover, the
rudeness of a husband, the burden of years, wrinkles, and the like.
This is the uttermost I would allow them in the sciences."[491]

The checked cultural influences outside the Royal Court reap-
peared in the literary atmosphere that surrounded the Hôtel de
Rambouillet, where the beautiful Marchioness, Catherine Vivonne,
displayed the taste of her Savelli and Strozzi ancestors and
inaugurated the movement which meant so much to the French
society of the seventeenth century.[492]   While Latin and Greek had
failed in their mission to the French woman, the modern languages,
together with the classical vernacular, which now developed, met
at their hands their full share of patronage.

The superficiality introduced by the Queen of Navarre, and the
spirit of such of her imitators as still mistook the shadow for the
reality were thus the targets of the satirist's wit.   Molière's
literary critics agree that he was not lacking in sincerity when he
characterized the woman of his taste as one who does not "make

[489] Cf. Cordier, *Colloquia*.   Edited by Avellanus, Lib. II, Col. L, p. 163.
Philadelphia, 1904.
[490] *Du Pedantisme.*
[491] *De trois commerces.*   Translated by Rector, in *Montaigne, the Education
of Children*, 164, note 118.   New York, 1899.
[492] Cf. Bourciez, in *Hist. de la Langue et de la Litt. française*, IV, 33 ff.

herself learned in order to be learned;" who "understands how to be ignorant of the things which she knows;" who "conceals her study and her knowledge; and refrains from quoting her authors and from expressing herself in high-sounding phrases."

The woman with the true humanistic instinct, with genuine interest, that is, in life and in the things of life, was still a living reproach to the *précieuses ridicules*. Like Cecilia Morillas, the Marchioness of Rambouillet had declined the King's invitation to a life of honorable service at the Royal Court, that she might devote herself to her own household and to the bringing up of her six children, among whom two daughters adorned the society which their mother had created, and the other three entered the convent.[493]

Not in such, but in the unlearned "*bas-bleus*, for whom marriage is a thing entirely too shocking, and maternity a base function,"[494] did Molière and Fénelon[495] find subject for regret.

[493] Cf. Crane, Int. to *La Société Française au Dix-septième Siècle*. New York, 1889.
[494] Le Breton. In *Hist. de la Langue et de la Litt. Française*, V, 62.
[495] Thornin, *Ibid.*, 443 ff.

CHAPTER V

NORTHERN EUROPE

The full and varied life of the North, replete with material and social interests, furnished a field for Renaissance culture rather broader in territorial extent than that of the South, but, from the viewpoint of the ideal classicist, somewhat narrower in scope. The enthusiasm for the New Learning which the Italian ducal courts fostered, early spread thence to the great trade centers of Germany and the Netherlands, and among the numerous municipal educational institutions thus brought into being or improved, were to be found schools for girls where Latin was taught in addition to German, arithmetic, music and the household arts.[496]

The earliest of these Renaissance schools were established under the direction of the Brethren of the Common Life, but no definite statistics of the foundations made previous of the time of Cardinal Cusa, are available. Under the direction of this great Catholic reformer, [497] girls' schools multiplied as later on they multiplied in Spain under the patronage of the great Ximenes. Here, as in Spain and Italy, the common schools in general were confided to the care of the different congregations of nuns,[498] but in some instances they were under the direction of laywomen. In Zanten, a school of this kind, established in 1497 by Cardinal Cusa was directed by Aldegundis von Horstmar. Eighty-four students were registered, including the daughters both of the nobility and the citizen classes. The historian asserts that the directress of this school had been trained under the Brethren of the Common Life, which assertion explains the nature of the curriculum offered.[499] A year before the opening of this school Adrian Potken was teaching Greek and Hebrew in the boys' school at Zanten[500] and if the girls did not share these advantages, the fact that they were taught Latin after the method of the Brethren, leaves no doubt as to their thorough classical training.

Outside of the convent there were in Germany and the Nether-

---

[496] Cf. Lorenz, *Volkserziehung und Volksunterricht im späteren Mittelalter.* Paderborn and Münster, 1887.

[497] Cf. Janssen, *Geschichte des deutschen Volkes*, I, 78 ff. Freiburg, 1897.

[498] Cf. Heimbucher, *Die Orden und Kongregationen der katholichen Kirche,* II. Paderborn, 1897.

[499] Janssen, *op. cit.*, I, 28; Lorenz, *op. cit.*, 78.

[500] Janssen, *Ibid.*, 87.

154

lands, as elsewhere in humanistic circles, learned women who shared the literary tastes of the men of their households. Margaret von Staffel, wife of the deputy Adam von Allendorf, wrote poetry both in Latin and in German and was the author of metrical lives of St. Bernard and St. Hildegard.[501] Catherine von Ostheim was remarkable for her knowledge of history and for her work in abridging the Chronicles of Limburg. In Augsburg Margaret Welser, wife of the humanist Conrad Peutinger, was celebrated for her learning in companionship with her husband.[502] All these women continued their reading in the classical languages with their house chaplains or other humanists, as was usual also in the courts of the nobles.

Intercourse with Italy, whether through intermarriages or in the interest of studies, brought the courts of the North into close touch with the early humanistic centers of the southern principalities. Through the marriage of Barbara von Brandenburg with Lodovico Gonzaga,[503] Mantua came to exert an influence on the Margrave Johann, in favor of humanistic learning, which resulted in the employment of Ariginus as secretary and schoolmaster at his court.[504] It does not appear that the princesses of Brandenburg shared largely in the training afforded by the presence of Ariginus, but under his successor, Vigilantus, the Electress Elizabeth, mother of Joachim II, became proficient in the classics.[505] As Vigilantus died in 1512, Elizabeth must have received her childhood training under that humanist.

In the Palatinate, and generally in the vicinity of the universities, the courts all possessed women remarkable for their learning. The Countess Matilda, daughter of Count Palatin Louis III, was herself a poet and a collector of German poetry. At her instigation the University of Freiburg was founded by her second husband, Archduke Albert of Austria, and that of Tübingen by Count Eberhard von Würtemberg, her son by her first husband.[506] It is significant also that the wife of this Count Eberhard was Barbara Gonzaga, daughter of Lodovico Gonzaga and Barbara von Brandenburg.[507]

---

[501] *Ibid.*, 98 ff.
[502] *Ibid.*
[503] *Supra.*
[504] *Monumenta Germaniae Paedagogica*, XXXIV, 61 ff. Berlin, 1906.
[505] Cf. *Ibid.*, 264, 330 ff; 474 ff.
[506] Cf. Janssen, *op. cit.*, I, 99 ff.
[507] Cf. Ady, *Isabella d'Este*, II, 33.

A revived interest in study at the court dates from the time when, under the influence of Petrarch, the Emperor Charles IV issued the provision of the Golden Bull, directing that all the princes of the empire be given instruction in the four languages spoken in the realm.[508]   In this provision there is no evidence that the education of the princesses was not contemplated, and the history of the later Renaissance women at the Imperial Court seems to warrant a traditional training for them similar to that of the princes.

The Hapsburg women especially combine in their personalities and characters all the characteristics of true Renaissance types. Margaret of Austria, daughter of the Emperor Maximilian I, for years Regent of the Netherlands, is one of the most perfect examples of complete education furnished by humanism.   Margaret was born in 1479, and upon the death of her mother, Marie of Burgundy, passed her early years, from three to twelve, at the court of Ann of Beaujeu, as the betrothed of Charles VIII of France.[509] Under these circumstances, she was thus early grounded in the qualities of mind and heart that befitted the future queen, in accordance with the ideas of the French Regent, herself so solidly established in all womanly graces and virtues.   On the breaking of the marriage engagement between Charles and Margaret, Maximilian recalled her to the Netherlands, where she spent four years under his care before setting out for Spain as the affianced bride of the Infante Juan, only son of King Ferdinand and Queen Isabel. In the correspondence which Margaret afterward held with her father, there is every evidence of a close intimacy of literary and artistic interests between the great patron of the Renaissance and his gifted daughter.   At one time Maximilian writes to ask Margaret to draw up a Latin letter to the Pope, stating the case of Guelder's claims;[510] at another, it is to chide her for taking the liberty to remonstrate with him for wishing to take part in a sectional Church council;[511] or again it is to thank her for her solici-

---

[508] Zeumer, "Die Goldene Bulle Kaiser Karls IV."   In *Quellen und Studien zur Verfassungs-geschichte des Deutschen Reiches in Mittelalter und Neuzeit.* Bd. II, hft. 2, p. 47.   Weimar, 1908.

[509] Cf. Hare, *The High and Puissant Princess, Marguerite of Austria.*   London and New York, 1907.

[510] *Correspondance de Marguerite D'Autriche avec ses Amis.*   Edited by Van den Bergh, Vol. II, Letter 170.   Leide, 1847.

[511] *Correspondance de L'Empereur Maximilian 1er, et de Marguerite d'Autriche.* Edited by Le Glay.   Vol. I, Letter 300.   Paris, 1839.

tude for his temporal needs and to exchange gifts of affectionate devotion. On this last subject, there is preserved a letter indicative of the manner in which these great rulers chose to "dignify their leisure." It begins thus:[512] "My good daughter: I have received by the carrier the beautiful shirts and tunics, which you have helped to make with your own hands. This gives me great pleasure, principally because it shows me how solicitous you are for my personal needs, especially since this season weighs heavily upon me. My poor body shall find great comfort in the soft contact and sweet odor of this beautiful linen, fitting garments for the angels in Paradise. And I hasten also to thank you with a picture of a future saint, done with my own hands."

Maximilian here probably alludes to a portrait of Margaret herself, as to that of a future saint.

In another letter, the Emperor asks his daughter to aid him in his historical collections by procuring for him the "genealogical tree of the kings of Spain and that of the kings of England," and a history of Spain, "La Valeriana."[513]

Margaret's stay in Spain as the three-month bride of the Infante Juan, and after the death of that prince, for a few years longer, afforded her the exceptional advantages provided at the court of Isabel, under the patronage of the great Queen and in company with her gifted daughters. Catherine of Aragon was still in Spain at this time (1598), and profited by the opportunity of exchanging with Margaret conversation lessons in Castilian for those in French.

Margaret's three years in Savoy as the wife of Duke Philibert, served further to widen her experience, and when, on the death of this second husband, she finally took up her life's task as Regent of the Netherlands (1507) she was equipped for the position as were few other women of her time.

The presence of Juana of Aragon in the Netherlands had prepared the way for her hapless sister-in-law, to whose care were soon to be confided three of the daughters of Juana and her eldest son, Charles, afterwards the Emperor Charles V. After the death of their father, Philip the Handsome, and the retirement of their mother, who had now completely lost her reason, Margaret took upon herself the guardianship of these children. In her household at the castle of Malines were combined the rich treasures of litera-

---

[512] *Ibid.*, II, App. No. 3.
[513] *Ibid.*, Vol. I, Letter 278.

ture and art bequeathed her by the House of Burgundy, and those of Hapsburg and Savoy, added to the magnificent gifts of tapestries and other furnishings, with jewels and plate, bestowed upon Margaret as the bride of the Spanish Infante.[514]

The library at Malines was stocked with manuscripts and printed volumes of the Greek and Latin classics, and with the best native productions of the Middle Ages and the Renaissance. Here Christine de Pisan could speak to the princesses from her pages of glowing manuscript which had been handed down by the Burgundian dukes, and to intensify the impression, there hung in the castle library a beautifully wrought tapestry representing the scenes of her *Cité des Dames*.[515]

Margaret's own poems, fresh from her pen, were further inspiration to her nieces,[516] and the little domestic circle shared in the sentiments expressed by Jehan Lemaire in his tender elegy over the death of the household pet, the green parrot presented by the Emperor Sigismund to Marie of Burgundy, Margaret's mother. This bird was the "Amant Vert" over whose personality modern critics have speculated, not without daring conclusions as to the motives and sentiments of the poet and the Regent, such as are often indiscriminately attributed to Renaissance influences.[517]

The perfect types of goodness and beauty reproduced in the persons of these young princesses are portrayed in their likenesses by Mabuse, to whom as to Dürer, both Maximilian and Margaret extended a liberal patronage.

Precisely who the tutors of Juana's daughters were is not evident from available sources, but the household of the Spanish princess must have been well supplied with literary women as well as learned men, and Margaret's charges might traditionally be given women for their tutors. Adrain Dedel (Utrecht), afterwards Pope Adrian VI, was tutor to Charles, as was later on Louis Vacca,[518] and according to some authorities, Vives himself devoted some time to teaching at this court.[519] Cornelius Agrippa sought Margaret's patronage by dedicating to her his eulogistic work on the nature of woman, *De nobilitate et praecellentiâ feminei sexus declamatio*, and by

---

[514] Cf. *Correspondance de L'Empereur Maximilian etc.*, II, 468 ff.
[515] *Ibid.*
[516] Cf. Marguerite d'Autriche, *Albums et œuvres poétiques de.* Edited by Gachet. Bruxelles, 1849.
[517] Cf. Hare, *op. cit.*
[518] *Correspondance de L'Empereur Maximilian 1er, etc.*, I, 35; II, 115.
[519] Cf. Hare, *op. cit.*

his services as annalist and secretary won the honor of pronouncing the Regent's funeral oration.[520] Lemaire also gave faithful service in the limits of his capacity,[521] and Erasmus encouraged the Regent in her literary projects.[522] The presence of Bianca Sforza at the court of Vienna as the second wife of Maximilian strengthened intercourse with Italy and helped to further there the interests of the liberal arts.

The after careers of the daughters of Juana are proofs of their accomplishments: Eleanor, the eldest, married successively Emmanuel the Great of Portugal and Francis I of France. At the court of Portugal she left a reputation for learning and virtue while in France she was equally the object of veneration. After the death of Francis I she retired into the Netherlands. Isabel, the second eldest, was lucklessly married to Christian II, of Denmark, whose career furnished her with matter for the exercise of her humanistic courage. Finally dying young and broken hearted, she left her children in the care of the Regent, who trained them as she had trained their mother.[523] Maria, the youngest daughter confided to Margaret, was married to Louis of Hungary, and after the death of her aunt became in her turn Regent of the Netherlands.[524]

The church at Brou, erected under Margaret's direction in honor of her second husband, Philibert of Savoy, to serve as his monument and her own, is a fitting memorial of Hapsburg womanhood in the days of Flemish Renaissance art and humanistic literary culture.

To mention of these learned women who adorned society in the literary centers established in the courts or the free cities of the North, must be added that of another type of woman, very conspicuous in the annals of the time as the ideal of culture in the convent. The large numbers of princesses who retired to these institutions of Germany and the Netherlands during the early period of the Revival is remarkable,[525] inasmuch as the mode of life in these convents was by this time largely regulated by the spirit of the Brethren of the Common Life[526] or of that of St.

[520] Cf. Catholic Encyclopedia, *Agrippa of Nettesheim*; Hare, *op. cit.*
[521] Cf. Thibaut, *Marguerite d'Autriche et Jehan Lemaire, etc.*, Paris, 1888.
[522] Cf. Altmeyer, *Marguerite d'Autriche*, 164. Liège, 1840.
[523] Cf. Ady, *Christine of Denmark, Duchess of Milan and Lorraine.* New York, 1913.
[524] Cf. Hare, *op. cit.*, 220.
[525] Cf. Heimbucher, *op. cit.*, II ; *Monumenta Germaniae Paedagogica,* XXXIV.
[526] Janssen, *ibid.*, I, 77 ff.

Francis,[527] the one with its strict asceticism of the *De Imitatione Christi*,[528] the other with that of the rigorous evangelical poverty professed by the Seraphic Saint of Assisi.

Johannes Janssen, in his monumental work, the *Geschichte des deutschen Volkes*, has conclusively shown that hard literary labor and deep spirituality characterize the life of these convent women, drawing his evidence from the virtue and intellect which they manifested during the struggle for their rights when the princes accepted the teachings of some of the foremost of the sixteenth century agitators, on the subject of monastic vows. Comparatively few nuns proved their lack of judgment and virtue by electing to abandon their way of life when urged to do so by the reformers, while hundreds made heroic resistance to even physical force at the attempt of the civil authorities to compel them to break their vows.[528a] The defection of Catherine von Bora and her associates proves the exception rather than the rule.[529]

Following Johann Butzbach, author of an unpublished history of literature, written in 1505,[530] Janssen makes mention of a number of German nuns, learned and virtuous, who published their works or held correspondence with the humanists of their day. Among these are Augustinians and Benedictines, as well as members of the later congregations, considered more strict in their mode of life. Gertrude von Coblentz, Mistress of the Novices in the Augustinian convent of Vallendar, and Christina von der Leyen, of the same order, in the Convent of Marienthal, are praised for their literary abilities. Barbara von Dalberg, niece of Bishop von Dalberg of Worms, was a learned Benedictine of Marienberg, and to another Benedictine nun, Aleydis Raiskop, Butzback dedicated his history of literature, while to still another nun of the same order, the artist, Gertrude von Buchel, he dedicated his work "Celebrated Painters." Aleydis Raiskop composed seven Latin homilies on St. Paul and translated a work on the Mass from Latin into German. A Latin correspondent of the great Trithemius, was Richmondis von der Horst, abbess of the Convent of Seebach.

---

[527] Cf. Heimbucher, *op. cit.*, II.

[528] Cf. Catholic Encyclopedia, *Thomas à Kempis*.

[528a] Janssen, *op. cit.*, II, 376 ff.; *Ibid*. III, 104 ff. Cf. "Briefe der Felicitas Grundherrin," in *Historisch-politische Blätter für das katholische Deutschland*, XLIV, 378 ff, 441 ff. München, 1859.

[529] Janssen, *op. cit.*, II, 299; 573 ff.

[530] *Ibid.*, I, 97 ff.

Ursula Canter, another nun, is praised for her extensive learning in theology, literature, rhetoric and the fine arts.

At Nuremberg, the Franciscan nuns, Charity and Clara Pirkheimer, were remarkably gifted and stanch in adhering to their spiritual and intellectual rights. The memoirs of Charity Pirkheimer, when abbess of the Nuremberg convent, and her letters to her brother, are valuable contributions to the history of Germany in the sixteenth century.[531] This nun had associated with her, Clarissa Apollonia Tucher, niece of the Nuremberg lawyer, Sixtus Tucher. This humanist, in his letters to his niece and her friend, exhorts them to disinterestedness in their studies and to the practice of virtue in keeping with their gifts of knowledge.[532]

Through the schools directed by these nuns and fostered by the Church, a general level of culture was attained by the women of the North during the early period of the Revival.[533]

The theoretical humanists who followed in the footsteps of Cardinal Cusa, labored like him in behalf of an education proper to fit the average girl for right living in the midst of the social enjoyment and material prosperity of these great industrial centers. In addition to the pedagogical works of the Brethren of the Common Life, applying to both sexes in common, there were produced at this period in the Netherlands other writings dealing exclusively with the problem of woman's education. Among the views thus expressed are those of Erasmus in the *Colloquies* and the *De Matrimonio Christiano*, and more especially those of Vives.

The *De Institutione Christianae Foeminae* is not considered as written for the Queen of England or for her subjects in particular, but rather as addressed to her to secure her patronage and in a special manner directed to the well-to-do burgher classes of the North. In its appeal to the masses this work supplements that of D'Arezzo, as it supplements it also in treating at length of the girl's training in early childhood and in general of the woman's conduct throughout life. Vives' insistence here upon the moral side of education has led some of his critics[534] to assert that the

[531] *Ibid.*, II, 377 ff.
[532] Janssen, I, 97 ff.
[533] Cf. "Literarische und künstlerische Thätigkeit in deutschen Nonnenklöstern im ausgehenden Mittelalter," in *Hist. politische Blätter für das katholische Deutschland*, CXVIII, 644 ff.
[534] Cf. Thamin, *Hist. de la Litt. et de la Langue Française*. Edited by Petit de Julleville. V, 444.

virtue of chastity alone found consideration in his principles
of pedagogy. A study of this work, however, in its historical
setting, and in its relation to the *De Officio Mariti* and the *De
Ratione Studii Puerilis* (for a girl), of the same author, shows
Vives' attitude towards the Renaissance education of woman to
be identical with that of the best exponents of the humanistic
ideals. The favorite argument of the opponents of a classical
education for the girl was the moral argument, in refuting which
Vives, with all his colleagues, sought to establish the value of a
deep and solid course in Latin and Greek and in auxiliary branches
of study as the best means of securing the girl from the vain and
dangerous allurements of social freedom. This Savonarola of the
North makes it evident that the woman of his contemplation must
be first modest and pure but that upon this foundation he would
raise the edifice of learning. He is not satisfied with the rôle of
theoretical reformer only—he would be the destructive critic
today but tomorrow society must yield him a place in the ranks
of her silent pedagogues, whose secret art alone had power to
charm the heart away from vanity and anchor it on the rock of
truth—where beauty and goodness meet.

In some of the prosperous communities of the North the humanist had before his eyes conditions similar to those existing in
Renaissance Venice or Genoa, or in Florence in her earlier days.
A stranger to the mode of life into which he was introduced on
leaving his native Valentia, he contemplated the scenes before
him with the eye of a severe moral critic and felt all the misgivings
of a true prophet of social reform. "Also your dearest daughter
Mary, shall read these instructions of mine, and follow in living,"
he says to Queen Catherine of Aragon,[535] but he presently adds,
"Which she must needs do, if she order herself after the example
that she hath at home with her, of your virtue and wisdom."[536]
But there were other princesses and other girls for whom he wished
to supply maternal precepts, putting the "good and holy women
in remembrance of their duty but slightly" and taking up
"sharply," those whom "teaching availeth but little," those who
"struggle with a leader and must be drawn."[537] In appealing to
this latter class, the humanist sought to win over to his cause every

---

[535] Introduction. Translated by Hyrde. Watson, *op. cit.*, 37.
[536] *Ibid.*
[537] *Ibid.*, 36.

Christian woman, that the regeneration of society might everywhere be wrought out through the ideal home.

Of the First Years

With all his colleagues, Vives follows Quintilian in his theories for the early training of the child, insisting upon the duties of the mother in nourishing both the body and the mind of her young charge, that the power of love and of the laws of imitation may be secured as aids in the after-training of the child. The responsibility of parents in exercising wise discrimination as to the proper moment to minister to the growing needs of the child's mental development, and care in studying the individuality of children, receive prominence here. Vives' remarks on the first exercises of the young child are significantly in keeping with the best modern psychological views. For the girl, "when she is of age able to learn anything," he recommends first, after the knowledge of God and of her relations with Him, practice in establishing adjustment to her physical environment, by means of exercises in household duties. The bearing of this passage on the subject of mental development is clear from the author's speculations as to the proper age at which to begin; whether with Quintilian at 4 or 5, or with Aristotle at 7. The author adds a warning to such parents as, with a view of preserving their children from physical exhaustion, only weaken them the more by injudicious hindrance in the use of wholesome exercises.

To mention of the physical benefits to be derived from such activity, Vives adds the moral advantages to be gained by a life secured from idleness—by the traditional handling of wool and flax, "two crafts yet left of that old innocent world." Alluding to the practice of queens in this particular, he says that rank should not rob any one of the advantage of these wholesome exercises, for "among all good women it is a great shame to be idle,"adding that Queen Isabel taught her daughters to spin, sew and paint.

Significantly also Vives classifies among the exercises proper to these first years, cooking and caring for the sick. He would have the girl begin betimes to learn to handle kitchen utensils and to prepare dainty morsels to please her father and mother and her brothers and sisters, especially in time of sickness, that she may later on do the same in her own household. He would not have her leave to the servants this delicate care. The presence of the daughter, in case of the mother's absence, he recommends as a help to order and economy among the servants. After denouncing such as loath the kitchen and find pleasure in handling "tables and cards," he concludes: "Therefore in my counsel a woman shall learn this craft, that she may in every time of her life please her friends, and that the meat may come more cleanly unto the table."

Here, too, is a warning against the danger of accepting theories contrary to tradition in the question of the girl's seclusion during the first years. "Let all her bringing up be pure and chaste the first years, because of her manners, the which take their first forming of that custom in youth and infancy." And he explains: "It is an ungracious opinion of them that say they will have the children to know both good and evil. . . . And, verily, fathers that will not have their child unexempt and ignorant of evil, be worthy that their children should know both good and ill, and when they repent them of their evil doing, should call yet unto remembrance, that they learned to do evil by their father's mind and will."

Vives introduces his discourse on the girl's studies with the remark that some are slow, others very apt, but that the former should not be discouraged and the latter should be spurred on and encouraged. He would have the girl learn to read by the aid of serious books, and to write by exercise in grave and sober sentences from the Holy Scriptures and the philosophers.

What Subjects the Girl Should Study

Before enumerating the books best to be read, the humanist inveighs against the bad books circulated in the vernacular and in translations, such as the Arthurian Legends in versions evidently out of keeping with those of Malory and Tennyson. These he places here in the same category with *Celestina*. To the works of this kind to be shunned for their viciousness and against which, he asserts, civil legislation should act, he adds those of another class, that is, those harmful only to literary taste and productive of frivolity. Of these he says: "As for learning, none is to be looked for in these men, which saw never so much as a shadow of learning themselves. And when they tell aught what delight can be in those things that be so plain and foolish lies! One killeth twenty himself alone, another killeth thirty, another wounded with a hundred wounds, and left dead, riseth up again, and on the next day made whole and strong overcometh ten giants, and then goeth away loaded with gold and silver, and precious stones. . . . I never heard man say that he liked these books, but those that never touched good books. . . . And as for those that praise them as I know some that do, I will believe them, if they praise them after that they have read Cicero and Seneca, or St. Jerome, or holy Scripture, and have mended their living better."

In the enumeration of good books which follows, Vives lays stress on the reading of the Bible and the Fathers and then the Greek and Latin classics, especially Plato, Cicero, and Seneca, adding, "and such others." In the *De Ratione Studii Puerilis*[538] he further recommends the historians and the standard poets, while in the *De Officio Mariti* he gives a further list, his object there being to point out matter for leisurely reading, rather than for close study.[539]

In connection with language and literature Vives would thus teach the girl philosophy and history with lessons in the use of common remedies for the infirmities of young children. Of other studies he here says expressly that he assigns no limit to the learning of a woman, any more than to that of a man. And again he asserts that "the woman's wit is no less apt to all things than the man's is," adding, "She wanteth but counsel and strength."

Of the woman's functions, for which education should fit her, he points out two; that of the mother and that of the teacher: "Let her learn for herself alone and her young children, or her sisters in our Lord." Earlier, speaking of what teachers are fitting for the girl he had said: "If there be found any holy and well learned woman, I had rather have her teach them." These passages explain what Vives further meant by asserting that it is not becoming to a woman to rule a school, that is, over men; to make public speeches, in the nature of disputations; or to teach, that is, to settle questions. Here his views are in perfect harmony with those of D'Arezzo. Eloquence, which he explains in the *De Officio Mariti* as logic, grammar, and politics, pertaining as they do to forensic eloquence, was distasteful to these theorists when found in a woman. In a number of passages Vives treats of the oral mastery of language, in contradistinction to speech-making.

---

[538] Watson, *op. cit.*, 144, 146.
[539] *Ibid.*, 302 ff.

In the *De Officio Mariti*, explaining the eloquence for which
Cornelia and other Roman ladies were praised, he says that they
were commended, not because they exercised themselves in carefully composed discourses, but because they had acquired the art
by the familiar custom of their fathers.   And he adds: "But now-
adays they call her eloquent, that with long and vain confabula-
tion, can entertain one. . . . And this they call the gentle
entertainment of the court. . . . And all such as were praised
of our elders for their eloquence, were most extolled and lauded,
for as much as they kept the language of their forefathers, sincere
and clean, as Cicero declareth in his book of an Orator."

Vives admired such women of his time as were able to converse
freely and modestly in the classical languages or in the vernacular
as is evident from his allusion to Juana of Aragon and to her sister
Catherine, of whom he says: "It is told me with great praise and
marvel in many places of this country" . . . that Juana "was
wont to make answer in Latin, and that without any study, to
the orations that were made after the custom in towns, to new
princes.   And likewise the English say by their queen."[540]   It is
against the artificiality of the unlearned maiden or her empty
talkativeness with the "young man little wiser than herself" that
Vives gives warning here: "When she speaketh, let her communi-
cation be simple, not affectate, nor ornate, for that declareth the
vanity of the mind."[541] And again: "Some be so subtle-minded,
that among their companions they babble out all at large, both
their own matters and other folks' nor have no regard what they
say, but whatsoever cometh on the tongue's end."   He says again,
that if a woman does not need eloquence he does not urge its
acquisition, but that nothing will excuse her from the acquisition
of wisdom and goodness.   He says it is no shame for a woman to
be silent but it is a shame to lack discretion and to live ill.   But he
adds again: "Nor I will not here condemn eloquence."

Vives' idea as to the subtleties of mathematics agrees also with
that of D'Arezzo.   He would have the woman leave deep speculation to men, but he assigns her a broad field for investigation
when he declares that "so much knowledge of natural things as
sufficeth to rule and govern this life withal, is sufficient for a
woman."[542]

[540] *Ibid.*
[541] *Ibid.*, 207.
[542] *Ibid.*, 196.

In the study of religion, the humanist again points out an un-
limited source of information: "The Lord doth admit women to
the mystery of His religion, in respect of which all other wisdom
is but foolishness, and he doth declare that they were created to
know high matters, and to come as well as men unto the beatitude,
and therefore they ought and should be instructed and taught, as
we men be." In her devotions, Vives would here again have the
girl pray in the vernacular or have care taken that she understand
the Latin prayers which she uses.

Training in Virtue and Morality

After the usual exhortations to Christian self-denial in the matter
of food and sleep, Vives forcibly points out the peculiar virtues
against which custom wages war and in which he would see the
young girl grounded from her tender years. The social maladies
which, in his keen criticism, the author here exposes are chiefly:
ignorance, vanity in dress, idleness, love of exciting pleasures,
frivolous and dangerous reading, and the outcome of all these—
unchastity. The remedy for these ills the author had shown in a
general way to be schooling under strong moral influences, but
both in the *De Institutione Christianae Foeminae* and the *De Officio
Mariti* he treats of the necessity of parental authority and teaching
as an essential condition of lasting social reform.

The two features in the girl's education, preeminently the work
of the home, Vives points out to be good sense in habits of dress
and personal adornment, and moderation in pleasure seeking.
The head of the family must secure to the women of his household
the advantages of learning, that they may find in books wholesome precepts of wisdom in these matters, and to this must be
added personal counsel and example and, if need be, gentle coer-
cion. Ignorance, Vives says, is the only cause why some women
are "studious and most diligent to adorn and deck themselves."[543]

Under the head of attire, the author gives detailed advice on
abstaining from beauty-shop practices and from the excessive display of gold and jewels, as well as from frivolous and dangerous
styles of dress. His remarks conjure up that pitiable automaton
of the image of Depravity, too often to be met with in our modern
thoroughfares.

[543] *Ibid.*, 200.

In treating of this class of vices, Vives begins with face-painting and hair-bleaching, ingeniously showing the folly of such practices and endeavoring to persuade the respectable girl from imitating others whose ignorance may excuse them. Here the humanist is the maternal counsellor, speaking heart to heart with the Christian maiden. "Verily," he says, "I would fain know what the maiden meaneth that painteth herself. If it be to please herself, it is a vain thing. If it be to please Christ, it is a folly; if it be to delight men it is an ungracious deed. . . . Methinks it much like, if thou wilt go about to win them with painting, as thou wouldst entice or attempt him with a visor. . . . Thou art but in ill case, if thou have nothing else to please him with, that shall be thy husband, but only painting."

In his discourse on dress, Vives exposes the social evil of extreme fashions, as of emanations from unwholesome quarters, making his meaning clear in such passages as: "Thine evil and unchaste raiment shall reprove thee." "But and . . . thou make thyself as a poisoner and a sword unto them that see thee, thou canst not be excused as chaste in mind." And answering the objections of such as may ask if one must be slovenly, he answers that such teaching is far from his purpose, laying down the maxim: "Let it not to be wondered on, nor let it be to be loathed."

Against the abuse of perfumes, of jewelry and the like, he draws arguments from the ancients and from the Gospel precepts, saying: "Then wilt thou say, we must needs do some things for the use of the world and customs. Now would I know, what custom must be followed, if thou name me wise men I grant; if thou say of fools why should they be followed? . . . Peradventure there is an evil custom brought up, be thou the first to lay it down, and thou shalt have praise of it; and other[s] shall follow thine ensample. And as the [ev]ill ensample is brought in of ill folks and established, so of good folks it shall be put away, and good brought up. . . . Now whose is that custom that thou talkest of, and of whom was it taken? Of pagan women. Why do not we then keep still our pagan's law? For if thou list to be called Christian, use manners according thereunto."

Among exciting pleasures, Vives condemns jousts, and social dances such as were prevalent in some countries where the custom of saluting partners on the lips drew down the indignant denunciations of the ladies of Italy and Spain. "In old times," says Vives,

"kissing was not used but among kinsfolk; now it is a common thing in England and France. If they do it because of Baptism, that they may seem all as brethren and sisters I praise the intent. If otherwise I see not whereunto it pertaineth to use so much kissing, as though that love and charity could none other way stand between men and women." This passage makes clear his meaning when he observes: "What good doth all that dancing of young women, holden up on men's arms, that they may hop the higher?" Of "the old use of dancing" for the development of bodily grace, he remarks that it is "clean out of use."

Throughout these treatises it is everywhere apparent that the humanist had at heart the training of the valiant woman of Proverbs—one judicious and strong, not cloistered in the home, but finding there her chief happiness and her first duty. "Her home shall be unto her as a commonwealth, and she must learn what her duty and office is at home, and what is her husband's. . . . She must learn also to contemn worldly chances, that is, she must be somewhat manly and strong, moderately to bear and suffer both good and evil." Speaking of the practice of devotion on the part of the maiden he says: "Let her pray unto the holy Virgin whom she shall truly represent."[544]

After a tender allusion to the power of sympathy and the love and reverence which he bears to his own mother and mother-in-law, Vives expresses the thought concerning the wife's true dignity common to all the moralists of his school: "Nor thou shalt not have her as a servant, or as a companion of thy prosperity and welfare only, but also as a most faithful secretary of thy cares and thoughts, and in doubtful matters a wise and hearty counsellor."[545]

With the breaking out of the movement for Church reform, outside of the Church, there appeared in the North a new attitude towards classical education. This attitude comprehended the training of the male citizen for the duties of clergyman or civil official, and in its practical outlook excluded, not only the average boy, but the girl of whatever ability or condition.

Representative humanists, such as Melanchthon and Sturm, and, generally, all the classicists associated with Luther, are silent on the subject of woman's higher education. While evidently not opposed to the girl's classical training, the early Reformation

[544] *Ibid.*, 88, note.
[545] "De Officio Mariti," *Ibid.*, 209.

humanists found it a sufficiently arduous undertaking to establish Latin schools for boys to replace the Church schools that were closed by the civil authorities. In consequence of this, the history of classical education in Germany, dating from the first two decades of the sixteenth century to the last two of the nineteenth, is the history of boys' high schools and colleges and of university courses open to men.[546]

After the work of destruction was completed, such convent property[547] as had not been appropriated by the princes or taken to endow the churches of the Reformers,[548] was applied to the use of boys' schools,[549] and Luther had to appeal to the civil authorities for aid to establish in each town a girls' school for the purpose of imparting there even catechetical instruction.[550]

It was unfortunate from the side of pedagogical theory, that Luther was not a humanist, inasmuch as his influence was far reaching and his views on education widely accepted after his death. In his writings there are occasionally to be found general statements in favor of higher education for the girl, such as his desire to see everywhere the "best" schools for both "girls and boys,"[551] and his advice that the more apt children be kept longer in school,[553] that they might be trained to become teachers. His plea also for the study of Hebrew and Greek as the keys to the proper understanding of the Scriptures,[554] could not consistently exclude the idea of such study on the part of the girl, since she as well as the boy, was to be put in a position to interpret for herself both the Old and the New Testament as the only guide of her religious belief and practice.[555] But the practical application of this principle is nowhere to be found in the scheme for education proposed by Luther. According to his plan the girl is to study the Bible in either Latin or German translations, thus accepting from others both the interpretation of the texts and the decision as to

---

[546] Cf. Rein, "Encyklopädisches Handbuch der Pädagogik," *Mädchener ziehung und Mädchenunterricht*; and, *Mädchengymnasien*. Cf. *Monumenta Germaniae Paedagogica*.

[547] Cf. Janssen, *op. cit.*

[548] Cf. Godfrey, *Heidelberg, etc.* London, 1906.

[549] *Ibid.*

[550] "An den christlichen Adel deutscher Nation von des christlichen Standes Besserung," *Sämmtliche Werke*, XXI, 320 ff. Erlangen, 1832.

[551] "An die Burgermeister und Rathherren allerlei Städte in deutschen Landen," *Ibid.*, XXII, 190.

[553] *Ibid.*

[554] *Ibid.*, 180 ff.

[555] Cf. Painter, *Luther on Education.* Philadelphia, 1889.

the genuineness of those texts. Moreover, she is to be given instruction in the Ten Commandments, according to a set form of interpretation, and even in the Creed, in like manner, although the latter was not claimed to be a portion of the Bible.[556]

In his *Address to the Nobility*, Luther says: "Would to God each town had also a girls' school, in which girls might be taught the Gospel for an hour daily, either in German or Latin."[557] After discussing the necessity of studying his catechism with his exposition of the Commandments, the Our Father and the Creed, he says: "We may find some boors and niggards even among the nobles, who pretend that henceforth neither pastors nor preachers are needed, since we have all that is required in books, and can learn it by ourselves, and who cheerfully let the benefices go to ruin and waste, so that both pastors and preachers suffer hunger and thirst enow, as perhaps is fitting for stupid Germans."[558]

Coming to definite terms as to what common schooling he would have provided for girls, he says expressly in the Letter to the *Mayors and Aldermen:* "It is not my idea that we should establish schools as they have been heretofore, where a boy has studied Donatus and Alexander twenty or thirty years, and yet has learned nothing. The world has changed and things go differently. My idea is that boys should spend an hour or two a day in school, and the rest of the time work at home, learn some trade and do whatever is desired so that study and work may go on together, while the children are young and can attend to both. . . . In like manner, a girl has time to go to school an hour a day, and yet attend to her work at home."[559]

This statement is followed by a recommendation that the brighter children be given more opportunities, since accomplished teachers, preachers and workers are needed, but in soliciting state and private aid for this purpose repeatedly throughout the letter, Luther speaks only of means to educate clergymen and civil officials. Similarly, in the *Sermon on the Duty of Sending Children to School*, he appeals to the consciences of parents to supply boys for these functions, with no mention of a higher education for girls.[560]

---

[556] Cf. "Grosser Katechismus." *Sämmtliche Werke*, XXI, 26 ff.
[557] Translated by Painter, *op. cit.*, 138.
[558] "Preface to Large Catechism." Translated by Wace and Buchheim in *Primary Works*. London, 1896.
[559] Translated by Painter, *op. cit.*, 199, 200.
[560] Cf. "Ein Sermon oder Predigt, dass man solle Kinder zur Schule halten." *Sämmtliche Werke*, XX, 7 ff.

Besides the obstacle to the girl's secondary education thus arising from lack of funds, another serious drawback now presented itself in the lack of suitable teachers.   Luther made efforts to secure the services of women for the catechetical schools, and there is evidence that some such teachers were employed.   On June 10, 1527, he addressed a letter[561] to "Frau Elizabeth Agricola, schoolmistress at Eisleben," the wife of Johann Agricola, a preacher in that town; and on May 2, of the same year, he had written to "Else von Kanitz, now at Eiche," inviting her to Wittenberg "to instruct young girls," saying, "that in beginning such work you may be an example to others.   You shall be in my house," he continues, "and at my table, so that you may be exempt from dangers and cares."[562]

To lessons in the Catechism, these teachers doubtless added instruction in German, according to the provision made by congregations after the example of Leisnig, whose constitution provided that: "The ten directors, in the name of the congregation, shall have power to call, appoint, and remove a school teacher for the young boys. . . .   In like manner the ten directors, out of the common treasury, shall provide an honorable, mature, and blameless woman to instruct young girls under 12 years of age in Christian discipline, honor and virtue, and at a suitable place to teach them reading and writing in German a few hours daily."[563]

The teachers who were to give the girl instruction in the Gospel were practically to be drawn from the reserved force of "ordinary pastors," instructed in Latin, which language they were to learn to read and write, and afterwards to take up a trade while waiting to be called upon "in case of need."   Speaking of the education of these less promising boys, Luther says: "For we need not only learned doctors and masters in the Scriptures, but also ordinary pastors who may teach the Gospel and the catechism to the young and ignorant. . . .   If they are not capable of contending with heretics, it does not matter."[564]

Luther finally clearly defines his position, announcing in theory what he had worked out in practice, prescribing for the girl an education in the vernacular, and leaving to the boy the study of other languages: "Even women and children can now learn more of God and Christ from German books and sermons (I speak the truth) than was formerly known by the universities, priests,

---

[561] *Letters to Women,* Let. IX.   Translated by Malcolm.   London, 1856.
[562] *Ibid.,* Letter VIII.
[563] Painter, *op. cit.,* 139.
[564] *Ibid.,* "Sermon on the Duty of Sending Children to School," 235.

monks, the whole Papacy, and the entire world. But even the ordinary pastor and preacher must be acquainted with Latin, which he can no more dispense with than the learned can dispense with Greek and Hebrew."[565]

In accepting Luther's plan, on the intellectual side, Germany deprived woman of her right to participation in that "general education" which, his followers claim, the principles of Protestantism render necessary by holding the Bible to be the only source of religious truth, and imposing upon Protestant nations the obligation "to place man in an independent position, and dignify him with the responsibility of ascertaining and performing his duty immediately in the sight of God."[566]

In thus having recourse to the expedient of departing from principles which, in their practical application, had proved merely Utopian, the movement compelled woman to yield her right to a share in the fruits of intellectual culture bequeathed by years of educational progress. In prescribing for the girl an elementary education in the vernacular as an aid in the study of religion, Protestantism here lost sight of the Renaissance ideal, while at the same time it did woman a service from the moral viewpoint. The crisis through which the northern nations were now passing was a dangerous one for her.[567] Participation in the new intellectual activities must have exposed the girl to all the inconveniences of free speculation as well as of silent acquiescence in the theories now put forward in the schools on the subject of moral responsibility.[568]

Modern educational theorists are able to point to the homes of northern Europe as to models of domestic order and virtue,[569] and this because the sixteenth-century movement failed to affect the time-honored customs of the Teutonic nations whose proverbial reverence for womanhood[570] rendered them proof against the very daring teachings concerning individual freedom, everywhere to be met with in the writings of Luther, side by side with his edifying discourses on the sanctity of the home and of parental duty and authority.

[565] *Ibid.*, 236.
[566] *Ibid.*, 72.
[567] Cf. Janssen, *op. cit.*
[568] Cf. Luther, *op. cit.*
[569] Cf. Schumann, "Die Mädchenerziehung im deutschen Mittelalter," in *Kleinere Schriften über pädagogische und kulturgeschichtliche Fragen*, I, 108 ff. Hannover, 1878.
[570] Cf. Janssen, *op. cit.*; Weinhold, *Die deutschen Frauen in dem Mittelalter*. Wien, 1851.

CONCLUSION

The history of the humanistic movement for the higher education of woman demonstrates the erroneous character of several important assertions on the subject of woman's education, as made by popular modern historical writers and writers of fiction, and widely endorsed by public opinion. Among these assertions are those pertaining to the status of woman during the Middle Ages and the Renaissance, as well as during the nineteenth century.

The high state of mental culture to which the woman of the fifteenth century attained in a half-generation, presupposes intellectual power and solidity of purpose, the two important results of true education. The third result, the acquisition of knowledge, might easily have followed, even if one rejects the important truth that, in the process of character formation and of intellectual development considerable positive knowledge is of necessity acquired. Had the cloistered women of the Middle Ages monopolized all learning, a miracle would have been required to convert so suddenly the wives and daughters of the early humanists into accomplished writers and thinkers. In like manner it is hard to conceive the attitude of these humanists towards woman as one created by a sudden impulse and directed towards a household drudge and unwilling handmaiden.

As the movement passes on from Italy into other countries the true cause of woman's Renaissance freedom becomes more and more apparent. If the modern concept of the results of the Revival of Learning is accepted, its mission was to emancipate the human mind from the slavery of authority. Regarded in this sense it fulfilled its mission only outside of the Church, and even there only to one half of humanity. In Italy and in the Iberian Peninsula it failed, while in the other countries here under consideration it met with but partial success. The result in Protestant countries was the independence of individual man and the more or less complete subjugation of woman to him, a subjugation through which, by the turn of events, she was forced to renounce many of her intellectual rights. In dechristianized countries the subjection amounted to degradation to the social status of the accepted neo-paganism, and as a logical consequence woman was forced to choose the alternative of stout resistance or blind submission.

174

Where the Renaissance movement continued to be guided by the principles which inspired it, woman continued to be free, and it is significant that precisely here the "woman question" came to be battled out by men. Christ set man the standard when He prescribed indissoluble monogamatic marriage and pronounced the state of consecrated virginity still higher than this, and His Church safeguarded woman's sacred privileges by guiding the intellectual movement of the fifteenth century along the sure paths of such established moral principles as these. The reiterated assertions as to her opposition to woman's higher education and, as a consequence, to woman's mission outside the home, have not been sustained by historical evidence. On the contrary, her unqualified sanction of the life of voluntary service embraced by millions of her daughters is the surest pledge of her confidence in their power. Furthermore, through the spirit of Christian democracy within the Church's bosom, inspiring as it did Christian benevolence both of heart and hand, there was secured to the daughters of the poor from the time of the Renaissance an education which popular opinion of today looks upon as possible only to the rich and powerful. In this spirit of Christian communion is found the explanation of the fact that, where the Church was free to carry on her mission, the blessings of Renaissance culture did not remain the sole possession of its original patrons, the noble and the wealthy. In whatever rank of society, woman stepped forth from the Middle Ages at the side of man not because his attitude towards her had changed nor because she herself had undergone a sudden metamorphosis. To him she was still the noble daughter of God and the emulator of the wisdom and graces of the Mother of Christ. To her he was to remain the official head of the family, and as such her superior; the other half of humanity, and as such her equal; the guardian of her God-given rights and the defender of her sacred privileges, and as such her acknowledged inferior. Such an acknowledgment every Christian man who has faith in the divinity of Christ is taught to make in the presence of the Blessed Virgin Mary whom he is supposed to be happy to call his Mother and proud to honor as his Queen.

BIBLIOGRAPHY

GENERAL

Bibliothek der katholischen Pädagogik. Freiburg, 1888.

Catholic Encyclopedia. Sixteen volumes. New York, 1907–14.

ERASMUS, DESIDERIUS. *Opera Omnia.* Ten volumes in 2. Lugduni Batavorum, 1703–1706.

GUGGENBERGER, A. *A General History of the Christian Era.* Three volumes. St. Louis, 1901.

HEIMBUCHER, MAX. *Die Orden und Kongregationen der katholischen Kirche.* Two volumes. Paderborn, 1896–97.

HÉLYOT, PIERRE, and BALLOT, MAXMILIAN. *Histoire des Ordres Monastiques, Religeux et Militaires.* Eight volumes. Paris, 1714–19.

HENTSCH, ALICE A. *De la Littérature didactique du Moyen Age s'addressant specialement aux femmes.* Halle, 1903.

McCORMICK, PATRICK JOSEPH. *Education of the Laity in the Early Middle Ages.* Washington, 1912.

McCORMICK, PATRICK JOSEPH. *History of Education.* Washington, 1915.

MONROE, PAUL. *Text-Book in the History of Education.* New York, 1912.

PASTOR, LUDWIG VON. *Geschichte der Päpste seit dem Ausgang des Mittelalters.* Six volumes. Freiburg, 1899–1913.

RASHDALL, HASTINGS. *Universities of Europe in the Middle Ages.* Two volumes in 3. Oxford, 1895.

RIO, ALEX. FRANÇOIS. *De L'art Chrétien.* Paris, 1874.

SANDYS, JOHN EDWIN. *History of Classical Scholarship.* Vol. II. Cambridge, 1908.

TAYLOR, HENRY OSBORN. *Classical Heritage of the Middle Ages.* New York, 1901.

VACANDARD, ELPHÉGE. *The Inquisition.* Translated by Bertrand L. Conway. New York, 1908.

VIVES, JUAN LUIS. *Opera.* Two volumes. Basileae, 1555.

WOODWARD, WILLIAM HARRISON. *Studies in Education during the Age of the Renaissance.* Cambridge, 1906.

ITALY

ADY, CECILIA M. *A History of Milan under the Sforza.* London, 1907.

AENEAS SYLVIUS. (Piccolomini, Pope Pius II). *De Liberorum Educatione.* Basileae 1551. Translated by W. H. Woodward in "Vittorino da Feltre and Other Humanist Educators." Cambridge, 1912.

BAUDRILLART, ALFRED. *The Catholic Church, the Renaissance and Protestantism.* Translated by Mrs. Philip Gibbs. New York, 1908.

BASCHET, ARMAND. *Recherches de Documents d'art et l'Histoire dans les Archives de Mantoue.* (Gazette des Beaux Arts, 1866.)

BERTONI, GIULIO. *La Biblioteca Estense e la coltura ferrarese ai tempi del duca Ercole I.* Toreno, 1903.

176

BURCKHARDT, JACOB CHRISTOPHER. *Civilisation of the Renaissance in Italy.* Translated by S. C. C. Middlemore. London, 1898.

CARTWRIGHT, JULIA. (Mrs. Henry Ady.) *Baldassare Castiglione, the Perfect Courtier, His Life and Letters.* Two volumes. London, 1908.

CARTWRIGHT, JULIA. (Mrs. Ady.) *Beatrice d'Este, Duchess of Milan; A Study of the Renaissance.* London, 1899.

CARTWRIGHT, JULIA. (Mrs. Ady.) *Isabella d'Este, Marchioness of Mantua; A Study of the Renaissance.* Two volumes. London, 1903.

D'AREZZO, LEONARDO BRUNI. *De studiis et literis.* Parisiis, 1642. Translated by W. H. Woodward in "Vittorino da Feltre and Other Humanist Educators." Cambridge, 1912.

DEL LUNGO, ISODORO. *Donna fiorentina del buon tempo antico.* Firenze, 1906.

DEL LUNGO, ISODORO. *Women of Florence.* Translated by Mary G. Steegmann. London, 1907.

DENNISTOUN, JAMES. *Memoirs of the Dukes of Urbino.* Edited by Hutton, Three volumes. London and New York, 1909.

DOMINICI, BEATO GIOVANNI. *Regola del Governo di Cura Familiare.* Edited by Donato Salvi. Firenze, 1860.

DONISMONDI, IPPOLITO. *Dell Istoria Ecclesiastica di Mantova. Parte Prima.* Mantova, 1612.

GREGOROVIUS, FERDINAND. *Lucrezia Borgia nach Urkunden und Korrespondenzen ihrer eigenen Zeit.* Stuttgart und Berlin, 1906.

GRUYER, GUSTAVE. *Vittore Pisano.* (Gazette des Beaux Arts, 1894.)

GUARINO, BATTISTA. *De ordine docendi et studendi.* Modena, 1496. Translated by W. H. Woodward in "Vittorino da Feltre and Other Humanist Educators." Cambridge, 1912.

HARE, CHRISTOPHER. (Mrs. Marian Andrews.) *The Most Illustrious Ladies of the Italian Renaissance.* London and New York, 1904.

JERROLD, (MRS.) MAUD F. *Vittoria Colonna, with some Account of Her Friends and Her Time.* London and New York, 1906.

KRISTELLER, PAUL. *Barbara von Brandenburg* (Hohenzollern Jahrbuch, 1899.)

LUZIO, ALESSANDRO, E RENIER, RODOLFO. *Mantova e Urbino: Isabella d'Este ed Elisabetta Gonzaga nelle relazoni famigliari e nelle vicende politiche.* Torino-Rome, 1893.

McCORMICK, PATRICK JOSEPH. *Two Catholic Medieval Educators.* Catholic University Bulletin. October, 1906; April, 1907.

MONNIER, PHILIPPE. *Le Quattrocento; essai sur l'histoire littéraire du XVe siècle italien.* Two volumes. Paris, 1901.

PIUS II, POPE. See Aenaes Sylvius.

ROSMINI, CARLO DE'. *Idea dell'ottimo precettore nella vita e disciplina di Vittorino da Feltre e de' suoi discepoli, Libri Quattro.* Milano, 1845.

SYMONDS, JOHN ADDINGTON. *The Renaissance in Italy.* Seven volumes. London and New York, 1900-3.

TIRABOSCHI, GIROLAMO. *Storia della Letteratura Italiana.* Nine volumes. Firenze, 1809.

VASARI, GIORGIO. *Le vite de'più eccellenti pittori, scoltori et architetti.* Three volumes. Bologna, 1647.
VEGIO, MAFFEO. *De Educatione Liberorum.* Translated by K. A. Kopp in "Bibliothek der katholischen Pädagogik," II. Freiburg, 1889.
VERGERIO, PIER PAOLO. *De Ingenuis Moribus.* Basileae, 1541. Translated by W. H. Woodward in "Vittorino da Feltre and Other Humanist Educators." Cambridge, 1912.
VESPASIANO DA BISTICCI. *Vite di Uomini Illustri del secolo XV.* Firenze, 1859.
WOODWARD, WILLIAM HARRISON. *Vittorino da Feltre and Other Humanist Educators.* Cambridge, 1912.
YRIARTE, CHARLES. *Isabella d'Este et les artistes de son Temps.* (Gazette des Beaux Arts, 1895.)
YRIARTE, CHARLES. *Venise: Histoire, Art, Industrie, La Ville, La Vie.* Paris, 1878.

SPAIN AND PORTUGAL

ALTIMIRA Y CREVEA, RAFAEL. *Historia de España y de la Civilizacion Española.* Two volumes. Barcelona, 1902.
ANTONIO, D. NICOLAO. *Bibliotheca Hispana Nova.* Two volumes. Matritri, 1788.
AUTON RAMIREZ, SR. D. BRAULIO. *Diccionario de Bibliografía Argonómica y de toda clase de escritos relacionados con la agricultura.* Madrid, 1865.
BYWATER, INGRAM. *The Erasmian Pronunciation of Greek and Its Precursors.* London, 1908.
FEIJÓO Y MONTENEGRO (FEYJÓO), BENITO JERÓNIMO. *Theatro critico universal.* Translated as "Three Essays, etc." by A Gentleman. London, 1778.
FITZMAURICE-KELLY, JAMES. *History of Spanish Literature.* New York, 1898.
FLÓREZ, FR. HENRIQUE. *Memorias de las Reynas Católicas.* Two volumes. Madrid, 1790.
FUENTE, D. VICENTE DE LA. *Historia de las Universidades, colegios y demás Establecimientos de Enseñanza en España.* Four volumes in 2. Madrid, 1884–89.
HUME, MARTIN A. S. *The Spanish People, Their Origin, Growth and Influence.* New York, 1901.
LATASSA Y ORTIN, FELIX DE. *Biblioteca Nueva de los Escritores Aragoneses que florecieron desde el año de 1500 hasta 1599.* Five volumes. Pamphlona, 1798–1802.
LEBRIXA, ANTONIO DE (LEBRIJA). *Introducciones Latinas—Contrapuesto el Romance al Latin.* Madrid, 1773.
LEBRIJA, ANTONIO DE. *Gramatica Castellana—Reproduction Phototypique de l'Edition Princeps* (1492). Preface by E. Walberg. Edited by Max Niemeyer. Halle, 1909.
MARIÉJOL, JEAN HIPPOLYTE. *Un Lettré italien à la Cour d'Espagne—Pierre Martyr d'Anghera, sa Vie et ses Oeuvres.* Paris, 1887.

MARINEO, LUCIO. *De Rebus Hispaniae Memorabilibus*—Alcalá (de Henares), 1533.

Ibid. Spanish Edition. *De las Cosas Memorables de España*—Alcalá (de Heneres), 1539.

Memorias de la Real Academia de la Historia. Vol. VI. Madrid, 1821.

PARADA, D. DIEGO IGNACIO. *Escritoras y Eruditas Españolas.* Madrid, 1881.

PRESCOTT, WILLIAM H. *History of the Reign of Ferdinand and Isabella.* Three volumes. Philadelphia, 1882.

RADA Y DELGADO, D. JUAN DE DIOS DE LA. *Mugeres celébres de España y Portugal.* Two volumes. Barcelona, 1868.

REYNIER, GUSTAVE. *La Vie Universitaire dans l'ancienne Espagne.* Paris and Toulouse, 1902.

TICKNOR, GEORGE. *History of Spanish Literature.* Three volumes. Boston, 1891.

ENGLAND

A Collection of State Papers Relating to Affairs in the Reigns of King Henry VIII, Edward VI, Mary and Elizabeth (1542–1570). Edited by Samuel Haynes. London, 1740.

Ibid. In Reign of Elizabeth (1571–1596) Edited by William Murdin. London, 1759.

ASCHAM, ROGER. *The Whole Works of.* Three volumes in 4. Edited by R. Giles. London, 1865.

BEWSCHER, FRED. W. *The Reformation and the Renaissance.* London, 1913.

GREY, LADY JANE. *Memoirs and Literary Remains of.* Edited by Harris Nicolas. London, 1832.

Historical Reprints. Edinburgh, 1886.

HOOKHAM, MARY ANN. *The Life and Times of Margaret of Anjou.* Two volumes. London, 1872.

Miscellaneous State Papers from 1501 to 1726. Edited by Philip Yorke. Two volumes. London, 1778.

MORE, CRESACRE. *The Life of Sir Thomas More.* London, 1726.

Original Letters Illustrative of English History. Edited by Henry Ellis. Three volumes. London, 1825.

Privy Purse Expenses of the Princess Mary. Edited by Frederick Madden, London, 1831.

Proceedings and Ordinances of the Privy Council of England, Vol. VII. 32 *Henry VIII to 33 Henry VIII.* Edited by Harris Nicolas, 1837.

ROPER, WILLIAM. *The Mirrour of Vertue in Worldly Greatness or the Life of Sir Thomas More, Knight.* London, 1902.

Select Statutes and Other Constitutional Documents Illustrative of the Reigns of Elizabeth and James I. Edited by George Walter Prothero. Oxford, 1898.

STRICKLAND, AGNES. *Lives of Tudor Princesses.* London, 1868.

STRICKLAND, AGNES. *Lives of the Queens of England.* Twelve volumes. London, 1842.

STONE, JEAN MARY. *The History of Mary I. Queen of England.* London, 1901.
The Loseley Manuscripts and Other Rare Documents—Henry VIII to Mary I. Edited by Alfred John Kempe. London, 1836.
Tudor Proclamations. Edited by R. Garnett. Oxford, 1897.
WATSON, FOSTER. *Vives and the Renascence Education of Women.* New York, 1912.

FRANCE

BRANTÔME, PIERRE DE BOURDEILLES. *Oeuvres Complètes.* Eight volumes. Paris, 1822-23.
Collection des meilleurs ouvrages françois composés par des femmes. Six volumes. Edited by Melle. Kéralio. Paris, 1787.
COLONIA, DOMINIQUE, DE. *Histoire Littéraire de la Ville de Lyon, avec une Bibliothéque des Auteurs Lyonnais, sacrés et profanes.* Lyons, 1728-30.
CORDIER, MATHURIN. *Colloquia.* Edited by Arcadius Avellanus. Philadelphia, 1904.
CRANE, THOMAS FREDERICK. *La Société Française au Dix-septième Siècle.* New York, 1889.
GOULART, SIMON. *Mémoires de l'Estat de France sous le règne de Charles IX.* Three volumes in 8. Meidelbourg, [Geneva], 1578.
GREGOIRE, LOUIS. *Dictionnaire Encyclopédique.* Paris, 1872.
Histoire de la Langue et de la Littérature française des Origines à 1900. Edited by L. Petit de Julleville. Eight volumes. Paris, 1896-1899.
LAIGLE, MATHILDE. *Le Livre des Trois Vertus de Christine de Pisan et son milieu historique et littéraire.* Paris, 1912.
Latin Themes of Mary Stuart, Queen of Scots. Warton Club No. 3. Edited by Anatoile de Montaiglon. London, 1855.
LEFRANC, ABEL JULES MAURICE. *Histoire du Collège de France, depuis ses origines jusqu'à la fin du premier empire.* Paris, 1893.
Lettres de Catherine de Médicis. Ten volumes. In Documents inédits sur l'Histoire de France. Published by Le Cte Hector de la Ferrière. Paris, 1880-1909.
LE VICOMTE DE MEAUX. *Les Luttes Religieuses en France au seizième siècle.* Paris, 1879.
MARGUERITE DE VALOIS. (d'Angoulême.) *L'Heptaméron des Nouvelles.* Paris, 1559.
MARGUERITE DE VALOIS. *Les Mémoires de la Roine Marguerite.* Edited by de Mauleon sieur de Granier. Paris, 1628.
MAROT, CLÉMENT. *Oeuvres.* Edited by Charles d'Héricault. Paris, 1867.
MAROT, JEAN. *Oeuvres.* Paris, 1723.
MONTAIGNE, MICHEL EYQUEM DE. *Essais.* Paris, 1652.
Nouvelle Collection de Mémoires pour servir a l'Histoire de France, depuis le 13e Siècle jusqu'à la fin du 18e. Thirty-two volumes. Edited by Michaud et Ponjoulat. Paris, 1835-39.

PISAN, CHRISTINE DE. *Oeuvres Poétiques de.* Société des Anciens Textes Français. Edited by Maurice Roy. Three volumes. Paris, 1886–96.

Recueil des Lettres de Marie Stuart, Reine d'Ecosse. Edited by Le Prince Alexandre Labanoff. Londres, 1844.

RUBLE, LE BARON ALPHONSE DE. *La Première Jeunesse de Marie Stuart.* Paris, 1891.

STEVENSON, JOSEPH. *Mary Stuart: a Narrative of the First Eighteen Years of Her Life.* Edinburgh, 1886.

WARD, CHARLES FREDERICK. *Epistles on the Romance of the Rose and Other Documents in the Debate.* Chicago, 1911.

NORTHERN EUROPE

ALTMEYER, J. J. *Marguerite d'Autriche, sa vie, sa politique et sa cour.* Liège, 1840.

CARTWRIGHT, JULIA (MRS. ADY). *Christina of Denmark, Duchess of Milan and Lorraine.* New York, 1913.

Correspondance de L'Empereur Maximilian I et de Marguerite D'Autriche, sa fille, Gouvernante des Pays-Bas, de 1507 à 1519, publiée d'apres les Manuscrits originaux par M. Le Glay. Two volumes. Paris, 1839.

Correspondance de Marguerite D'Autriche avec ses Amis 1506–1528. Two volumes. Edited by L. Ph. C. Van den Bergh. Leide, 1847.

Encyklopädisches Handbuch der Pädagogik. Seven volumes. Edited by Wilhelm Rein. Langensalza, 1895–99.

GODFREY, ELIZABETH. *Heidelberg. Its Princes and Its Palaces.* London, 1906.

HARE, CHRISTOPHER (MRS. ANRDEWS). *The High and Puissant Princess Marguerite of Austria.* London and New York, 1907.

Historisch-politische Blätter für das katholische Deutschland. One hundred and fifty-two volumes. München, 1838–1900.

JANSSEN, JOHANNES. *Geschichte des deutschen Volkes, seit dem Ausgang des Mittelalters.* Eight volumes. Freiburg, 1897.

LORENZ, S. *Volkserziehung und Volksunterricht im späteren Mittelalter.* Paderborn and Münster, 1887.

LUTHER, MARTIN. *Sämmtliche Werke.* Sixty-seven volumes. Edited by J. K. Irmischer and E. L. Enders. Frankfurt am Main und Erlangen, 1828–70.

LUTHER, MARTIN. *Letters to Women.* Collected by K. Zimmermann. Translated by Mrs. Malcolm. London, 1865.

MARGUERITE D'AUTRICHE. *Albums et oeuvres poétiques de.* Edited by Emile Gachet. Bruxelles, 1849.

Monumenta Germaniae Paedogogica. Forty-five volumes. Berlin, 1886—

PAINTER, F. V. N. *Luther on Education.* Philadelphia, 1889.

SCHUMANN, J. GOTTLOB. "Die Mädchenerziehung im deutschen Mittelalter." In *Kleinere Schriften über pädagogische und kulturgeschichtliche Fragen, I.* Hannover, 1878.

THIBAUT, FRANCISQUE. *Marguerite D'Autriche et Jehan Lemaire de Belges, ou De Littérature et des Arts aux Pays-Bas sous Marguerite D'Autriche.* Paris, 1888.

ZEUMER, KARL. "Die Goldene Bulle Kaiser Karls IV." In *Quellen und Studien zur Verfassungsgeschichte des Deutschen Reiches in Mittelalter und Neuzeit.* Weimar, 1908.